# Reclaiming the Common Good

Wyn Mellor

Simon P. Woodman, Rev. 11.15

Henrietta Atkins

Siarz Barrow

# Reclaiming the Common Good

## How Christians can help rebuild our broken world

A collection of essays collated and edited by Virginia Moffatt

DARTON·LONGMAN+TODD

First published in Great Britain in 2017 by
Darton, Longman and Todd Ltd
1 Spencer Court
140–142 Wandsworth High Street
London SW18 4JJ

ISBN 978-0-232-53315-6


A catalogue record for this book is available from the British Library

Typeset by Kerrypress Ltd, St Albans
Printed and bound in Great Britain by Bell & Bain, Glasgow

# CONTENTS

# Notes on Contributors

**Virginia Moffatt** is a writer and community activist. Beginning her career in Lambeth L'Arche community, she spent thirty years working in the voluntary sector and local government to improve the lives of adults with learning disabilities. She has a BSc in Biology from the University of York, an MSc in Voluntary Sector Organisation from the LSE and a Diploma in Creative Writing from the Oxford Department of Continuing Education. In recent years she has campaigned on welfare issues, worked for the belief and values think tank Ekklesia, for whom she is now an associate, and as a Practice Manager at a GP surgery. She currently works for a Catholic multi-academy. Virginia's first novel, *Echo Hall*, will be published by Unbound in 2017. She lives in Oxford with her husband Chris Cole, Director of Drone Wars UK, and their three children.

**Dr Patrick Riordan SJ** teaches political philosophy at Heythrop College, University of London since 2002. Prior to that date he worked at the Milltown Institute of Theology and Philosophy in Dublin. He has also worked in the Philippines. His latest book is *Philippine Common Goods: A good life for all* (Davao City: Ateneo de Davao University Press, 2016). Other publications include *Global Ethics and Global Common Goods* (London: Bloomsbury, 2015) and *A Grammar of the Common Good* (London: Continuum, 2008). He has published articles on human dignity, natural law, business ethics, and just war theory in the context of terrorism.

**John Moffatt SJ** grew up in North London. He is a Roman Catholic priest in the Society of Jesus (Jesuits). He has worked in secondary education and university chaplaincy since joining the order in 1982. He has written a guide for modern people who want to make sense of Catholic theology entitled *The Resurrection of the Word* (available from Way Books) and intermittently posts articles on the website 'Letting the Porcupine Out of the Bottle'. He currently lives at the Hurtado Jesuit Centre in Wapping.

**Simon Barrow** is Director of the beliefs and ethics think tank Ekklesia and a member of the Iona Community. He was formerly Assistant General Secretary of Churches Together in Britain and Ireland and he has also worked extensively in current affairs journalism and theological education. He has co-edited the books *Scotland 2021* (Bella Caledonia / Ekklesia, 2016), *Consuming Passion: Why the killing of Jesus really matters* (DLT, 2005) and *Christian Mission in Western Society* (CTBI, 2001) among others.

**Bernadette Meaden** is an Associate of the belief and values think tank Ekklesia, and in recent years has written extensively for Ekklesia on social justice issues, particularly welfare reform and its impact on the poorest and most disadvantaged members of society. She is a freelance writer who has contributed to many publications on political, social and religious issues. She is the author of a book on the UK Christian peace movement, Protest for Peace, and recently contributed to *Scotland 2021*, a collection of essays looking at Scotland's political future.

**Dr Simon Duffy** is Director of the Centre for Welfare Reform, an independent think tank that works to improve the welfare state, and secretary to the international cooperative Citizen Network. Simon is a philosopher and social innovator, best known for his work on self-directed support and citizenship. He has set up and led a number of organisations including Inclusion Glasgow and In Control. Simon's writings include Keys to Citizenship, Women at the Centre, The Unmaking of Man and Unlocking the Imagination. He was awarded the RSA's Prince Albert medal for social innovation in 2008 and the Social Policy Association's award for outstanding contribution to social policy in 2011. His doctorate is in moral philosophy where he set out to defend the reality of the Moral Law.

**Rev. Vaughan Jones** is an ordained minister at Union Chapel Islington, a Congregationalist church which, besides being an active congregation, is a major music venue and project for people experiencing homelessness. He was the founding Chief Executive of Praxis, a voluntary organisation working with refugees, asylum seekers and other vulnerable migrants including survivors of human trafficking. In that capacity he has over 30 years' experience developing and managing projects including advice, housing, language supports, employment advice and training and community development. He currently assists the Migration Matters Trust in developing research and policy, promoting evidence-based approaches to migration. He is also a Trustee of the Refugee Council.

Vaughan has a Master of Theology degree in Pastoral Theology from Heythrop College, University of London.

**Savitri Hensman** was born in Sri Lanka and came to England as a small child. She lives and worships in a diverse inner-city area and, like many others in the UK, has relatives and friends from various parts of the world. An Ekklesia associate, she is a writer and activist and works in the fields of service user and public involvement and community development. She is the author of *Sexuality, Struggle and Saintliness: Same-sex love and the Church*, which was published by Ekklesia in 2016.

**Ellen Teague** is a London-based Catholic journalist who writes and campaigns on justice, peace and ecology issues. She is a member of the JPIC team of the Columban Missionary Society in Britain and both campaigns for them on environmental justice and edits their newsletter, *Vocation for Justice*. She also writes regularly for *The Tablet*, *Messenger of St Anthony* International Edition and Redemptorist Publications, collaborating closely with organisations involved in the National Justice and Peace Network of England and Wales (NJPN). She is a member of the NJPN Environment Working Group and has been speaking at diocesan days in England on *Laudato Si'*.

Interest in environmental justice was sparked while working as a volunteer teacher in Africa in the 1980s and then for CAFOD as their campaign coordinator on the 'Renewing the Earth' campaign. She has produced several study programmes for Christian groups, including 'Paint the Church Green', 'Our Earth, Our Home', Green assemblies for primary schools, and the Columban study programme on *Laudato Si'*. Ellen is also an assessor for the Live Simply Parish Award in England and Wales.

She is married with three sons.

**Edward P. Echlin** is an ecological theologian, Honorary Research Fellow at Leeds Trinity University, and a Visiting Scholar at Sarum

College, Salisbury. He is author of numerous books and articles, including *Climate and Christ, A Prophetic Alternative* and *The Cosmic Circle: Jesus and Ecology* (Columba Press).

**Henrietta Cullinan** is a peace activist and writer. She was born in London. She studied Architecture and then Philosophy before raising a family and working in further education, teaching adult literacy and English. She recently travelled to Kabul, Afghanistan as a member of a peace delegation with Voices for Creative Nonviolence UK.

**Susan Clarkson** was born in Bradford in 1946. Susan has been a member of a Roman Catholic religious order but left in 2010. She lived in Catholic Worker communities in the USA and Britain from 2001 to 2015. During this time she took part in nonviolent direct action in the USA and Britain, being part of the Riverside Ploughshares action in 2003. In 2012 she went to Kabul to visit the Afghan Peace Volunteers with Voices for Creative Nonviolence UK. Susan has been a Quaker since 2013 and is particularly interested in the work of Quakers in Russia, which she has visited several times.

**Rev. Dr Simon Woodman** grew up in Sevenoaks in Kent, and has degrees from Sheffield, Bristol and Cardiff Universities. He is the Co-Minister of Bloomsbury Central Baptist Church in the West End of London, and the Baptist Chaplain at King's College London. He has previously been a market stallholder on Camden Market, a Baptist minister in Bristol, a tutor at South Wales Baptist College, and a lecturer at Cardiff University. He has written extensively on the book of Revelation, and is co-editor of the *Baptist Quarterly*. He is married to Liz.

# Introduction

## Virginia Moffatt

On a recent trip to Gladstone's Library in Hawarden, I came across a set of essays by W. H. Fremantle, on the subject of the role of the church in the world. The book was part of William Gladstone's personal collection, and it was clear by the annotations in the margins, it was one that had an impact on the former Prime Minister. On the opening page, the great man had marked a sentence, describing the role of the Church:

> as having for its object to imbue all human relations with the spirit of Christ's self-renouncing love, and thus to change the world into a kingdom of God.[1]

It was no surprise to me that Gladstone, a politician who devoted his life to making the world a better place for everyone, should have embraced this sentiment. And it seems to be a suitable starting point for this collection of essays, which offer some reflections on how Christians can help promote a vision for the 'common good' in the world today.

The concept of the 'common good' was devised by Aristotle and, since the development of Catholic Social Thought, has always been of particular interest to Christians engaged in social justice issues. In recent years, it has had particular resurgence, perhaps in response to a sense that things are not as they should be. Thus in 2010 the Catholic Bishops of England and Wales framed their 2010 election paper around the common good,[2] the 2016 National Justice and Peace Conference took democracy and the common good as its subject,[3] and the Christian arts festival Greenbelt 2017 has also chosen the common good as its theme.[4] Meanwhile, the organisation 'Together for the

Common Good'[5] has been set up to bring people of different views together to build a movement for the common good. In recent years their publications, *Together for the Common Good: Towards a national conversation*[6] and *A Faithful Presence: Working for the common good*[7] have provided helpful reflections on what building the common good might mean for us here in the UK.

This new book of essays is intended to bring a fresh perspective to the discussion, which we hope will assist in this national conversation. The idea for the project emerged from a conversation I had with David Moloney, Editorial Director of Darton, Longman and Todd, during which we reflected how, despite our best efforts, it often feels like we are losing the battle to create a world based on common good principles. We agreed that it would be timely to produce a book that not only articulated why this has happened, but provided some insights into how the common good could be reclaimed. Accordingly, I have gathered together a range of individuals committed to working for peace and justice in a variety of fields, and asked them to provide a perspective based on their specialist knowledge. I am very grateful to all my fellow writers, for responding so positively to my request, despite short notice in some cases, and personal issues and work demands in others. It has been a privilege and a pleasure to bring together their fascinating ideas and excellent analyses.

When we began this book, we hoped it would provide a challenge to mainstream thinking on issues such as welfare, austerity, migration, the environment and peace and security. Believing that the next election would not be till 2020, we anticipated that it might provide useful insights into debates about how to bring about positive change to the UK and the world. But Theresa May's surprise decision to hold a snap election in 2017 has dramatically changed the political landscape. The Labour Party's unexpected resurgence, the rise of young people engaging in politics, a rejection of the politics of smear and fear, have resulted in a hung Parliament rather than the predicted Conservative majority. The Prime Minister's authority is weakened, particularly since she will have to rely on the Democratic Unionist Party to govern. Brexit negotiations are just beginning and will be complex and difficult. At the time of writing, it is unclear whether May will remain in post for long and another election may be called, perhaps even as early as autumn 2017. We are faced with a period of uncertainty. While most of us would undoubtedly prefer stability, uncertain times can actually be helpful in creating opportunities for change. After decades of political consensus, we are entering into a period where everything is up for discussion. We are beginning to ask ourselves what kind of a society do we want to be? What kind of world do we want to live in? One that works for a few, or one that works for the common good? The publication of this collection asking such questions couldn't be more timely.

The essays are divided into four parts. In the first, 'What is the Common Good?', Patrick Riordan SJ outlines the history and principles of the common good, from Aristotle to Catholic Social Teaching, demonstrating with clarity why it is so important that Christians embrace this philosophy.

In Part Two, 'Service and Society', three pairs of essays focus on the UK. Where the first of each pairing reflects on the current situation with regard to the common good, the second suggests ways in which it could be reclaimed. Thus in Chapter 2, John Moffatt SJ provides us with an elegant explanation of how the success of the post-war government in building a society that worked for all was gradually eroded by external pressures, such as oil crises, collapse of industry and the rise of free-market economics. Taking this theme up, Simon Barrow argues that in many ways the idea of the 'common good' has become uncommon. He suggests that when the life of the Church is ethical and driven by the right ethos, it demonstrates the 'common good', and that it not only needs to articulate this vision for the world, but ally itself with those who share such a vision.

The next chapters deal with the system of benefits. Bernadette Meaden gives us a detailed history of the development of the welfare safety net, demonstrating how Christians such as William Temple were integral to its foundation. She describes how Margaret Thatcher embraced the ideas of Hayek, aiming to reduce the amount spent on welfare, and how successive governments have created a false image of people on benefits being 'scroungers' and 'skivers', leading to people being left in extreme poverty. Simon Duffy then explains how we need to return to Temple's original vision, to create a vision of welfare that both meets people's basic needs but also empowers them to take control of their lives. He proposes basic income as one of the mechanisms by which we could achieve this.

In the final two chapters in this section, I explore how austerity and market policies have put public services under such extreme pressure that many are stretched to the point of collapse. I propose that rather than rolling back the state, it is time to roll back the market, reinvest in public services, and develop wealthy communities that benefit everyone.

Part Three, 'People and Planet', considers how we also need to be promoting the common good on the world stage. Migration is one of the most pressing issues of our time, and in his thoughtful chapter Vaughan Jones discusses how, while migration is positive for some (those who work in well-paid industries), for those moving for work or fleeing war or oppression, the situation is very different. He argues that the demonising of the second group of migrants misrepresents their positive contributions to the communities in which they settle. Savitri Hensman reflects on the richness migrants bring to our culture, reminding us that the Bible frequently makes clear that we have a duty to welcome refugees and strangers. She outlines a positive vision for how we might fulfil this obligation, which not only means ensuring better treatment of migrants, but also tackles the fears that people may have about immigration.

These are followed by two essays focusing on the environment. Ellen Teague lays out the threats the Anthropocene age pose to the life of the planet, threats that include climate change, extraction industries and nuclear weapons. She outlines how Christians and people of all faiths and none are working to save our environment for future generations. Edward P. Echlin reflects on how we can enact the common good when we recognise we are living in a bioregion and have a responsibility to consider the environmental impact of our activities. He describes how focusing on the 'Joy of Enough' helps us make sustainable lifestyle choices and live more simply.

Finally, we turn to issues of peace and security. While war can never be seen as being part of the common good, the 'just war theory' has been an attempt to conduct war in a moral way. In a very personal essay, Henrietta Cullinan discusses the implications of just war theory, before exploring the impact of war on the people of Afghanistan, the costs of Trident and the effect of drones. She concludes that rather than succumbing to a modern vision of 'the forever war' we need to respond to the Pope's call to live lives of active nonviolence. Susan Clarkson demonstrates how such lives are possible, through the examples of two inspiring communities. She describes the work of the Catholic Worker Movement, and the Centre for Creative Nonviolence in Afghanistan, both of which provide a challenging and hopeful vision for a more peaceful world.

The final section, 'Our Mission', suggests how Christians might take these ideas forward. In his essay, 'A new Jerusalem: building a vision for the common good', Simon Woodman explores the book of Revelation and the metaphor of 'new Jerusalem'. Although there are a number of ways to read this (some controversial in the light of the ongoing conflict in Israel/Palestine) Simon's interpretation is as an image for the Church Militant. This is designed to challenge us to choose whether to live as citizens of Babylon (Rome) or new Jerusalem (the Church). So in this way it is not a gift that comes from God in the future, but a vision of the people of God living in the present under the rule of Christ. In a previous essay, Simon states:

> It is significant that the new Jerusalem is seen by John descending from heaven, with this image carrying a rhetorical function which is not usually noted. Having initially drawn his audience through the open door into the heavenly realm (Rev. 4.1), John has shown them heaven's perspective on their earthly situation. Here at the end of his visionary work, he returns them back to the earth as the new Jerusalem, transformed through their participation in his symbolic scheme (Woodman 2008: 235–6). Having experienced John's representations of the divine judgments on the satanic empire, and having seen both the effects of empire and its ultimate fate, John's audience find that when they return from the heavenly vision to the earth, everything is different. No longer do they look at the empire which surrounds them and see strength, beauty and righteousness; rather, they see weakness, corruption and judgment. Those who witness the vision of the burning of Babylon become those who are already living the proleptic reality of the new creation, because they have been freed from their ideological slavery to Babylon. John's vision of the new heaven and earth therefore has a timeless aspect to it, with the one seated on the throne declaring in the present tense 'see, I am making all things new.'          (21.5; cf. Isa. 43.19)

This vision of the new heaven and the new earth, with the new Jerusalem at their centre, is therefore primarily a vision for the here-and-now of John's audience. It presents

them with a challenge that they are to be those who give
testimony to the in-breaking kingdom of God, those who
live as citizens of new Jerusalem rather than as citizens of
Babylon. The renewal of the created order is therefore not
solely something to be anticipated at some decisive point
in the future, as the divine answer to the environmental
destructions wrought by empire. Rather, it is to be found
in the present as the idolatrous claims of the satanic empire
are exposed, opposed and rejected, and as humanity
responds to the prophetic witness to the existence of an
alternative to slavish devotion to the beast of empire.'[8]

In other words, 'new Jerusalem' is a vision for an alternative reality
brought into being by people working for the common good. It is not
the first time that this metaphor has been invoked by those wishing
to ensure social change. I was pleased to discover as we were putting
these essays together that in the 1940s both Winston Churchill[9] and
Clement Attlee[10] were also inspired by the idea of a 'new Jerusalem',
as they attempted to rebuild post-war Britain. In this modern age of
austerity, mass migration, environmental concerns and threats of war,
and in the light of the 2017 General Election, it seems entirely fitting
that we revisit this idea to help us re-imagine the world in which
we live.

The image of new Jerusalem has also inspired our choice of front
cover. In 1993, I was working in South London for a charity supporting
adults with learning disabilities (formerly Southwark Consortium,
now Choice Support). A colleague of mine, Gaby Mitchell, had a role
coordinating community projects, and commissioned a local artist,
Stan Peskett, to create a mural on the side of one of the houses that
Choice Support manages. The house is close to Peckham Rye, where
the poet and artist William Blake once had a vision of the new heaven
and new earth described in the book of Revelation. Stan chose this
theme for his mural, and over a bank holiday weekend worked with
local community members, adults, children and people with learning
disabilities, to create a stunning piece of art that is still there today. It
seems to me that both the image (with its beautiful oak tree, a symbol
of the healing of the nations, as noted in Simon Woodman's closing
chapter) and the event itself, sum up exactly the message of this book.
The local community came together with a common purpose, creating

a beautiful work of art that can be enjoyed by all, and still brightens the area today, a vision of hope in troubled times.

Of course, in a book like this, there will inevitably be omissions. There was not room to include essays on the economy and a debate as to whether capitalism is dead [11] or needs reformation. Nor was there a chance to discuss specific sectors such as health and education in more detail. The impact of Brexit and Donald Trump's presidency are both subjects that could fill a book of their own, as is the importance of standing in solidarity with oppressed groups, disabled people, people of colour, the LGBTQI community and women, in their continuing struggles for equality. Despite these omissions, it is our hope that *Reclaiming the Common Good* will inform, challenge and inspire readers, so that together we can reclaim the common good for a better today and brighter tomorrow.

## Notes

1.  W. H. Fremantle, 'The world as the subject of redemption: being an attempt to set forth the functions of the church as designed to embrace the whole race of mankind', eight lectures delivered before the University of Oxford in the year 1883 on the foundation of the late Rev. John Bampton MA, Canon of Salisbury (New York: Longmans Green, 1895).

2.  Bishops' Conference of England and Wales, *Choosing the Common Good* (Stoke on Trent: Alive Publishing, 2010).

3.  The National Justice and Peace Conference is held each year at Swanwick Conference Centre. The title of the July 2016 conference was 'Democracy and the Common Good'.

4.  The Greenbelt Arts Festival, takes place each year at Boughton House, Northamptonshire. The theme of the 2017 conference is 'The Common Good'.

5.  Together for Common Good website, http://www.togetherforthecommongood.co.uk/

6.  Nicholas Sagovsky and Peter McGrail (eds), *Together for Common Good: Towards a national conversation* (London: SCM Press, 2015)

7.  Hilary Russell, *A Faithful Presence: Working for the common good* (London: SCM Press, 2015).

8.  Simon Woodman, 'Can the Book of Revelation be a gospel for the environment?' in Matthew J. M. Coomber (ed.), *Bible and Justice: Ancient texts, modern challenges* (Chesham, Bucks: Equinox Press, 2011), pp. 189–90.

9.  Sir Michael Barber, 'Rab Butler's 1944 Act brings free education for all', BBC website, 17 January 2014, http://www.bbc.co.uk/schoolreport/25751787

10. John Bew, 'Clement Attlee: an unromantic hero', *New Statesman*, 26 September 2013.

11. Paul Mason, *Postcapitalism: A guide to our future* (London: Allen Lane, 2015).

# PART 1

# WHAT IS THE COMMON GOOD?

# 1. The History and Principles of the Common Good

## Patrick Riordan SJ

How can we talk meaningfully about common goods in a world which provides so much evidence of the absence of goods in common and of commitment to shared projects? Is it unrealistic to reflect on the common good where the reality of our lives is diversity, plurality, disagreement and conflict? My task in this chapter is to address this question, and to do so by recovering the principles and criteria of the common good as these have been discovered and articulated in human history. It will only be possible to pick out some significant moments from over two thousand years of human experience and political, philosophical and theological reflection on the common good. I focus on four: Aristotle, the first thinker to link politics and the common good; medieval Christianity, which used Aristotle's language to say something he could not have understood; modernity, which rejected the Aristotelian and Christian agreement that there is an ultimate good in common; and finally twentieth-century Catholic Social Thought.

### Aristotle

The notion of common good is originally philosophical, introduced by Aristotle in his *Politics*. As Aristotle sees it, human action is always for some good, or something that is perceived to be good. The maker of flutes sees something worthwhile in the product, in enabling good and beautiful music, and allowing the excellence of the performer to appear. Flute maker and flute player cooperate: they act together for a good in common. Among the goods at stake in their activity is their own perfection and excellence, even if they don't think about this. Aristotle is aware that there are many instances of cooperation, and many organisations and institutions facilitating collaboration, whether business, sporting, cultural or religious, each of which has its distinctive activities oriented to their various purposes, constituting their common goods. For him, then, common good is not only or primarily designated in the singular as *the* common good. There are as many common goods as there are forms of cooperation. For him also there remains always a valid question whether the good pursued in collaboration by some people is a genuine good, and whether it is truly for their good, i.e. that its achievement would accomplish their excellence or perfection. For instance, the pirates of Somalia cooperate for their good in common, but is enrichment achieved through theft really good, and does it make them better or excellent people?

Aristotle introduces the singular, with definite article when discussing the good for the sake of which the political community cooperates. Against the background of the Greek city state such as Athens he considers that the highest possible good of cooperation which best perfects the collaborators is the good achieved in politics. As the city is taken to represent the highest possible form of cooperation, so its good is taken to be the highest possible good. Aristotle labels *the* common good as 'the good life'. This is beyond survival, life itself, for which much cooperation is needed. In trying to say what exactly constitutes the good life, Aristotle relies on a contrast with alternative views of politics. The political association is more than a set of non-aggression pacts, it is more than a mutual guarantee of rights, and it is more than a set of contracts for the exchange of goods and services, all possible forms of association recognised in his day. But what that 'more' is, Aristotle does not explain in detail. However, he does provide some pointers which allow us to understand in outline what he means. He points out that communities based on non-aggression or mutual benefit in trade are not interested in fostering the character and virtue of the citizens of partner cities. But in the mature political community which he advocates, the legislators in pursuing the common good would be primarily concerned about the moral development of citizens, and would make laws with the purpose of training the citizens in virtue. By 'virtue' Aristotle means the capacity for noble actions, for excellence in the performance of distinctive human actions, among which he lists the activities of friendship and the doing of justice as a member of the citizen body. The context whereby only native-born male property owners could be included among this group reminds us that the virtues in question are very different from those of medieval Christianity.

Aristotle had surveyed the constitutions known in his world, and he was quite aware that few of them if any lived up to the high standards he had formulated for the common good. In every case, however, a constitution of a city encapsulated some conception of the good, and of the good life. The basis for political community, he believes, is the sharing of a view of what is good and worthwhile, what is noble and just, and what is lawful. Without agreement on such fundamentals, an association of people would not constitute a political community. Just as we could hardly imagine a tennis club without a commitment by its members to the sport of tennis, so also he thought, we could not conceive of a *polis* without agreement among its citizens about the shared vision of the good life. Harmony and agreement are at the heart of his account of the common good. Still Aristotle conceded that there are many possible conceptions of the good life, each with its own characteristic form of constitution, and a corresponding criterion of justice. So for instance, in oligarchy, the unifying vision regards the good life as a life devoted to the pursuit and enjoyment of wealth. In a city like Sparta, renowned for its military prowess, the characteristic virtues to be fostered in the citizenry are military virtues.

Aristotle enquires whether rule is exercised for the common good, the good of all, or only for the good of the rulers. This allows him to distinguish between good and bad extremes. Rule by one for the common good is termed monarchy; rule by one in the interest of the ruler only is tyranny. Aristotle's objection to democracy as he understands the term is that it is rule by the many in their own interests, and not in the interests of all.

It is possible to formulate two criteria for the common good, based on Aristotle's own distinctions. If the *telos*, the purpose of the political community, is to be a *common* good, then it could only be such if it does not systematically exclude any individual or any group of persons from a fair share in the good for the sake of which they cooperate. This is the first criterion, modelled on Aristotle's concern that rule be for the good of all, and not merely for the good of the rulers, whether one, few, or many. And if the *telos* is to be a common *good*, then it could only be such if it does not systematically exclude or denigrate any genuine dimension of the human good. This second criterion is modelled on Aristotle's evaluation of different constitutions in terms of their conceptions of human good, whether expansive or constricted.

...relied on the phrase translated as 'always more than' to identify the conception of the human good which would be satisfactory and comprehensive without being able to say exactly what it is. It is something striven for in political life; it would be more than a mutual guarantee of rights, or a set of non-aggression pacts, or treaties to exchange goods and services. The common good, the good life in Aristotle's sense, names something which is already known, but only vaguely. It names something yet to be fully discovered, but the two criteria help in the process of discovery, since the common good will have to satisfy these conditions.

Many aspects of Aristotle's view seem to be incompatible with politics today. The expectation of harmony and agreement about the good is at odds with our experience of politics as predicated on conflict. His expectation that the law-makers in his city should be concerned about the moral training of citizens would be rejected in our context in which individual autonomy is highly valued, and the attempt to legislate morals is dismissed as paternalism. Similarly, the notion that human fulfilment is achieved by participating in politics and that such fulfilment is the ultimate human good would likewise be rejected in our time as jeopardising individual freedom. However, Aristotle's discussion is sufficiently programmatic that elements of it can survive to guide our discussion of other conceptions of the common good. The key ideas are the heuristic nature of the concept, pointing to what is only partly known and still in the process of being discovered, and the two criteria of non-exclusion of persons and the non-exclusion of dimensions of the human good. Incidentally, it is the application of these two criteria to Aristotle's own thought which allows for the correction of his prejudices.

## Medieval Christianity

The reception of Aristotle's philosophy within Christian theology provoked many new questions for believers. What is the common good of Christians? Is it the same as the common good of all humanity? Is the Church's common good the same as the common good of the political community, and if not, how are they related? This was not the first time that the Christian faith was confronted with Greek philosophy. In his letters St Paul draws on the common stock of Stoic philosophy especially with relation to political matters in characterising the new community he was instrumental in founding and organising. In the Letter to the Philippians Paul borrows Stoic ideas to explain what is involved in the Christian life. It is a life which has a goal, and that goal is to be a participant in an ideal community, and Jesus is the model for all who strive for this goal. Paul writes: 'our commonwealth is in heaven, and from it we await a Saviour, the Lord Jesus Christ, who will change our lowly body to be like his glorious body, by the power which enables him even to subject all things to himself' (Philippeans 3:20–21). The Greek word which is translated in the Revised Standard Version as 'commonwealth' is *to politeuma*, which has at its root the idea of *polis*, or city, political society. Sometimes it is translated as 'citizenship', giving 'our citizenship is in heaven'. Paul borrows the Stoic idea of an ideal community transcending the actual and inadequate and failing communities in history to explain what the community of the faithful is, a society by analogy with an ideal city. He borrows other popular teachings, retaining their form and giving them new content. He reworks the traditional political concepts of *oikos* (household), *polis* (polity) and *basileia* (kingdom).

These terms are the conventional ones used for speaking about political reality, even after the forms in which they originated had ceased to exist. Still, with the memory of how the Greek city state functioned with its assembly of citizens, the language was available for Paul to give new meaning to *ekklesia*, the assembly, now referring not to the gathering of citizens of Rome, or of Athens, but to the citizens of a new *polis*, gathered in the houses of the Roman believers (Romans 16:5). This Greek word, originally purely political in meaning, has through its adoption by Paul and its usage through the centuries become the Latin term for Church, *ekklesia*, and survives in the English word ecclesiastic, and related terms.

The Letter to the Ephesians is Pauline in tone and content even if it may not have been written by Paul. But it relies on the familiar Greek political terms to explain to the Gentile converts their membership as believers in the community of the Church. 'So then you are no longer strangers and sojourners but you are fellow citizens with the saints and members of the household of God' (Ephesians 2:19). The theme of unity in the Body of Christ is important in this letter and the implied equality of all within the community, in which Gentiles or latecomers are on equal terms with Jewish converts, a theme of equality resonating elsewhere in Paul's writings (Galatians 3:28).

Many of the terms used by Paul such as household, city, kingdom, polity and assembly had been used by Aristotle in his *Politics*. And when his writings were rediscovered in the thirteenth century Christian theologians realised that they had to distinguish clearly between the Greek conception and the Christian vision of the common good. The clarity of Aristotle's thought made it very useful for saying how the Christian understanding of the common good differed from Aristotle's even if Aristotle's own language was the best suited for doing so.

Aristotle maintained that the highest good of cooperation was that achieved in the *polis*, the political community. Christians following the example of St Paul writing to the Philippians would have to deny this, and offer their view that as God is the highest good, so for humankind the attainment of heaven is the highest good. This is already the reality of Christian existence in history, that believers seeing themselves as citizens of that heavenly city are on their way as pilgrims to a destiny offered to them as gift, as grace. A political system which claimed to be the highest good of human cooperation would have to appear as idolatrous for Christians, claiming for itself something which only the Kingdom of God could be.

The moral purpose of politics and legislation according to Aristotle was of course attractive to Christian believers, but following Augustine they had to deny that human instruments on their own could make people good. The unsuitability of the state as moral educator was first remarked by Augustine in his *The City of God*. This fifth-century document can be taken as representing the abandonment of the classical expectation of moral consensus as found in Aristotle. Unlike the Greek philosophers who hoped for harmony and unity, Augustine expects the political arena to be conflictual. He explains this in terms of the radical tension throughout all of human affairs between the 'City of God' and the 'earthly city'.[1] The radical disorder brought about by the rebellious assertion of human will means that human action and human structures are largely motivated by the *libido dominandi*, the desire to dominate others, and by the pride whereby one seeks to make a name for oneself and achieve a place in posterity by successful participation in the affairs of one's city. As a result, the status of the political community was relativised. It was no longer to be seen as the forum in which the common good or the supreme good would be pursued and achieved; only in the context of the City of God, in Augustine's sense, could the highest good for humans be realised. The most that political institutions could hope to achieve is an inferior good, which Augustine refers to as 'temporal peace and justice'. But while this good of security and civil peace might be seen as an inferior good it was nonetheless truly good and a common good for all those who would participate in maintaining and indeed benefiting from political community.

That only God by his grace could make people good required a rejection of some of Aristotle's key ideas. In the place of Aristotle's magnanimous great-souled man, the Christian saw the figure of the broken and suffering Christ as the model of virtue. The Greeks could never conceive of humility as a virtue, but for Christian believers it was central to their discipleship, in lives modelled on Christ.

Thomas Aquinas attempted to integrate his Christian heritage in which Augustine was the outstanding teacher with Aristotelian reflection on political reality. The success of his achievement is illustrated in the discussion of the purpose of civil law, and whether it is to make people good, as Aristotle says, or to control and limit the destructiveness of sin, as Augustine suggests. Aquinas manages to combine the insights of his two authorities, accepting both that the law's purpose is to make people good, and that the law is an instrument of control for the purposes of social peace. This he does by qualifying the goodness which is the proper object of *humanas* distinct from God's law. Agreeing with Augustine he recognises that the goodness of citizens which can be achieved by means of human law is not their ultimate good, but is nonetheless truly good. This distinction is evident in his discussion of the effects of law. He admits that law makes its subjects good: 'the proper effect of law is to make those to whom it is given good, either simply or in some particular respect'.[2] In response to an objection he clarifies what might be the particular respects in which citizens are to be good. Outward compliance might be sufficient to qualify as good in terms of the civil law, but it could not suffice to qualify as morally virtuous. 'The common good of the political community cannot flourish unless the citizens be virtuous, at least those whose business it is to govern. But it is enough for the good of the community that the other citizens be so far virtuous that they obey the commands of their rulers.'[3] It is quite acceptable to Aquinas that this be achieved by means of the coercive force of the civil law, even if there are many citizens who can be law-abiding without the threat of punishment. For them the directive force of the law is what guides their actions.

> Since some are found to be depraved and prone to vice and
> not easily amenable to words, it was necessary for such
> to be restrained from evil by force and fear in order that
> they might at least desist from evil-doing and leave others
> in peace, and that they themselves, by being habituated
> in this way, might be brought to do willingly what
> hitherto they did from fear and thus become virtuous.
> Now this kind of training which compels through fear of
> punishment is the discipline of laws.[4]

With this and similar distinctions between the goodness which is the
aim of divine law (the commandments, the law of love) Aquinas can
speak of different common goods. The common good of any political
community, including its peace, stability and well-being, is to be
served by its civil laws, but inevitably it is limited as a common good
for two reasons: the deficiencies of the authorities, and the inadequacy
of the means. Human rulers lack the knowledge and the competence
needed to guide people towards their divine destiny, something only
possible by God-given grace. And the instruments of human law-
making and judgement cannot look into the hearts of people but can
only observe and so condition external behaviour. But it is the turning
of the heart, the love with which the good is done, which signifies for
the Kingdom of God the ultimate common good.

The ideas borrowed from Aristotle served well to present the
Christian vision in terms of common goods. In contrast to Aristotle,
who saw the ultimate common good as realisable in a political
community in history, Aquinas, following Augustine, saw the ultimate
common good as the Kingdom of God, already present through
history, but realised fully only beyond history. At the same time, the
notion of common good which Aristotle could see as applicable to all
forms of cooperation – action together is for some good in common
– allowed Aquinas and his contemporaries to acknowledge the
distinctive common good of the political community, without having
to endorse it as the highest possible good in common.

## Common good in modernity

Armed conflict between proponents of different ultimate goods
provides the background to the usual story of the emergence of
liberal political thought in the modern period. The political turmoil

of the period led to the assertion of the sovereignty of the state, and ultimately the national state. Sovereignty meant the denial of any higher authority, whether in Church or Empire, so that political rulers were not to acknowledge any higher common good than that which was achievable in their politics. Even religious and moral law should be subject to their authority.

This was a central argument of Thomas Hobbes, the English philosopher who formulated the purpose of the state (he called it commonwealth) in his writings, especially *Leviathan*. He explicitly denied that there could be any agreement on what was good in itself, or a common good as truly worthwhile. In fact, he is responsible for establishing the idea, which has survived him in much of modern and postmodern thought, that to say something is good is not to say anything about the thing in question, but about the speaker or agent who strives for that thing. If I say that Shakespeare is a good dramatist, then, according to Hobbes, that means that I like and value Shakespeare, but it doesn't tell you anything about the Bard. In the absence of agreement on what is good, society could only exist and be stable if sovereign authority would establish and enforce public order. For Hobbes anyone would have an interest in having such a system of law and order since it would provide them with the security to get on with their lives and pursue whatever it was that they thought worthwhile. Such a system would be vulnerable to disruption by enthusiastic religious preachers and so Hobbes insisted that the civil authorities would have to vet such teachers and only license those to preach and function whose doctrine would not disturb the public peace.

The logical structure of Hobbes's system draws the focus away from ultimate ends or common goods and directs it towards the necessary means. People want different things from life, but everyone wants to have the means which will enable him or her to pursue their goals without interference from others. Those means will include liberties and security from murder and theft, and for these appropriate structures of civil authority and law enforcement can be supported. In a sense, one could say that the common good in this way of thinking is not an end but a means, or condition for the pursuit of the end. But Hobbes would warn us against thinking that the means as good is in some sense truly good, or valuable in itself, or that it could not be replaced by alternative means which could also be effective.

John Locke was another important political thinker who, like Hobbes, shaped modernity, in England and America, as well as in Europe. Although usually positively compared to Hobbes for his more optimistic view of human nature and for his advocacy of limited government, the structure of his argument is similar to that of Hobbes. Like him, Locke focuses on the political and legal instruments which are required to enable individuals with their families to pursue their own interests. The major difference is that Locke has a more expansive account of those interests. Where Hobbes emphasises security, Locke articulates the natural rights to life, liberty and possessions, which, as moral claims, also limit the legitimate authority of political rulers. The similarity of their thought is that the basis for agreement in society (recall Aristotle's idea that it is agreement on what is good which makes a political community) is commitment to secure the means or conditions allowing individuals to pursue their own good as they conceive of it.

John Stuart Mill's renowned defence of liberty, at the heart of our inherited respect for the freedom of speech, denies the entitlement of public authorities to regulate behaviour for the good of people, or in that sense for the common good. Unlike his predecessors Mill was aware of the importance of fostering a public debate about the human good, what he called utility in the broadest sense, as the interests of humans as progressive beings capable of development. However, this aspect of his thought has been neglected and he continues to be read as a defender of individuals' freedoms in the face of possible constraints, both social and political, imposed in the name of a common good.

The key structure in modern thinking of seeking agreement on means rather than ends and so avoiding discussion of an ultimate common good is found in the writings of the most influential twentieth-century political philosopher, John Rawls. In his various publications, on justice within a state (*A Theory of Justice*, 1971), on politics in a pluralist society (*Political Liberalism*, 1986) and justice in international relations (*The Law of Peoples*, 1999), Rawls argues for the relevant structures by appealing to what people would choose to have as means and conditions, whatever their ultimate goods might happen to be. But while the focus is on means, and avoids considering the good as such, much less the common good, it is noticeable that there is a trajectory in the thought of modern thinkers summarised here in the series Hobbes, Locke, Mill and Rawls. There is an increasing appreciation of what is involved in providing the means and conditions for people to pursue their good alongside an acceptance that it is not within the competence of a state either to decide what the ultimate good for people consists in, or to act to achieve such an ultimate good.

## Catholic Social Thought

The modern denial of an ultimate common good as a basis for politics was anticipated in the Christian and medieval rejection of Aristotle's idea that the political community could attain the highest good. The recognition that the civil community had its own common good, more restricted than that of the Kingdom of God, left open how exactly the basis of agreement for the political community could be formulated. For Christians, however, for whom both kinds of common good continued to be important, the question remained as to how the two could be combined. This challenge was taken up in a major way by the Second Vatican Council in the Catholic Church in the 1960s.

The disciples of Jesus believe that following him through death to resurrection they are invited to enjoy the vision of God in the company of all the saints. What exactly this will be like we cannot know, beyond the assurance that it will exceed our wildest dreams (1 Corinthians 2:9). Christian writers have tended to concentrate on the shadow side, the problems that will be solved, the injustices that will be resolved, the poverty and deprivation that will be overcome in abundance. The images from the Hebrew Scriptures also stress the dynamic of deliverance from slavery and subjection in Egypt and of return from exile in Babylon. More positively, images of banquets and abundance, and of vindication and justice are also mined from these Scriptures to communicate the hope of Christians.

In announcing a common good, Christian writers have named this as the shared goal of all of God's children, to see the Lord face to face in heaven, to receive and enjoy salvation. St Paul reminded his friend Timothy and the readers of his letters that it is God's will that all people be saved (1 Timothy 2:4). That is the destiny offered to all men, women and children, and which they are invited to accept in freedom. The Second Vatican Council in its 'Dogmatic Constitution on the Church', *Lumen gentium*, repeated this promise and situated the mission of the Church in this context: to communicate the universal call of all to holiness, and to assist in providing the resources that Jesus makes available to his pilgrim people on their way to this destiny.

This reformulation of Paul's message contains the same elements: it is offered to all, everyone without exception, and it is based on a promise which requires confidence and trust in the one promising rather than detailed comprehension of what is promised.

In Christian tradition the supreme common good was identified as God, and the vision of God, the ultimate goal of Christian striving and the fullness of life prepared by the Creator for his creatures. It is noticeable, however, that in the twentieth century, beginning with Pope John XXIII's encyclical letter *Mater et magistra*, 'Mother and Teacher' (1961), the common good came to be used in speaking not primarily of the ultimate goal of human striving, but of the conditions and resources that would facilitate the achievement of that purpose. The point of the shift of emphasis became clearer in the context of the general realignment of Catholic thought in the mid-twentieth century. The Church saw the need to shift from a defensive and fearful stance to a more positive engagement with the world. As the opening words of *Gaudium et spes*, the 'Pastoral Constitution on the Church in the World of Today' put it, the Church identifies herself with and shares in 'the joy and hope, fear and anxiety of the men and women of today'. The Council wanted to address all men and women, and not just believers in Christ, or in God, but all, including atheists. Hence the recognition that while all of these addressees will not share the same ultimate vision, they might nonetheless be able to agree on what conditions and resources would help people achieve their vision of the good life, whatever it might be. 'The common good embraces the sum total of all those conditions of social life which enable individuals, families, and organisations to achieve complete and effective fulfilment' (*Gaudium et spes* §74).

Published in 1965, the Pastoral Constitution draws on the earlier language of Pope John's encyclical to focus on the set of conditions for human fulfilment. Undeniably the theme of fulfilment both for individuals and for communities is at the heart of the statement, but the focus is on conditions. Here we see the opening to the world of the Council: the desire to have a basis for cooperation with people of good will, who might not share in the Church's ultimate convictions but still can be partners in working for human development.

The full set of conditions which would enable persons and groups to achieve their fulfilment is what the Council sees as the common project of humankind. This extends across the full range of human activities and human aspirations. No list, however long, would be exhaustive, and that is not just because it is hard to think of everything. It is also because human ingenuity is constantly creating new possibilities and so new conditions, coming up with new fields of endeavour, new areas of scientific exploration and new possibilities of medical and surgical intervention and care. Accordingly, the complete set of conditions for human flourishing, including economic, social, cultural, legal, political, international and global, reveal how complex the challenge is. And in each of these areas we can expect lively debate about what needs to be done.

One such debate concerns workers. Since the engagement of Pope Leo XIII with the phenomenon of modern capitalist economic systems in *Rerum novarum* (1891) the popes have repeated the insistence that human work not be treated just as a factor of production which has a cost, a cost which employers are constantly motivated to minimise. Workers are persons who by their willing cooperation contribute to the communal projects of meeting human need and providing the cultivated, manufactured and built environment in which human life can flourish. Culminating in the letter of Pope John Paul II explicitly devoted to the topic of work, *Laborem exercens*, 'On Human Work' (1981), the popes have maintained a constant insistence that work and the status of the worker is at the heart of the social question. Unemployment, the lack of opportunity to work, is fundamentally undermining of the sense of dignity and self-worth of human beings, who rely on their work to provide for their families and who without the earnings that come from honest work are unable to meet their obligations. Now in the twenty-first century a new term, 'the precariat', has been coined to identify the phenomenon that increasing numbers of people in employment are unable to earn sufficient to meet their needs, and that in the context of widening inequality between the extremes of wealth and poverty. This is clear evidence of the absence of a common good in the economy, in which enormous wealth for some is produced alongside poverty for many others.

Such a scandalous situation calls for solidarity. Pope John Paul II wrote in his encyclical letter *Sollicitudo rei socialis*, 'On Social Concern' (1987), that solidarity 'is not a feeling of vague compassion or shallow distress at the misfortunes of so many people, both near and far. On the contrary, it is a firm and persevering determination to commit oneself to the common good; that is to say to the good of all and of each individual, because we are all really responsible for all' (*Sollicitudo res socialis* §38). Pope John Paul is clear about the need on the part of the Church and all Christians for a firm commitment to changing the circumstances which deprive people of their humanity and deny them the prospect of a decent life. In the Catholic tradition of upholding the common good the focus can be directly on those groups which are vulnerable to exploitation or discrimination. Hence the adoption of the language of preferential option for the poor. The Church wants to place itself at the side of those who are victims, who suffer, who bear a disproportionate burden either as a result of natural catastrophe or human irresponsibility.

Solidarity is paired with another important principle related to the common good, namely, subsidiarity. The principle of subsidiarity insists that assistance motivated by solidarity should not replace the efforts of recipients themselves to address their problems and find solutions. It entails a willingness to help, with an expectation that those being helped take responsibility to find and implement their own solutions to their problems. In a hierarchically structured governance system the principle of subsidiarity requires that the higher level authorities assist but do not replace those operating on the ground. This is opposed to all centralising tendencies which are inclined to draw all power to the centre of institutions or organisations, depriving the so-called grass roots of opportunities to manage their own affairs. Of course, it should apply to the Church itself also.

In his 2009 encyclical letter, *Caritas in veritate*, 'Love in Truth', Pope Benedict writes: '*The principle of subsidiarity must remain closely linked to the principle of solidarity and vice versa*, since the former without the latter gives way to social privatism, while the latter without the former gives way to paternalist social assistance that is demeaning to those in need'. By 'social privatism' Benedict means the attitude that everyone should be left alone to mind their own business, and by its opposite, 'paternalistic social assistance', he means the paternalistic attitude of acting on the assumption that one knows what is best for others. This statement is made originally in the context of reflection on international development aid. There are two important values which are to be respected, and disregard of one in favour of the other can lead to distorting or objectionable outcomes.

## Conclusion

This brief survey of the notion of common good reveals the diversity of meanings for the term. Some use it to speak of an ultimate good in common, but among those Aristotle locates that good within the political while Augustine and Aquinas and recent popes locate it in the Kingdom of God, the fulfilment of which is beyond history. However, in both cases there is something heuristic about the term, since the advocates of both the immanent and transcendent visions of common good are unable to say exactly what the ultimate common good consists of. On the other hand, there are modern voices which deny an ultimate good in common whether immanent or transcendent. Their focus for agreement in political life is on the necessary conditions for a secure and stable system. Only means or conditions can suffice as common good in the political context. The distinction between the common good as end and common good as means does not require a separation or polarisation. Both the medieval Christians and recent Catholic Social Teaching combine the two. It is assumed that every individual and every group espouses some view of their well-being, either implicitly or explicitly. While in our pluralist situation there is unlikely to be agreement between people and cultures as to what exactly constitutes human fulfilment, we may perhaps be able to work towards agreement on the whole range of means and conditions we need to put in place to enable persons and their communities to thrive. We can formulate criteria in relation to those conditions for fulfilment. Pope Paul VI in his 1967 letter *Populorum progressio*, 'On the Development of Peoples', succinctly summarised the common good as 'the integral development of every person, and of the whole person'. The fulfilment of every person: that's the first criterion that no one be excluded; integral fulfilment of the whole person: that's the second criterion, that no dimension of human well-being be systematically excluded from our shared concerns in social collaboration. These criteria can also be identified in the principles of solidarity and subsidiarity. Solidarity, that we commit to the cause of those excluded, and subsidiarity, that in the name of caring for them we don't deprive people or groups of their autonomy.

## Questions

- Does Aristotle's idea of the common good of politics presuppose that everybody agrees on the common purpose?
- Is the political common good to be identified with the highest common good?

- Can people committed to common goods cooperate with fellow citizens who deny any goods in common?
- What common ground can people who are divided by their faith or ultimate commitments find for cooperative political engagement?

## Notes

1.  St Augustine, *The City of God*, ed. David Knowles (Harmondsworth: Penguin, 1972). Cf. also: R. A. Markus, *Saeculum: History and Society in the Theology of St Augustine* (Cambridge: Cambridge University Press, 1970).
2.  Thomas Aquinas, *Summa Theologiae*, part II–II question 92, article 1.
3.  Thomas Aquinas, *Summa Theologiae*, part II–II question 92, article 1, response to 3rd objection.
4.  Thomas Aquinas, *Summa Theologiae*, part II–II question 95, article 1. http:// w2.vatican.va/content/benedict-xvi/en/encyclicals/documents/hf_ben-xvi_enc_20090629_caritas-in-veritate.html §58, emphasis in original.

# PART 2

# SERVICE AND SOCIETY

# 2. Whatever Happened to the Commmon Good?

## John Moffatt SJ

Andrew Marr has this to say about Clement Attlee's Labour government of 1945–51:

> It created the national health service. It brought in welfare payments and state insurance 'from the cradle to the grave'. It nationalized the Bank of England, the coal industry, which was then responsible for 90% of Britain's energy needs, and eventually the iron and steel industry too...[1]

Add housing, feeding, dismantling an empire and a war machine (though they did develop an atomic bomb), the astonishing list goes on, and all against the background of a near-terminal financial crisis. Here we have an exemplary case of government working for the common good.

And now? Well, we have had seventy years of the welfare state. Most of these have been years of economic growth. So why are there an increasing number of homeless people among the glittering new buildings owned by the super-rich – whose employees fetch and carry for them on zero-hours contracts, unprotected by union or by law? Why, when you walk past foodbanks or boarded-up shop fronts, do you hear stories of disabled people driven to suicide by the profit-making company subsidised by government to process their claims 'efficiently'? And while politicians of Left and Right retire into lucrative consultancies or directorships, why does an ugly, xenophobic public discourse distract the victims of austerity policies from the true authors of their misery?

It is important not to over-romanticise the past – or to over-demonise the present. Though a significant number of people live in very harsh circumstances in modern Britain, though working life is becoming harder and more precarious for many more and though inequalities of income and assets are rising fast, few of us (I suggest) would want to return to the Britain of 1945 and the years of post-war austerity. Nevertheless it feels as though something important has been lost. Hence our question: whatever happened to the common good?

## Find myself a city to live in

We could begin by asking, what exactly *is* this common good that we have lost? But those of you who have read Patrick Riordan's article[2] will recognise that a question about 'exactly' is misplaced. 'The common good' isn't an 'exactly' kind of thing. A better way of thinking about it is as a guiding idea, drawn from our existing experience, that tells us where to look. It is a notion that we recognise when we see it incarnated in political reality. It's a little bit like the term 'great art' in that respect. As there are multiple ways of realising 'great art', so too 'the common good', reflects the multiple ways we humans can organise our lives together and the varying conditions under which we have to do so.

The starting point, then, for understanding the sort of thing we are looking for, is to think about human organisations or societies. Patrick has explained how Aristotle (one of the key sources for the language of common good) took as his frame of reference city states, the standard political unit of the eastern Mediterranean in his day. They were tiny in comparison with modern mega-cities, let alone nation states. But for Aristotle, they were the minimum units that allowed human communities to be self-sufficient. The combination of activities, from farming, to fishing, to trade and from political administration to land management created the conditions for each citizen to flourish within his sphere of activity – trade and family life. However, for Aristotle it is not just about trade. His common good is achieved when the city's members live well in every sense, when they flourish materially *and* ethically in a society held together with ties of friendship and shared value.

Patrick Riordan has elsewhere[3] teased the picture out with the modern example of a university. I would like to play with that idea a little. Universities have a sort of self-sufficiency – people eat, work, live within their confines. There is a great diversity of activity needed to make a university work, from teaching, researching, leading, to repairing, cooking and cleaning. Those who are part of it can take institutional pride in doing their bit, without having to understand every vital function or activity – without, usually, having much of a voice in the decision-making that affects the whole. There are of course disputes, squabbles, rivalries, but so long as most people are happy to get up and go to work in the morning, students learn, lecturers are stimulating, research is innovative, the paint on the walls is fresh, any visitor walking around and dipping in will recognise the place to be flourishing. Most people are performing their different activities willingly and well, and thus contributing to the flourishing of all.

Such an institution has its 'tone'. Where relationships are stable and defined by trust, loyalty and mutuality, organisations can feel good to be in and that in itself is part of the flourishing. But things can go wrong. Some people get ill or stop pulling their weight. Some leaders handle delicate situations badly. New demands for efficiency conflict with traditions of institutional friendship. The tone changes – and with it the quality of the organisation's flourishing. Anyone who has worked in state-sector organisations over the last forty years may recognise some of these elements. They usefully draw our attention to the flourishing of individuals in what I want to call their 'ecotopes'.

## Ecotopes

By 'ecotope' I mean industries considered as a working environment together with dependencies. It could include small-scale industries conducted by a large number of independent, widely scattered people, like pop-up kitchens, artisanal bakeries and micro-breweries, or large-scale industries like coal-mining, mobile phone manufacture and universities. The boundaries of an ecotope are not perfectly defined, but for our purposes it is important that it is associated with a fairly specific identifiable product. The coal industry provides an easily identifiable ecotope, the energy industry one less so. But it also has an outward spread in the sort of community life and dependent economic and social activities that grow up around it (housing, village shops, brass bands). The word is not ideal but I want to use it partly as a nod to a key idea in Pope Francis's *Laudato Si'*, that human systems should not be considered in abstraction from the other life-systems of the planet,[4] and partly because it reminds us that working environments are also part of the living environments of human beings and that their quality therefore matters.

The problem with an ecotope, like a biotope, is that it is vulnerable to changes in the wider environment. As long as the relationship with the wider environment is stable you can tinker with a given ecotope, improve it, make life better for the people who work within it, and the community dependent on it. But when that stability is undermined you have a choice between protecting the ecotope from the environmental changes – which may well take its toll on neighbouring ecotopes – or managing a transition which may ultimately threaten the existence of the ecotope, with human consequences far wider than loss of jobs.

So here is a first suggestion. In 1945 it appeared that the primary task of a government was to improve the lot of their citizens considered as workers, against the backdrop of existing ecotopes. However, in the post-war years, the national and global environment supporting those ecotopes changed and changed rapidly. The consensus about government priorities changed with it. We live with the results.

## Prehistory

It is important to remember that that political consensus was itself the end point of a long and complex process of growth in popular empowerment. At the end of the eighteenth century, government intervention in employment disputes was limited to arresting or shooting rioting workers. But a hundred years later, thanks to the early efforts of a motley crew of socialists, utilitarians and Nonconformist Christian entrepreneurs, compassion for the poor had achieved an effective political status. The results ranged from basic health and safety legislation to gradual extensions of the vote. This trajectory continued into the twentieth century and Orwell, writing in 1941,[5] could claim that the British working class were better off in almost all ways than they had been thirty years before. He attributes this not just to wage rises, but to technological advances which had benefited the whole community.

The spurs to reform in Britain were clearly pragmatism as much as any new-found love of suffering humanity. The moneyed classes did not want a revolution *as well as* not wanting to be cruel or inhumane.

And that may reflect a fundamental truth of political reform: i much easier to persuade people to do the right thing if it has obvious benefits for them as well. (That needs to be factored into any serious discussion of progress towards a common good.) But however complex the motivation, we can see improving the lot of workers in their ecotopes as a dominant government concern in the first half of the twentieth century. How deep was the solidarity? Orwell's sardonic description from the war years of England as 'a family with the wrong members in control' suggests it was not unambiguous.[6] Perhaps, then, 1945 was about putting the right members in control, voting for Attlee, and an end to those five giants identified by Beveridge: want, disease, squalor, ignorance, idleness.

## So whatever happened to the common good?

One answer is, nothing. No government of the last seventy years would claim to have been acting in the sole interests of a particular financial class, however much they might have appeared to be doing so. The ideal of free education, free health care at the point of use and state protection of citizens from the effects of sickness, unemployment, poverty and homelessness retains a political solidity, in spite of serious erosion, up to the time of writing.

So a second answer is that 'the common good' has been substantially re-imagined since 1945. The arrival of Margaret Thatcher in office in 1979 set a new political tone and a new framework for thinking about and achieving national flourishing or prosperity. On her watch, government would no longer be about redressing the economic injustices of the past or about reducing inequalities between citizens. It would be about creating (*ex nihilo* where necessary) a land of economic opportunity.

Thus government should no longer concentrate on protecting existing ecotopes, but instead foster an entrepreneur-friendly environment in which ecotopes could wax and wane, spring up and die on their own merits. There might be human collateral damage on the way, but that was the price of economic progress for society as a whole. Contrast 1945. Then *everyone* (at least officially) had to make do and mend as the price of a better future.

The change of tone involved a shift in how we saw ourselves. We were no longer to see a Britain filled with the victims of social injustice.

Rather we were to see a Britain of free agents, some of whom might be failing to grasp the opportunities for social mobility. In 1945 social solidarity was an essential component of the flourishing state. From 1979 solidarity was jettisoned in favour of raw economic progress and 'tough love' structures promoting initiative over-dependency.

## From workers to consumers

Marr says of the talented, visionary and diverse Labour leadership team under Attlee: 'they believed in a socialist society, but few of them seemed to be able to agree in detail what that meant.'[7]

Perhaps the seeds of the 1979 transformation were already sown in that post-war settlement. It was after all a compromise. There had been no communist revolution. Even the moves towards welfare state and the nationalisation of health care and of key industries were merely a natural extension of the British state's activities during the war years. But the economics was not radical. The Keynsian pathway to full employment was investment. And the gradual nationalisation of trains, coal, steel and eventually cars was not just a symbolic act of management 'on behalf of the people'.[8] Many of those key industries were already struggling.

But alongside the ambiguities of the shared project, that government was, as Andrew Marr's account shows, desperately vulnerable to events.[9] A week after VJ day, a sudden hole in the accounts opened up when President Truman cancelled the wartime lend-lease arrangement. The sudden crisis took the economist John Maynard Keynes on a desperate, protracted and only partially successful begging mission to the USA. Two years later it was a cold winter, freezing the newly nationalised coal stocks. Similar shocks awaited later governments, from untimely deaths to nasty surprises in the special relationship with the USA, from political and financial scandals to a sudden hike in oil prices, a tumbling pound and rampant inflation.

All the while, government control of rail, coal and steel not only set a management challenge, but also made the government, as employer, the natural object of blame in case of dispute. Unions fought to protect and improve their ecotopes, the government tried to make them more efficient, meanwhile passengers stood waiting on platforms, and lights went out. And all this against the distorting background of Cold War paranoia and proxy war. In spite of the genuine, underlying growth of a fairer and more prosperous society, solidarity was under strain long before 1979.

It is interesting to compare Orwell again:

> However much one may hate to admit it, it is almost certain that between 1931 and 1940 the National Government represented the will of the mass of the people. It tolerated slums, unemployment and a cowardly foreign policy. Yes, but so did public opinion.[10]

Something similar could be said of the electorate that grew tired of industrial disputes and allowed a new political and economic agenda to take root over the next eighteen years.

During those years we were gradually taught to admire entrepreneurs, buy shares, own our homes and choose our state schools. We became more aware of our rights as consumers. Successive governments had to develop increasingly sophisticated (and energy intensive) ways of showing that the services they and others provided met our needs (or demands). Our dominant self-image changed. The majority of us were no longer our worker-selves fighting for justice shoulder to shoulder against a predatory, super-wealthy elite. We became our consumer-selves looking to the government to guarantee quality goods, on the shelves at a reasonable price.

## The *Herald of Free Enterprise*

But how can a war on union power, cutting taxes paid by the rich, reduction of public spending and the selling off of state assets *possibly* be regarded as working for the common good? The answer is, surprisingly easily, if you accept wholeheartedly a streamlined and modernised version of the free-market theories of Adam Smith and his successors, as did the new wave of economists and political thinkers of the 1970s.

The outline of Smith's big idea is that as long as a government can guarantee a free and fair market for goods, goods will find their 'natural' price according to the balance of supply and demand, owners will get a 'natural' profit and labourers will get a 'natural' wage. As long as owners pursue profit, moving capital to new enterprises as needed, as long as workers judge that they can afford to work on the terms available, and as long as consumers continue to buy what they need at the best price, everybody wins. Because, in the market, many agents with many talents are competing, each taking on their share of the risk of commercial failure, it is through the market that the resources available will find their way to those who need them by the most efficient and fairest route, without any one person being in control. For Smith, owner, worker and consumer are weighed against one another in a Newtonian balance of interests. The sums come out most equitably in the free market.

It generates the ethical paradox that though everyone acts in their own interests nevertheless everyone benefits, meaning that moral values of selflessness and other-interest, which most people (including Smith himself) tend to think are crucial to social living, appear to be unnecessary to increasing collective wealth. Indeed, in his *Theory of Moral Sentiments,*[11] Smith acknowledges the 'natural selfishness and rapacity' of the rich, while claiming that an invisible hand leads them to make 'nearly the same distribution of the necessaries of life' as if the earth had been fairly divided from the start.

Something of that last hypothesis clearly lies behind the 'trickle-down theory' of social benefit made famous by Ronald Reagan and one can see the attraction for plutocrats and politicians. The latter need feel no qualms about deregulating markets on behalf of their campaign donors and the former need feel no guilt about the relentless pursuit of profit. In *The Truth about Markets,*[12] John Kay quotes Milton Friedman, redefining the ethical relationship between business and society in this direction: 'the social responsibility of business is to maximise its profits'. Kay goes on to say, 'This position is acceptable to many business people because it puts few restrictions on their behaviour. The corollary is the general contempt amongst intellectuals for business and those who engage in it.'

Not all intellectuals, however. Immediately before the Reagan era, in *Anarchy, State and Utopia,*[13] the Harvard philosopher Robert Nozick developed a theory of government that went even further and turned the long-standing allergy of wealthy Americans to paying taxes into a natural right. He argued that the task of the state was simply to protect property and to ensure that contracts were fulfilled. It could legitimately raise taxes for defence or policing, but beyond that, taxes were immoral. Thus any attempt to redistribute wealth by taxation is of itself unjust. In the USA, echoes of this argument underpin Tea Party rhetoric and Republican policy today.

But here, at any rate, we can see the philosophical and economic ideas behind a radical shift in government policies. We back away from trying to run businesses on behalf of the state. Instead we set up (supposedly) competitive markets, allow people to spend more of their money in the way they want, and let 'nature' take its course, in the quiet confidence that whatever the outcome is, it will be the best outcome. Whatever promotes profit and for whomever that profit is promoted, whatever ecotopes and dependent communities vanish on the way, everything, ultimately, contributes to a common good made visible in the annual Gross Domestic Product.

However, when the ferry *Herald of Free Enterprise* sank in 1987 with the loss of 193 lives, in a buccaneering pursuit of profit at the expense of safety procedures, it raised a powerful symbolic question about the sufficiency of market liberalisation to provide for all human needs.

## Where are we now?

John Maynard Keynes, writing in the 1930s, had this to say about the dangerous attraction of abstract models of human realities:

> Too large a proportion of recent 'mathematical' economics are mere concoctions, as imprecise as the initial assumptions they rest on, which allow the author to lose sight of the complexities and interdependencies of the real world in a maze of pretentious and unhelpful symbols.[14]

Something of the same could be said for the ideological and formulaic free-market thinking that flourished in the 1980s. But the brutalisation and disruption of societies that its crude implementation brought across the globe has prompted promising new shifts in the economic consensus.[15] Smith himself (far more humane than some of his disciples) says, 'no society can surely be flourishing, of which the far greater part of the members are poor and miserable',[16] and most nowadays recognise that GDP says little about the quality of life of individual citizens or communities.

John Kay has articulated a more subtle way of thinking about the complex interplay between government and citizen, entrepreneur, worker and customer. He talks about 'embedded markets'.[17] The idea acknowledges that the free-trading networks on which every society depends have an irreducibly personal dimension, which includes shared history and common values (trust, reliability, integrity, pride in quality). There are vital elements that money can't buy, things that market liberalisation can swiftly destroy, but not swiftly replace.

Furthermore, when networks flourish they are themselves dependent on things which entrepreneurship alone *cannot* most efficiently guarantee: the health, happiness and education of workers, the health, happiness and buying power of consumers. Alongside these are the invisible social virtues, nurtured and supported within a given community, that enable shared enterprise and collective flourishing to take place. The right 'tone' underpins flourishing networks, but does not come about by accident. The principled argument that the state should not be allowed to run anything begins to look as absurd as the argument that the state must run everything, if what we are interested in is a society in which all citizens can flourish. Here may be a starting point for reflection: in the concept of the 'embedded market', modified free-market thinking offers space for a more human economics of the common good.[18]

But we may also recognise that most national governments are, on their own, increasingly vulnerable. Virtual wealth is created globally at a dizzying pace by computerised trading in shares and financial products, and by the aggressive marketing of loans to us, but it disappears the moment debts are called in. Capital can be shifted from one tax jurisdiction to another at the press of a button. Creating the conditions for the transnational, economic giants to invest in a country can mean compromising on hard-won worker rights and protections. Attempts to control inequality can simply lead the economically powerful to relocate their wealth. Those ecotopes that a government successfully enables to exist in its territories are vulnerable to the pace of technological change. Each new shift in the complex of technologies and consumer aspirations can, in the space of a few years, wipe out a whole way of life.

There are other, internal political problems. Key areas for which governments are now held responsible (health, education and social care) are irreducibly labour intensive and so suffer from 'Baumol's cost disease': while other industries become increasingly efficient as technology improves, areas of work dependent on human activity will in comparison become ever more inefficient. This brings a political temptation to be disingenuous, undermining sound thinking about areas once thought crucial to the common good, and leads to the contemporary dehumanised systems for weeding out the (politically useful) 'scroungers'.

But that political dishonesty is itself fed by the incompatible wants of us, the voters and citizens. We want well-stocked supermarket shelves, but we don't want migrant workers to pick the fruit we are not prepared to pick, or Far Eastern workers to take the jobs we *do* want abroad. We want all our hospitals and schools to be outstanding, but we neither want to do demanding work made unliveable by politically driven target-setting nor do we want to pay the taxes that might make the targets feasible. We want national pride and independence, at the same time as we want levels of comfort and security that can only be guaranteed by international cooperation and solidarity. We want the state systems to treat us kindly and well when we are in need, but we also want them to punish harshly the criminals, scroungers and wrong sorts of migrant that inhabit our newspapers.

## Ecotopes and ecology

Nothing that has been said so far deals with more profound global questions about the sustainability of standard models of economic progress. Pope Francis's encyclical on 'the care of our common home' reminded us that any new models of civic friendship must include concern for all life on the planet and especially for those peoples whose simple and sustainable ways of life are threatened by our dominant assumptions about development and prosperity.[19] Tim Jackson and others like him propose new economic models of 'prosperity without growth'.[20] These challenge us further: are we working to improve the existing system, to make our embedded markets fairer (already hard enough), or (infinitely harder) are we working to create a radically new economic system for a radically different global society?

Certainly many of us (especially those in the younger generations) are becoming more aware of our interdependence across the globe. We can acknowledge that the way we consume affects both our ecotopes (and around them the communities in which we live and find meaning) and our biotopes – the very conditions of life on earth. Less positively, we all continually run against the barrier that the system we might want to reform is not just where we meet our material needs, but is also the home in which we are who we are. This means that the hardest questions lie within us. Do we, together, really want this? And if not, what do we actually want?

For we humans have a strange moral-make up. We all act in our self-interest but are also capable of compassion and generosity. We can compete as individuals and we can strive together as a team. We consider compassion more admirable than self-interest, yet do not consider it intrinsically unreasonable or immoral to act in the interests of ourselves, our family, our colleagues or our people (indeed it can be perfectly moral to do so). But to all of us comes the time when the voice of selfless compassion conflicts with the voice of self-interest. It is then that our ethical depths are tested. Can we act not just acceptably, not just understandably, but *admirably*? As individuals, as families, as communities, as nations?

And here our circumstances make a difference. It is perhaps easiest for us to be our generous selves either when things are going so well for us and ours that compassion enhances our relationship with the world, or when things are going so badly for all of us that we need each other to survive. It is much harder when we see others flourishing at our expense, or our way of life (worse, that of our loved ones) is threatened by competitors. It is not simply wealth or simply poverty, but social poverty and inequality that breed division, revolutions and repressive states.

This takes us back to the *context* of the common good. Human associations, however unequal or dysfunctional, evolve mechanisms that allow people to live together in a balance of personal freedoms, while controlling the socially and personally destructive powers of our darker nature. But if we want more, if our intuitions about social flourishing include the values of compassion, tolerance, fairness and solidarity, then our elusive common good will will rely not just on publicly enforced rules of behaviour but on the shared commitment of 'us' to practise and promote the admirable way of life our rules merely define. The majority of citizens must *want* to lead *this sort of* good life.

As we have indicated, this is easier when communal lifestyles are (globally) autonomous and stable, much harder when, as in our world, they are subject to constant turbulence from external forces. Nevertheless, in spite of our Western aversion to being moralised at and our political preference for the cold consolation of impersonal statistics and mechanical equations, there are good grounds for thinking that we do all need community, shared value and relationship if we are genuinely to flourish.

Perhaps, then, the general answer to our original question will be something like this: the consensual framework for the common good of 1945 has been superseded because of wider changes in the human ecology of the planet. The consensual framework for 2045 is still emerging. For that framework to foster the best of our common human values, it will need to be complex, collaborative, well informed, transnational. And all of us will need individual and collective moments of conversion on the way.

## Questions

* How do we become 'we'? How do we come to develop and share values for the common good?
* How do values, nurtured in local communities, become effective in transforming national debate?
* How, as individuals, do we identify the fulcrum points in our immediate environment where each of us can nudge social evolution in a better direction?
* How do we cope with divergent beliefs about human reality, value and strategy in a democratic society?

## Notes

1.  Andrew Marr, *A History of Modern Britain* (London: Pan Books, 2008), p. 61.
2.  Patrick Riordan SJ, 'The history and principles of the common good', in this publication, pp. 11–26.
3.  Patrick Riordan SJ, *Global Ethics and Global Common Goods* (London: Bloomsbury, 2015), pp. 54ff.
4.  Pope Francis, *Laudato Si'* (Vatican website, 2015), e.g. §5, quoting John Paul II on 'human ecology'.
5.  George Orwell, 'England, Your England', in *Selected Essays* (Harmondsworth: Penguin, 1957), p. 88.
6.  Ibid. p. 78.
7.  Marr, op. cit, p. 25.
8.  From a National Coal Board slogan of 1947, Marr, op. cit, p. 69.
9.  Marr, op. cit, pp. 8–16, 67–70.
10. Orwell,op.cit, p. 76.
11. Adam Smith, *Theory of Moral Sentiments*, 1759 edn (Online Library of Liberty: OUP, 1976), p. 251.
12. John Kay, *The Truth about Markets* (London: Penguin, 2004), p. 315.
13. See Robert Nozick, *Anarchy, State and Utopia* (Oxford: Blackwell, 1974).
14. John Maynard Keynes, *The General Theory of Employment, Interest and Money* (Miami, FL: BN Publishing, 2008), p. 187.
15. See e.g. Kay, *The Truth about Markets*; Ha-Joon Chang, *Bad Samaritans* (London: Random House, 2008).
16. Adam Smith, *Wealth of Nations* (Oxford: Oxford University Press 2008), p. 78.

17. Kay, *The Truth about Markets*, pp. 337ff.
18. For further exploration of the relationship between market economies and the common good from the perspective of Catholic Social Teaching, see Nicholas Sagovsky and Peter McGrail (eds), *Together for the Common Good: Towards a national conversation* (London: SCM Press, 2015), especially Griffiths (pp. 139–52) and Longley (pp. 183–96). See in particular Griffiths on the limits of markets, pp. 148ff.
19. *Laudato Si'*, §13
20. See Tim Jackson, *Prosperity without Growth: Economics for a finite planet* (Abingdon: Routledge, 2009).

# 3. The Uncommon Good

## Simon Barrow

'It's time our political representatives stood up for the common good.' That demand, or something like it, has been repeated on innumerable occasions in different contexts across recent decades in British public life. However, the language of 'the common good' has become increasingly dislocated in popular political and media discourse from its grounding in the virtue ethics of Aristotle and his successors, from the social and public choice theory of modern political theory, and from theological roots that stretch out from Aquinas to contemporary Catholic Social Teaching, as set out in Patrick Riordan's chapter. Indeed, the Christian contribution to common good thinking and action is something largely unknown outside (and often within) the religious sphere these days, in spite of its huge influence in post-war European polity and the practice of subsidiarity – broadly, the exercise of power in as close proximity as possible to those impacted by it.

This dislocation from a reasoned, socially embedded and character-shaped set of traditions – the retreat from public philosophy, let alone public theology – is the first sense in which I wish to speak of the 'goods' often associated with the phrase 'common good' as increasingly less common, or even uncommon. What I wish to do here is to explore different dimensions of this dislocation, and to take on board some of the critiques that may justifiably be levelled against 'common good' notions in their various theorised and untheorised forms. I also want to point towards the tasks of moral, political and religious repair, reconstruction and re-imagination which may be required to confront the increasingly complex challenges facing attempts to advocate and practise a 'good life' for all in our increasingly fractured world.[1]

## Incentives and barriers for the common good

Some years ago, when taking part in a conference on social theory, education and different belief systems at the University of Rennes in France, one of my hosts made an off-the-cuff remark of the kind that stopped me in my tracks. The kind of comment that, whether one is aware of it or not at the time, begins to reorient the way you view the world from your particular vantage point. 'The English', she observed pithily, 'are a peculiarly un-theoretical people.' That observation made me smile at the time. When I moved to Scotland seven years ago, it came back to haunt me. Finding myself caught up in a blossoming of public debate around the 2014 Scottish independence referendum, I began to notice a thirst for ideas, for praxes and for 'ways of seeing' (as John Berger put it) that I had struggled to find much coinage for down south. The difference in scale and intensity between public spheres in Scotland and those in England partly accounted for that, no doubt. From 2012 to 2014 the town hall meeting was more or less reinvented across Scotland. Like it or not (some did, some didn't) the issues facing the country in or outside the United Kingdom suddenly began to be talked about in pubs, clubs, at the shops, at football matches. Interestingly enough, this was less so in the churches, in spite of an imaginative, constructive and bipartisan programme called 'Imagining Scotland's Future'. This was pioneered in the third sector, and derived from participative civic techniques developed in Iceland and picked up by the Church of Scotland.

The thing I really noticed during what commentator Gerry Hassan once called 'Scotland's democratic moment' was that there was a genuine thirst in many quarters, perhaps more noticeably among pro-independence supporters, for fresh ideas, new perspectives and innovative policies towards a socially inclusive, environmentally responsible, economically more equal and nuclear-weapon-free future. 'Act as if you are in the first days of a new nation' was one aphorism that gained popularity. 'Another Scotland and another world is possible' was another one. At the heart of this kind of thinking and advocacy was a definite idea of 'a commons' that resides within particular communities, within Scotland as a relatively small-scale 'imagined community' (Benedict Anderson's description of nationhood) and within a world order where the desire to re-route globalisation was heartfelt but generally progressive, rather than insular or backward looking. This was a heartening experience. For a time at least – while retaining a profound awareness of the deep inequalities that scar Scotland, along with England, Wales, Northern Ireland and many other nations – it seemed credible and possible to talk of a fresh vision of a 'common good' in this place. For me that was in stark contrast to the evident vacuities of 'the Big Society' and the 'We're all in this together' slogans coming out of Westminster at the time. Particularly since they were driven by a Conservative-led coalition government that was, at the very same time, slashing welfare, stripping back the state, and encouraging voluntarism and privatism in place of any shared sense of social security (especially for the most vulnerable) at a time of economic shock. A similar critique could be mounted against Theresa May's 'Shared Society', where the nature and structure of what is to be shared is left opaque (and largely unfunded).

In contrast to these deliberately thin and rhetorically lightweight versions of the common good, I experienced from 2012 to 2014 a willingness among many in Scotland, beyond their aspirational slogans towards a fairer and better country and society, to dig deep into the realms of social action, popular economics, ecology, beliefs and values, communal experience, art and culture, and even interpersonal psychology. They did so as part of a search for the common territory that would enable a different kind of Scotland to emerge, with beneficial consequences for neighbours and for the world, as well as for ourselves. This was a particularly civic-driven reality, and it certainly wasn't for everyone (raising questions as to how 'common' the goods that were talked about and advocated really were). As the political journalist Iain Macwhirter wrily observed: the Yes campaign in the independence referendum was rather like a festival of ideas. But the viability of any festival, he warned, is not simply a matter of enthusiasm, but of 'how many people have actually bought tickets?' In the end, the vote on 18 September 2014 demonstrated that more people had chosen *not* to buy tickets to the independence dream. The regrettable tribalism of party politics in Scotland then seemed to reassert itself fairly quickly, albeit reshaped by a massive surge towards the SNP as a party simultaneously of governance (in Scotland) and insurrection (within the United Kingdom). Since then the energy and vitality seems to have dissipated significantly. The territory for envisioning and sharing goods has shrunk noticeably following the 2016 EU referendum. It seems that common bases for action can be eroded outside a 'campaign' context, when the stark prose of governing and being governed reasserts itself over a more aspirational politics.[2]

## The erosion and creation of 'a commons' for 'the good'

The relevance of all this to rethinking our wider understanding, advocacy and practice of 'the common good' is that it poses sharp questions about the gaps that exist between the visionary, the practical and the mundane in the public sphere. Most people, most of the time, do not spend their moments discussing politics, economics, beliefs and 'the good society'. The cares, burdens and many distractions of modern life exercise a much closer magnetic field on individual and family life than the enticements of what my associate from Rennes called 'theory' (meaning not so much disconnected or abstract thinking, but the attempt to bring ideas and convictions to bear on the construction of common projects within the realm of the societies we live in). In this sense, she suggested, the English (and not just the people of England, but many in Scotland and well beyond) are 'un-theoretical'. This is because thoughts about 'the common good' can only really be sustained and developed when there is, actually, some level of commonality upon which we all do indeed depend, which we all share in, and which helps shape our attempts to agree, disagree and negotiate. In other words, the reality of community (or its absence) in some sense prefigures theories of communal life, its enhancement or fragmentation.

So it was in Scotland that some of the people who came together during the debates that both preceded and followed the 2014 independence referendum gave strength and energy to something called Common Weal. Common Weal is a combination of a think tank, a social movement and a communications network. It is one of a number of initiatives in Scotland aiming to offer fresh insight into the possibilities of the country and its constituent parts through policies, forums, gatherings and an online news service. Nevertheless, as I have already suggested, despite the burst of energy that produced Common Weal, it and other civic movements have found it a tough business to sustain themselves and move forward. The one thing they have in their favour is that they recognise, in ways that I did not experience during my many years living in England, that goods which can be held in common indeed require the creation of 'a commons' through which they can be constructed and shared. But the problem is that our 'commons' are increasingly disappearing. The worlds of politics and commerce are dominated by transnational players. Supermarkets regularly squeeze out corner shops. Many forms of institutional religion are receding or struggling with no obvious replacement on the horizon. Bars and restaurants are taken over by chains. Even public spaces and parks are increasingly commercialised, and many people living in the urban environment have lost touch with the land and with reality outside 'the central belt'. Moreover, the veneer of multiculturalism in our societies has not often built the kind of inter- and cross-communal solidarities which the very notion of a 'common good' (one that is shared rather than restricted) implies.

The struggle to make what is common broad enough to provide a theatre for what is more than a merely parochial good is demonstrated (before we even get into the matter of the fragmentation of public philosophies, ideologies and beliefs) in our own post-war political, social and economic history. So the consumer era of atomisation and individualism in which we now live stands in stark contrast to a time when the language of unity of purpose and intent had much more common currency; that of the wartime era. This is not something we should simplify and romanticise in the way that talk of 'the Blitz spirit' can so easily do. But it does highlight the fact that a spirit of common purpose can create bridges across social, cultural and other divides.[3]

So in spite of the qualifications we might need to entertain in saying this, in Britain the quest for a politics that 'brings people together' can be indeed be traced back to the aftermath of 1945, when the drive to 'win the peace' after a time of devastating destruction raised the necessity of a fairer and more equal sharing in the post-war boom. This drove the country (then very much more of a United Kingdom in conception and culture) away from wartime austerity towards both a national health and social security system and a consumer-led phase of industrial prosperity in the 1950s and 1960s. That period of growth and optimism was, however, soon confronted by the looming Cold War. Then came the huge oil shocks of the early 1970s, the escalated Thatcherite de-industrialisation of the 1980s that preyed on the dissipation of old systems of production and control. This produced, in turn, the unequal 'loadsamoney' boom of the 1990s and the exponential new tech expansion of the 2000s. Then finally came a new age of austerity: one that dawned with the speculation-driven financial collapse of 2008 and the constraints imposed by increasing (but belated) awareness of the seriousness of global climate change. On the back of all that, we now face the brokenness of free-market dogma across the globe (a flawed neoliberal model of internationalism); the uncertainty, social dislocation and economic destabilisation of Brexit; the possible break-up or refiguring of the United Kingdom; and rise of demagoguery and insularity signalled by the election of Donald Trump on a minority share of the vote in the United States. Alongside this has developed a tide of far Right forces opposing a generous understanding of 'the commons' in Europe and beyond.

## The common and the good are under real threat

Put in these terms, the challenges that lie ahead appear particularly daunting. The plural, democratic and liberal capitalist order that Francis Fukuyama once predicted as 'the end of history' is under pressure as never before. A new hostility to migrants, 'foreigners' and 'outsiders' is evident in a world of almost permanent insecurity – something picked up in the contributions of Vaughan Jones and Savitri Hensman to this book. Resurgent nationalisms of an ethnocentric, aggressive and exclusive variety have been multiplying. The collective life of communities, regions, nations and supranational or intermediary structures has to deal with a whole series of challenges. These include the dominance of corporations over politics and multilateral agency; a variety of democratic deficits within and between nations; forced migration resulting from war, poverty, human rights abuses and climate change, and the horror of broken or failed states in the Middle East and other parts of the world. Meanwhile, we cannot be certain of the kind of China and Russia that are emerging as renewed powers in a once bipolar (Cold War) world. The collapse of the Iron Curtain gave way to a mono-polar successor (the 'New American Century'). This in turn has been strained by the multipolar complexity – and the struggle against it embodied in Trump and Brexit – that marks a profoundly disordered globalism driven by unstable financialisation. These are just a few of the disturbing trends that pose severe questions to the very notion of 'common' and 'good' in the early twenty-first century, let alone the combining of those two ideas into ways of humanising our lives. That is, to practices and policies that lead decisively towards sharing rather than hoarding, conservation rather than squandering, equality rather than inequality, peacemaking rather than warring, and hoping rather than hiding.

However, the threat to the coherence of a case for 'the common good' comes not just from the receding of the philosophical or religious systems mentioned at the beginning, the fragmentation of a variety of social orders, the divisions resulting from both commercialisation of most aspects of life, and the break-up of hegemonic political blocs and systems. It also resides in the collapse of the metanarratives (big, overarching stories) that have given common, though not uncontested, meaning to 'the good' in the past. These range from Christianity to Marxism. Even Humanism is now challenged by the trans- and post-Humanism of the cyber-tech society. What has happened in each of these cases amounts to a parochialisation of formerly hospitable belief systems (religious and non-religious) reinforcing the reality of the divisions that often take primacy over common projects. It is the latter that I want to say a little more about before suggesting some paths forward.

## We are not necessarily 'all in this together'

I have already suggested that the ability to talk meaningfully about 'the common good', and to instrumentalise it in practical terms, depends upon some existing 'commons', which offer the space and the language to give it content and traction. I have suggested that there are many factors that have eroded such 'commons', while also showing that in small ways (exemplified by the Common Weal project in Scotland, with which I have been peripherally engaged, and also the Iona Community, of which I am a member) it is possible to nurture the kind of terrain that is operationally required for the purposes of good. However, it is not possible to do that, on either a small or larger scale, without confronting the kind of deep divisions that make 'common life' and goods held in common (both material and spiritual) inaccessible to access for a large number of people. Those divisions are ones framed by money, power, class, race, gender, sexuality, dis/ability, education and culture. To speak of, or to seek to develop, a 'common good' which either ignores or wishes away such divisions is as dishonest as it is impractical. Indeed, when it becomes about merely ameliorating injustice rather than transforming it, it is downright undesirable. Economic factors loom especially large among the factors undermining easy claims to commonality. The failure to recognise has been a key weakness in much of the 'common good' rhetoric emerging from 'traditionalist' quarters in recent years, not least sections of the Christian community (more accurately *communities,* plural). Bereft of any thoroughgoing analyses of power imbalances, which need to be intersectional rather than reductive (to class, race, gender, etc., alone), 'the common good' can become simply a way of masking oppression and replacing collective action and solutions with privileged private philanthropy. As Augustine warned us, 'charity is no substitute for justice withheld'. Therefore, I would strongly suggest, any proposition about the common good needs to be, at the same time, a proposition about justice (if it is to be politically both visionary *and* realistic) and also a proposition about love (if it is to be truly human, seeing good as deeply personal and fulfilling). At the same time, it has to be acknowledged that the requirement for a justice that does love and a love that does justice presupposes a process of equalisation and interdependence in that 'commons' that seeks to do good. Otherwise it will end up merely imposing a factional vision through power, whether in the name of democracy or some other arrangement for rendering mere strangers accountable to each other in a mainly formal, abstract sense.[4]

## Uncommon Christian practices for making 'the good' more common

From the earliest times, Christians, to take one specific group of people who can act together, have had a way of talking about and acting out a 'common good' in which justice and love mutually dwell in each other. This way of acting and talking may be called 'church' ('the assembly', or, in Greek, the *ekklesia*).[5] By this term I do not mean a mere building or an institution. Nor do I mean an arrangement, as in much historic Christendom, by which institutional advantage is gained by conferring blessing on governing authority in an uncritical and often politically collusive and spiritually enervating way. No, by church as *ekklesia*, I mean a community distinguished by a moral and practical commitment that takes the levelling, sharing, subverting, forgiving, welcoming, right-doing and peacemaking way of Jesus Christ as constitutive for its own life – and correspondingly for the life it seeks to offer to and bestow upon others, without denying them their difference and identity. Understood in such a way, 'church' (which is inescapably global as well as inescapably local in the forms it needs to take) does not *have* a social idea and practice, it *is* a social idea and practice. In particular, following the logic of theological ethicist Stanley Hauerwas, who has sought to make this point on many occasions, the Church constituted as a both a sociological and spiritual reality in the broken and restored body of Christ understands itself not as a state that must defend itself by force, but as a community created by the truth of nonviolence: the unique, uncontrollable and inimitable life-giving of God which we call resurrection.[6]

Resurrection life (living beyond the fear and claim of death) is the only kind of revenge permitted to the Christian. It is the realisation that death, and particularly unjust death imposed by the sword, does not have the final word if God is as God is in Jesus (as Bishop David Jenkins once put it). That means the ethic, the ethos and the good that should be made common by the life of the Church for the sake of the world (not for its own sake) cannot be partial, restricted, tribal or mean. It can only be open, hospitable, humble and gift-bound. It will also be, in a world of factionalism, consumption and power, fragile and sacrificial; as well as creative and constantly in search of inspiration, the sustaining power of the Spirit. Its good will not instantly appear 'common', then. Indeed, the kind of concrete practices that flow from this kind of self-understanding of a community, and the virtue-specification and character-building needed to create and maintain it, will look very odd and *uncommon* to many people. These practices would include welcoming strangers, loving enemies, forgiving wrongdoers, foregoing profit, and questioning social and cultural norms. This is what Catholic divine Dorothy Day stood for when she said that 'the Gospel takes away our right forever to discriminate between the deserving and the undeserving poor'. Simon Woodman's chapter makes a not dissimilar set of connections and distinctions here, I should point out.

Now I am very conscious that for some readers I may have seemed to have leapt, in the last two to three paragraphs, from a rather pragmatic and *realpolitik*-familiar set of discourses about the common good in its social, political, economic and cultural/global senses, to a set of assertions about the Church as an exemplary social reality which sounds more like mystical theology than sociological prescription. In one sense, I acknowledge that to be true. The first thing that a church (and *the* Church), as a community of believers, has to do in *receiving* a vision of common good is to understand its own distinct and awkward birthing, nature and calling. That is, to recognise itself as founded in the life, death and new life embodied by a first-century Palestinian teacher, prophet and healer. This is, admittedly, a pretty odd (and increasingly uncommon) thing to do – even if, as Christians should, one justifies it on the basis that something decisive about the life of God, and the life of human beings in the world, is surprisingly but essentially disclosed in the life of this 'marginal Jew' (to use John P. Meier's term).

The second thing a church (and *the* Church), as a community of believers, has to do in *developing* a vision of common good is to think, in context, what forms it might properly take so as to be able to discharge the kind of mission that such a community of the common good should have. That means to live and act hopefully, alongside those who are disenfranchised, marginalised and despairing. And to do so in a world where the rich, strong, self-sufficient and violent are constantly in the business of grasping and using power in such a way as to *create* the disenfranchised, marginalised and despairing – quite apart from proliferating war and despoiling the planet. This means that the Church needs to see itself as being in a constantly revolutionary situation, rebelling against 'the powers that be' and 'politics as usual', and suspended between forms of common life that are alternatingly settled (to offer security) and sojourning (to keep moving forward). This is a scriptural spirit of adventure that orients us towards a good not fully revealed, and a commonality found in surprising places and alliances. It is in many respects the opposite of the kind of 'rescue packages' the Church is often trying to create as the Christendom system, in which it has until recently been axial, continues to collapse; and as the true identity of Christianity and the Christ it serves comes into deep question.

The third and final thing a church (and *the* Church), as a community of believers, has to do in *offering* a vision of common good is to make allies in unlikely, unexpected places and to recognise that none of the goods it holds and seeks to make common are its possessions or are unique to its polity. Often the truth is the opposite, in fact. So, for example, the Church has in different times and places preached human dignity or human rights while denying dignity and rights to its own people and failing to see or acknowledge the dignity and rights bestowed by those of other faiths or no religion. In that sense the Church is in danger not just of being un-theoretical but, in an inter-textual way, unscriptural too. Jesus made friends among those often regarded as unworthy or unclean. He disputed the self-arrogation of institutional religion. He was killed by a combination of state and religious power outside the gates of the city. And he was raised to new life by a power of good not controllable by earthly rulers in whatever guise. This is extremely important because, though I want to commend in this chapter an unswerving mission of the Church to enact a social ethic of economic sharing, welcome, forgiveness and peacemaking (those, I think are the four cardinal virtues required by a community facing the challenges of the twenty-first century), this should in no way be taken to imply a superiority, either morally or theologically, to others. Specifically, it should not be used to marginalise or dismiss those others who may believe in and practise such goals on other bases than historic Christianity (or any other variety of religion). God is larger than the boxes we try to keep God in, and the goodness that needs to be made common is much larger than we commonly think. This is another way of recognising that a genuine 'common good' is frequently *uncommon*, but nonetheless capable of being recognised, honoured, formulated, practised and shaped into usable but flexible forms, often from the edges of conventional systems rather than at their centre.

Lastly, then, there remains, in the midst of my problematising of too simple a notion of 'the common good', a question about how the practices and intentions of the Church as a specific community with a particular understanding of 'the good' might connect with struggles for commonality and goodness elsewhere. Also how it might make advocacy for such a widespread good consistent with its own internal life and behaviour. Here I think the language of 'the common weal' (which is, after all, the name of an American Catholic magazine as well as a movement/think tank in Scotland) is profoundly helpful. In popular parlance the term means 'the benefit or interests of all members of a country or community'. Another way of understanding it is as a question. *What is it that we need to hold in common in order actually to be people who have equal share in a community?* The immediate answers might include food, water, shelter, health, education, livelihood, art and culture. What we need to do, then, is to develop policies and institutions that make all those things as accessible and shared as possible, and to look at what kind of economy and environment can make this realisable. That partly involves attenuating, reforming and remoulding what we already have within our grasp (however long or short that grasp may be). But it also involves experimenting, innovating and recasting things in radically new or surprising ways

– a financial transaction tax, a universal basic income, a 'green new deal' economy, a social investment bank network, an agreement on the abolition of WMDs and the conversion of military industry to peaceful production, for example. The key, it seems to me, is that such policies and practices need to be developed out of the experience of those living at the cutting edge of the concerns they address (not least the poorest and most vulnerable). Also, they should be piloted and developed out of the expertise of people actively seeking to chart new possibilities (from conflict transformation to cooperative enterprise) from the ground up, rather than from the top down. In this way, and through a set of often uncommon inclinations, vision and practices, the goods that the world needs to flourish, rather than just survive, can truly be made more and more common.

## Questions

- What are the social, cultural and religious factors which have undermined a coherent understanding of 'the common good'? How, where and by whom might they be restored?
- What is your understanding of 'the good life'? What shapes and informs it, and how can it be shared and developed beyond your own social milieu or political/spiritual belief framework?
- Is it possible to talk about a 'common good' that includes a very poor person and a multi-millionaire? What is it that we need to hold in common in order to be people who have equal share in a community?
- What practical actions, projects and policies can churches and civic groups in your locale pursue in order to exemplify and promote an achievable 'common good'?

## Notes

1.  Jim Wallis, 'Whatever happened to the "common good"?', *Time* magazine, 4 April 2013.
2.  Simon Barrow and Mike Small (eds), *Scotland 2021* (London: Ekklesia/Bella Caledonia, 2016).
3.  James Richards, 'The Blitz: Sorting the myth from the reality', http://www. bbc.co.uk/history/british/britain_wwtwo/blitz_01.shtml, 17 February 2011.
4.  Nick Glunt, 'Michael Sandel: Equality is the key to the common good', *The Chautauquan Daily*, 8 July 2011.

5.  'Why the name *Ekklesia*?', Ekklesia think tank FAQ, http://www.ekklesia. co.uk/about/faqs/10, accessed 20 February 2017.

6.  Gary Dorrien, *Reconstructing the Common Good: Theology and the social order* (Maryknoll, NY: Orbis Books, 1990), compared with Stanley Hauerwas, *The Peaceable Kingdom: A primer in Christian ethics* (Notre Dame, IN: University of Notre Dame Press, 1983).

# 4. The Shrinking Safety Net

Bernadette Meaden

## Early Christian approaches to welfare

*If anyone is left out and deprived of what is essential, then the common good has been betrayed.*[1]

Early Christian communities had a strong sense of the common good, which was expressed in very practical ways. They viewed the well-being of every single member of their community as a collective responsibility, and went to great lengths to ensure that everybody's material needs were met. Those who owned land and property sold it and gave the proceeds freely, to be distributed to those who were in need. 'There was not a needy person among them, for as many as were possessors of lands or houses sold them ... and distribution was made to each as any had need' (Acts 4:34–35).

So every individual had their security guaranteed by their community – they had *social security*.

The Church Fathers reflected this approach, making statements which to modern ears sound strikingly radical. St John Chrysostom (344–407) said, 'Not to share our own wealth with the poor is theft from the poor and deprivation of their means of life; we do not possess our own wealth, but theirs.' Basil of Caesarea (330–379) said, 'If every man took only what was sufficient for his needs, leaving the rest to those in want, there would be no rich and no poor.' So, early Christians believed that their faith required much more of them than charitable donations to the needy; it required the radical sharing of material goods. As St Augustine (354–430) said, 'Charity is no substitute for justice denied.' The sharing of wealth was considered an act of justice, returning to the poor what in God's eyes was rightfully theirs, but had been denied them by an unjust human system. In Catholic Social Teaching this approach is referred to as 'the universal destination of goods', and is explained thus: 'God destined the earth and all it contains for all men and all peoples so that all created things would be shared fairly by all mankind under the guidance of justice tempered by charity.'[2]

## Historic approaches to welfare in the UK

In the United Kingdom, laws relating to the relief of poverty evolved over many centuries, a process which has continued up to the present day, with its ongoing process of welfare reform.

Right up to the twentieth century, people living in poverty relied heavily for assistance on the Church in some way – whether from the monasteries, or, after the Reformation, from a more codified system administered at parish level.

The 1601 Poor Relief Act obliged each parish in England to provide for its poor, elderly and infirm inhabitants. The resources to do this came from the Poor Rate, a sort of compulsory local income tax, which was levied according to a parishioner's ability to pay. Assistance could be given in various forms, from straightforward cash payments to food, fuel and clothing. This was referred to as 'outdoor relief' as it was received in the community – recipients were not obliged to enter an institution like a workhouse to receive help. It has been described as the most generous and geographically ubiquitous system in the world at that time.

This system evolved gradually until 1832, when a Royal Commission under the chairmanship of the Bishop of London was established to review all the legislation in this area and investigate how it was being administered, with a view to reducing expenditure. Leading members of the Commission were thought to be influenced by the views of Jeremy Bentham and Thomas Malthus, who asserted that giving assistance to the poor would enable them to survive and have children, and thus increase the problem of poverty, so it is not surprising that the Commission's recommendations were harsh, far removed from the generous, egalitarian approach of early Christianity.

The Commission took the view that poverty was largely caused by the laziness and immorality of individuals. Providing relief to the poor only encouraged them to be idle, and giving more help to families only encouraged the poor to have children. Accordingly the

Commission proposed that outdoor relief should be made illegal, so it would be impossible for a person to get any assistance outside of a workhouse. Conditions in the workhouse should be made very like prison, unpleasant enough to deter all but the most desperate from seeking help.

The proposals became law with the passing of the 1834 Act for the Amendment and Better Administration of the Laws Relating to the Poor in England and Wales. The system of workhouses thus introduced changed gradually over time, but remained in some form even into the twentieth century. Until 1948, welfare provision was largely 'residual', seen as being only for the poor, a safety net for those with no alternative, and carrying with it a powerful stigma.[3]

## The post-war consensus

The welfare state established after the Second World War can be seen as a clear departure from this approach, and more closely based on Christian principles. Poverty was no longer viewed as shameful, or the fault of the individual. Welfare support would be provided in a comprehensive manner for the population as a whole, in the same way as public services like roads or schools, so the stigma associated with it was greatly reduced.

Most people are aware that it was the Beveridge Report, published in 1942, which led to the establishment of the modern welfare state and comprehensive social security. But perhaps fewer people are aware that Beveridge was strongly influenced by the work of William Temple, Archbishop of Canterbury from 1942 to 1944. In his book, *Christianity and Social Order*, Temple outlined a vision of a post-war society in which the innate dignity of every person would be honoured.[4]

Having seen the effectiveness of a centralised collective war effort, many in the Church took a very positive view of what the state could potentially do in peacetime to secure the welfare of its people. In 1941, William Temple declared: 'The state is a servant and instrument of God for the preservation of Justice and for the promotion of human welfare.'[5]

Accordingly, the Church was very supportive of the ambitious programme of legislation which, between 1945 and 1948, set about establishing a system which would provide social security for all. Benefits included family allowance, sick pay, unemployment pay, a marriage grant, maternity grant-and a death grant. Literally, cradle to grave security. And importantly, in a marked departure from the stigmatising and judgemental systems of the past, such support was now to be seen as a right or entitlement, part of being a valued citizen deserving of a decent and dignified life. This met with such approval from the Church that the Lambeth Conference in 1948 passed Resolution 19, which stated:

> We believe that the state is under the moral law of God, and is intended by him to be an instrument for human welfare. We therefore welcome the growing concern and care of the modern state for its citizens, and call upon Church members to accept their own political responsibility and to co-operate with the state and its officers in their work.[6]

On 10 December 1948, the principles underpinning the welfare state were echoed and enshrined in the United Nations Universal Declaration of Human Rights. Article 25 says:

> (1) Everyone has the right to a standard of living adequate for the health and well-being of himself and of his family, including food, clothing, housing and medical care and necessary social services, and the right to security in the event of unemployment, sickness, disability, widowhood, old age or other lack of livelihood in circumstances beyond his control.
>
> (2) Motherhood and childhood are entitled to special care and assistance. All children, whether born in or out of wedlock, shall enjoy the same social protection.[7]

The years from 1945 until the late 1970s are regarded as the period of the 'classic' welfare state, characterised by a broad consensus of support among the public, and politicians from both major parties. There were of course critics from both Left and Right, but the basic ideas and principles of the welfare state faced no significant challenge.

The welfare state continued to evolve and expand, as society changed and awareness of different needs improved. In 1968, for instance, a survey by the Office of Population Censuses and Surveys found that among the 3 million disabled adults living in private households there was evidence of widespread poverty, and significant

extra costs incurred as a result of living with a disability.[8] This led to
the introduction of new benefits to help disabled people meet such
costs, including Attendance Allowance, Mobility Allowance and, later,
Disability Living Allowance.

## Challenging the welfare consensus

The broad consensus of support for the welfare state continued more
or less unchallenged until the 1970s, when it was disrupted by events
and ideas both national and international.

One such event, the oil crisis of 1973, in which the price of oil
quadrupled, led to economic and political turmoil. In Britain an
economic slump brought high levels of unemployment and inflation.
The Keynesian social democracy which underpinned welfare states
was perceived to be failing, which provided an opportunity for an
alternative approach to gain ground. The alternative emerged from the
University of Chicago, where Friedrich Hayek and Milton Friedman,
updating the classical liberalism of the nineteenth century, helped
create the neoliberal politics which has dominated the Western world
ever since.

Hayek fervently believed in the free market and the liberty of
the individual. He thought that attempts to pursue social justice or
reduce inequality in terms of income and wealth were incompatible
with individual liberty. Income redistribution and measures such as
progressive taxation were considered a threat to liberty and must
therefore be rejected. The state should play a minimal role in people's
lives. Milton Friedman believed that the free market was more
effective than the state at solving social problems. Competition and
choice were vital to economic progress. These ideas were embraced
by political kindred spirits Ronald Reagan and Margaret Thatcher,
and so took hold on both sides of the Atlantic.

Neoliberalism, with its small state, low tax, privatising and
deregulating agenda is highly conducive to the interests of rich
individuals and corporations, and so was propagated through well-
funded think tanks and privately owned media outlets. Eventually,
neoliberalism became so pervasive that it was even accepted, to a
greater or lesser degree, by traditional parties of the Left, and brought
radical change not just to economics but to almost every area of society
and culture.

There is a story that following her election as leader of the Conservative party in 1975, Mrs Thatcher interrupted a speaker who was advocating that the party should take a consensual 'middle way' on a variety of policy issues. Taking a copy of Friedrich Hayek's *The Constitution of Liberty* out of her bag she reportedly slammed it onto the table and said, 'This is what we believe!'

Given Mrs Thatcher's admiration of Hayek, it is not surprising that in 1982 she and her Chancellor, Geoffrey Howe, commissioned a policy paper to facilitate radical cuts to public spending. Measures included introducing a charge for state schooling and replacing the NHS with private medical insurance. When presented to cabinet the proposals caused uproar, and when leaked to the press caused a public outcry. Mrs Thatcher was obliged to publicly disown the proposals, stating that 'the NHS is safe with us', but Treasury papers released from the National Archive show that behind the scenes, the Prime Minister and Chancellor continued to work to keep the ideas alive.[9]

While such radical proposals did not succeed at the time, they served to fracture the post-war consensus and break a taboo, allowing people to think the unthinkable. No longer could the fundamental elements or principles of the welfare state be taken for granted – it was now conceivable that a government could dismantle or significantly weaken them.

As Florence Sutcliffe-Braithwaite has written, for Margaret Thatcher, 'The aim was not to abolish the welfare state entirely, but to chip away at it, leaving social security as a last resort for the very poorest minority, and making it irrelevant to those on middle and high incomes, who would choose private provision instead. In this, Thatcher was successful. When journalist Nicholas Timmins started his 'biography of the welfare state' in 1993, the welfare state seemed so attenuated that many of his friends "joked that I had better be quick about it before the thing disappeared". The contention that Thatcher failed to achieve her mission to destroy the welfare state starts from a false premise; she never intended to do so. However, she was largely successful in residualising welfare, and efforts to do so went along with an increasingly harsh rhetoric about those reliant on social security.'[10]

One significant change Margaret Thatcher did succeed in making was to break the link between the value of social security benefits and earnings. This meant that instead of cash benefits rising in line with national prosperity when the economy grew, they increased in line with prices, so their value has fallen steadily in comparison to the incomes of those at work. Numerous other changes in the 1980s and 1990s reduced entitlements to benefits, but this didn't reduce spending as a whole, because high unemployment and an ageing population meant that demand continued to rise. Spending was only kept in check by spreading resources more thinly between larger numbers of claimants.

Under the Conservative government of John Major (1992–97) the changing approach towards claimants was increasingly reflected in policy. The various unemployment benefits were replaced with a single Jobseeker's Allowance. In order to receive it claimants had to sign a Jobseeker's Agreement, which specified what was required of them. If they failed to comply with these requirements their benefit would be sanctioned – reduced or suspended. This marked the beginning of a shift to conditionality in the benefits system.

The New Labour government which took office in 1997 continued this approach, emphasising work as the route out of poverty and introducing schemes like the New Deal for the Long-Term Unemployed, and the New Deal for Young People. In 2008, in an attempt to reduce the numbers of people claiming out-of-work sickness and disability benefits, New Labour introduced Employment and Support Allowance (ESA), which replaced Incapacity Benefit, Severe Disablement Allowance, and Income Support for people unable to work due to illness or disability.

To receive ESA, new claimants had to undergo the newly introduced Work Capability Assessment. This purely functional assessment takes little account of diagnosis or prognosis, or symptoms like pain and fatigue. It has, therefore, produced some extraordinary outcomes, finding seriously ill people fit to work, many of whom have died shortly afterwards. When the assessment was rolled out to existing claimants in 2011, it was expected to reduce the claimant count by around 1 million, on the assumption that many claimants were not genuinely ill or disabled. The wrongness of this assumption is evidenced by the high proportion of 'fit to work' decisions successfully appealed against, and the fact that after many millions of assessments being carried out, the number of claimants remains almost unchanged.[11]

## The impact of the coalition government

When the coalition government took office in 2010, it quickly introduced a 'triple lock' for the state pension, a guarantee that it would increase every year by either the rate of inflation, average earnings or 2.5 per cent, whichever was the higher. Thus pensioner incomes were largely insulated from the radical reforms to come, described as 'the biggest shake-up of the welfare state in sixty years'.
Changes included:

- A much tougher benefit sanctions regime for unemployed, sick and disabled claimants. In 2014, after this system had been operating for two years and the effects were clear, the Joint Public Issues Team wrote: 'The DWP guidance repeatedly acknowledges that the sanctions it administers are expected to cause deterioration in the health of normal healthy adults. This undermines a foundational principle of the welfare system. It is precisely because of the damage caused by poverty on human well-being that the welfare state exists. We would argue that any human society should be disturbed by a statutory system that deliberately causes harm to another human being. At the heart of our Christian understanding of social justice is that human society should make provision for the weakest and most vulnerable. It is alarming to discover a welfare system that deliberately sets out to exploit a person's vulnerability in order to achieve control and compliance.'[12]

- The abolition of Disability Living Allowance, to be replaced by Personal Independence Payments, with the intention of reducing the number of entitled claimants and so reduce expenditure by 20 per cent.[13] Up to December 2016, with the reassessment process ongoing, 230,000 disabled or ill people had had their support reduced or completely withdrawn.

- The so-called 'bedroom tax', whereby tenants in social housing who were deemed to have one or more spare bedrooms faced a reduction in Housing Benefit, leaving them with a shortfall on their rent if they could not move to a smaller property.

- The flagship welfare reform policy, Universal Credit, aimed to simplify the benefits system and 'make work pay'. Designed with an in-built delay of several weeks or even a couple of months before a claimant receives payment, it has become associated with increased hardship, particularly a sharp increase in rent arrears. Claimants transferring to Universal Credit can fall into debt which they may never get out of. In June 2016, social housing bodies said that 79 per cent of tenants on Universal Credit were in rent arrears compared to 31 per cent of other tenants. They also reported, 'an increase in demand for money and debt advice services, foodbanks and hardship funds' with 'tenants increasingly using loan sharks and pay day loan companies'. Universal Credit has also introduced 'in-work conditionality' whereby people who are in low-paid work and receiving UC can have their benefit sanctioned if they do not comply with various conditions.

- From April 2017, many people who become unfit to work due to illness or disability will receive the same benefit payment as a healthy non-disabled person claiming Jobseeker's Allowance.

- The overwhelming effect of these and other reforms has been negative, bringing increased stress and hardship for those on the lowest incomes, and for some of the most vulnerable people in society. Indeed, the impact on disabled people has been so serious that in 2016 the United Nations Committee on the Rights of Persons with Disabilities conducted an inquiry into the UK and found 'reliable evidence that the threshold of grave or systematic violations of the rights of persons with disabilities has been met in the State party'.[14]

Across the UK, foodbanks have proliferated. There has been a rise in the number of children living in absolute poverty, a rise in the number of disabled people living in absolute poverty, a rise in rough sleeping and homelessness, and a rise in 'survival crime' where people steal food because they are simply starving. Foodbanks even ask for donations of female sanitary products because of what has been labelled 'period poverty'.

The situation is set to get worse, almost entirely due to political choices and policies. In its Living Standards 2017 report, the Resolution Foundation said:

Very significant cuts to working-age welfare of over £12 billion are a key component of what looks set to be falling living standards for almost the entire bottom half of the working-age income distribution between this year and 2020–21. The result is the biggest rise in inequality since the late 1980s.[15]

The Child Poverty Action Group is predicting a 50 per cent rise in child poverty over the same period.

Apart from the loss of support in material terms which these policies have brought, there has also been a loss in social and spiritual terms for the nation as a whole. Much of the public has been persuaded to take a negative view of social security and those who receive it, on the basis of false beliefs shaped by inaccurate media coverage and political spin. In our national life we have lost a sense of social solidarity, empathy with those in need, and mutual respect regardless of economic status. For those affected by this change in attitudes, not only have many lost a sense of dignity and worth, but they have also lost any certainty that society will provide them with a degree of security. Many disabled and ill people, for instance, live in fear of their next assessment, as they contemplate losing the support that enables them to survive.

The way empathy, trust and respect for people in need has been eroded in such a relatively short time has been remarkable. In 2012 academics at the University of Kent published a report, 'Benefits stigma in Britain',[16] which looked at public attitudes towards benefit claimants and how such attitudes were influenced. They found that 'outlandish slurs against benefit claimants as a group have become an accepted part of the political language, and the default setting for public attitudes is widely seen as one of suspicion and resentment'.

Looking at press coverage of benefit claimants they concluded,

> it is perceived deservingness which drives benefit stigma, and public discourse around social security in the UK seems almost to be designed to make claimants seem undeserving ... A particularly worrying aspect is that there now seems to be a feedback loop between politics, media coverage and public attitudes: over the last three years politicians of all parties have sought to calibrate their statements to reflect what they say members of the public have told them ... In other words, the public discourse of welfare in the UK seems to be caught in a vicious circle.

That was an eventuality Beveridge never anticipated when he set out his plan for a stigma-free social security system.[17]

Some organisations and churches, while responding to the need created by certain welfare policies by setting up foodbanks, homeless shelters, etc., have also have striven to counteract the negative and misleading coverage of benefit claimants. The Joint Public Issues Team (Church of Scotland, Baptist Union of Great Britain, Methodist Church and United Reformed Church) has been particularly good at this. Significant reports like 'The lies we tell ourselves: ending comfortable myths about poverty'[18] and 'Time to Rethink Benefit Sanctions'[19] have made extremely valuable contributions to the debate. It is, however, very difficult to compete with tabloid headlines, and a whole genre of television programmes which have come to be known as 'poverty porn'. The most notorious of these programmes, Channel 4's *Benefits Street,* is now seriously quoted by eminent journalists as the source of their proclaimed knowledge about the lives of benefit claimants.

So changes to social security have been made acceptable to the British public because they have been persuaded that many people receiving benefits are either fraudulent or undeserving. They have also been persuaded that spending on social security is out of control, while the Office for Budget Responsibility says that 'the government is on track by 2020–21 to spend the lowest amount on welfare, as a percentage of GDP, in 30 years'.

As the amount spent on welfare is deliberately reduced as a share of our national wealth, many politicians are keen to persuade us to rely more heavily on private insurance against such misfortunes as unemployment, sickness or disability. This takes us even further away from the collective provision and solidarity of social security and ever closer to an individualistic approach. If a situation develops where a significant percentage of people have private insurance cover, and the welfare state is only for the very poorest, then something precious in our national life will have been lost. Since its inception, the mutuality of the welfare state has bound us together. We paid our taxes and National Insurance, and although for much of our lives we were paying for the help and support that other people received, we knew that at some point we too may need support. In that sense, we really were all in it together, supporting each other.

But if a growing section of the population begins to feel they have no need of the welfare state, that it is merely provision for an uninsured underclass, then there will be very little impetus to defend it and very little desire to pay taxes to support it.

In an article in *The Lancet* in December 2016, Simon Szreter and others wrote that to view welfare spending as an unproductive drain on the economy was 'historically obsolete'. They argued that, 'there should be an end to setting the goal of economic growth against that of welfare provision. A healthy and prospering society needs both. We suggest that they feed each other.' They concluded: 'This country's history shows that long-term prosperity has been served best when the interests of the poor and the wealthy are not mutually opposed in a zero sum game. Investment in policies that develop human and social capital will underpin economic opportunities and security for the whole population.'[20] Some Christian thinkers, like Phillip Booth, argue that welfare provision can give the state too great a role in people's lives. They advocate an approach that complies more with the Catholic principle of subsidiarity, which holds that matters should be dealt with by the smallest, lowest and least centralised competent authority, closest to the people involved.

Of course, when it comes to providing support to help people cope with difficulties in their lives, this is very true. Community-based grass-roots schemes can be far more innovative and flexible than a one-size-fits-all centrally administered approach. However, as Simon Duffy writes, 'The dilemma here is that these kinds of powerful social innovation, inspired by the commitment of ordinary men and women to social justice, are often perceived by the powerful as providing further evidence for the incompetence of the state or the limitations of public services. This then leads to further privatisation or the justification of even deeper cuts to public services. This is a bitter pill to swallow.'[21]

Perhaps the biggest danger of applying the subsidiarity principle to welfare provision is that it risks abandoning the redistributive role which only the state can play, leaving poorer people and areas to fall back on their own inadequate resources. The UK government is currently making moves in this direction, and problems and injustices are already becoming apparent.

Having made very large cuts to national funding for social care, the government has said that local authorities can make up the shortfall by increasing council tax. Obviously, Councils in prosperous areas will be able to raise far more money than councils in deprived areas. The government also proposes passing responsibility for Attendance Allowance, a benefit paid to people over 65 who need help with personal care, over to local authorities, to be funded by local business rates. Again, poorer areas will be placed at a disadvantage by a move that, as Age UK says, 'would create a postcode lottery of support for older disabled people'.

In his essay, 'Pluralism and the Common Good in a Market Economy',[22] Phillip Booth writes: 'Unemployment insurance, health, pensions, and so on – can be provided by a rich tapestry of commercial, mutual and charitable organisations. In the tradition of Catholic Social Teaching, it is not the role of the state to displace these initiatives, but to support them.' He goes on to describe the 'rich tapestry' of health provision before the Second World War, in which private insurance, friendly societies and direct payments covered the majority, while 'Less than 15 per cent relied on free services provided charitably, through the goodwill of doctors or funded by government.'

This situation, which Booth seems to find broadly acceptable, with the state only needed to step in and try to fill the gaps, sounds like a nightmare scenario for a person on a low income with a serious health condition. The potential for humiliation and/or neglect seems all too vividly apparent. When it comes to basic human needs like health care and an income adequate to feed, clothe and house oneself, centralised universal state provision, available as of right, seems far more conducive to human dignity. One man's rich tapestry is another man's postcode lottery.

Only the state can even attempt to tackle inequality. As Pope Francis says in *Evangelii gaudium*[53]: 'Just as the commandment "Thou shalt not kill" sets a clear limit in order to safeguard the value of human life, today we also have to say "thou shalt not" to an economy of exclusion and inequality.'[23]

Pope Francis is quite clear about the primary role and responsibility of the state, saying, 'This imbalance is the result of ideologies which defend the absolute autonomy of the marketplace and financial speculation. Consequently, they reject the right of states, charged with vigilance for the common good, to exercise any form of control. A new tyranny is thus born, invisible and often virtual, which unilaterally and relentlessly imposes its own laws and rules.'

In a modern economy, applying the principle of subsidiarity to welfare provision may risk failing the poorest and most vulnerable, by allowing inequality to grow and leaving injustice unchallenged. As Pope Francis says,'I encourage financial experts and political leaders to ponder the words of one of the sages of antiquity: "Not to share one's wealth with the poor is to steal from them and to take away their livelihood. It is not our own goods which we hold, but theirs."'

An adequate, comprehensive, redistributive and stigma-free system of social security can empower the disadvantaged, discharge our collective responsibility to care for one another, and ultimately make a better country for all of us. It is essential for the common good.

## Questions

- Do you think Britain has become better or worse at looking after the poorest and most vulnerable people in society?
- The majority of children in poverty are now in working households. How should we solve the problem of in-work poverty?
- What do you think of changes in the benefit system in the last few years? Are 'welfare reforms' having the intended effect?
- Are foodbanks a good thing? Why do you think they are necessary?

## Notes

1.  Bishops' Conference of England and Wales, 'Choosing the Common Good – 2010', 2010.
2.  Pope Paul VI, *Gaudium et spes*, Papal Encyclical, 7 December 1965.
3.  The Workhouse website, 'The New Poor Law', http://www.workhouses.org.uk/poorlaws/newpoorlaw.shtml
4.  William Temple, *Christianity and Social Order* (London: Shepheard-Walwyn, 1942).
5.  William Temple, *Citizen and Churchman* (London: Eyre and Spottiswoode, 1941).
6.  The Lambeth Conference, Resolution 19, 1948.
7.  The Declaration of Human Rights, Article 25.
8.  Tania Burchardt, 'The Evolution of Disability Benefits in the UK: Re-weighting the basket, Centre for Analysis of Social Inclusion', CASE Paper 26, June 1999.
9.  Gavin Gordon, 'Margaret Thatcher's secret plans to dismantle welfare state almost prompted a Cabinet "riot"',*Independent*, 25 November 2016.
10. Florence Sutcliffe-Braithwaite, 'Margaret Thatcher, individualism and the welfare state', *History and Policy*, 15 April 2013,

http://www.historyandpolicy.org/opinion-articles/articles/margaret-thatcher-individualism-and-the-welfare-state

11. Jon Stone, 'Appeals against "fit to work" decisions more successful than ever before', *Independent*, 10 September 2015.

12. Joint Public Issues Team, 'Time to rethink benefit sanctions', a report by Church Action on Poverty, the Baptist Union of Great Britain, the United Reformed Church, the Methodist Church, the Church of Scotland, the Church in Wales, March 2015.

13. Disability Rights UK Pip Reform Briefing http://www.disabilityrightsuk.org/news/2016/march/dr-uk-pip-reform-briefing

14. Committee on the Rights of Disabled Persons, United Nations, Officer of the High Commissioner Report of the Inquiry Concerning the United Kingdom of Great Britain and Northern Ireland carried out by the Committee under article 6 of the Optional Protocol to the Convention CRPD/C/15/R.2/Rev.1, http://www.ohchr.org/EN/HRBodies/CRPD/Pages/InquiryProcedure.aspx

15. Adam Corlett and Stephen Clarke, 'Living Standards 2017: the past, present and possible future of UK incomes', Resolution Foundation, 31 January 2017.

16. Ben Baumberg *et al.* 'Benefits Stigma in Britain', Elizabeth Finn Care, University of Kent, 2012.

17. Ben Baumberg *et al.* 'Scroungers, fraudsters and parasites: how media coverage affects our view of benefit claimants', *New Statesman*, November 2012.

18. Joint Public Issues Team, 'The lies we tell ourselves: ending comfortable myths about poverty', a report by Church Action on Poverty, the Baptist Union of Great Britain, the United Reformed Church, the Methodist Church, the Church of Scotland, the Church in Wales, Joint Public Issues Team, February 2013.

19. Joint Public Issues Team, 'Time to rethink benefit sanctions'.

20. Simon Szreter *et al*, 'Health, welfare, and the state – the dangers of forgetting history', *The Lancet*, Vol. 338, No. 10061, pp. 2734–35, 3 December 2016.

21. Simon Duffy, 'Trump, a morbid symptom', *Huffington Post*, 2 February 2017.

22. Philip Booth, 'Pluralism and the Common Good in a market economy', in Nicholas Sagovsky and Peter McGrail (eds), *Together for the Common Good: Towards a national conversation* (London: SCM Press, 2015).

23. Pope Francis, *Evangelii gaudium*, Papal Encyclical, 24 November 2013.

# 5. A New Vision for Welfare?

Simon Duffy

## The problem of welfare

The term 'welfare state' was coined by Archbishop William Temple as part of his passionate advocacy for social justice during the 1930s.[1] The Church of England, under his leadership, played a critical role in preparing the ground for the post-war developments of the welfare state: social security, free education, the NHS and many other social and economic improvements.[2]

Today we live in an age where these changes are taken for granted or disparaged. The idea of the welfare state is no longer honoured and the use of the term 'welfare' is increasingly pejorative.[3] Since the 1980s the institutions of the welfare state have largely been under siege and since 2010 the UK government's austerity programme has seen severe cuts in public services, especially targeted on disabled people and those on lower incomes.[4]

Quite what is driving this assault on the welfare state is a matter of controversy. Leaders like Margaret Thatcher and David Cameron made their case for these changes using a mixture of ideological and economic argument, whereas Tony Blair and Gordon Brown presented their policies as an effort to 'modernise' the welfare state.

However, it is important to recognise that while the UK and the USA have led the assault on the welfare state, similar changes are underway in other countries, even in Scandinavia, where the welfare state model was most firmly established. This is not to legitimise these changes, but it is important to understand the way in which wider social and economic changes in the world are influencing changes in the welfare state.

One of the most important factors has been the end of the Cold War. There is no doubt that part of the consensus that sustained the post-war welfare state was a pragmatic awareness by the Right that a commitment to social justice would be necessary to hold back internal pressures for revolutionary change.[5] The collapse of communism did not just mean the end of an external threat, it also marked the end of the fear of internal revolution.

It is no accident that these changes have also been paralleled by the weakening role of trade unions and other forms of collective organisation: churches, working men's clubs and political parties have all become increasingly weak. The individual is atomised, privatised, provided with work or benefits, but much less connected to any wider social structures or systems of political influence.

It is also important to recognise that the national economy has changed radically. The development of the welfare state was combined with economic policies that saw the state maintain high employment rates by means of high levels of public spending. Whether or not this approach is sustainable, it was clear that by the 1980s this policy was changing. The UK government no longer accepted that it should increase demand by means of public spending. At the same time banks were given greater levels of freedom to create credit and promote economic activity. Increasingly it is the financial services industry (what in older times was known as usury) that has come to dominate economic life.

In tandem with these internal changes the world economy has also changed. Less-developed countries can now compete with or overtake Western economies, establishing new industries at lower costs. It is not just the old heavy industries producing steel, ships, cars and trains that have been undercut. Today the latest technology is also produced in countries with lower wages or by the use of robotics. The old welfare state had relied on these companies to provide pensions, sickness benefits and other welfare services. Today these occupational arrangements have radically declined and most individuals rely primarily on the state system; only a minority purchase their own private pensions or contribute to other forms of social insurance.

Another social system that had helped maintain the welfare state is the family; but family structures have also changed. Women achieved significant social progress by being able to access similar work opportunities as men. Increasingly women are expected to both work (often for less pay) and to provide care for children or older relatives. This has put more pressure on families, which now tend to be both smaller and more dispersed. This is not an argument for gender inequality; it is just to observe that gender equality has not led to an effective redistribution of incomes, work roles or family roles and a balanced approach for both genders.

There has also been a significant decline in the quality of public discourse and democratic life. The optimistic ideas and beliefs that initially inspired the welfare state have declined; this vacuum seems to have been filled by consumerism and by a rather empty form of liberalism. Modern liberalism is sometimes renamed neoliberalism, but it is hard to distinguish what is actually new about neoliberalism; instead it seems to have merely reduced human life to production and consumption. Discussion of public policy is increasingly coarse in tone and simplistic; the decline in consensus about the welfare state seems to have opened up a rhetoric of stigma. It is increasingly seen as acceptable to talk in the most disrespectful terms about people who are out of work or disabled. It is likely that this negative rhetoric about fellow citizens adds further impetus to the attack on the welfare state, particularly as there seems a tendency to forget that many universal and valued systems are part of the welfare state.[6]

## Sustainable solutions

Restoring the welfare state and rediscovering our commitment to the common good cannot rely on some simplistic return to a hallowed past. We cannot wind the clock back to 1945; we must identify a new kind of welfare state, one more fitting to our current reality and one that is more sustainable, and more defensible by future generations. To this end it is worth more clearly distinguishing the inner essence of the welfare state from its outer shell, the systems and institutions that were largely developed in the post-war years and with which it is now commonly identified.

The inner essence of the welfare state is the principle that the state, as an instrument of justice, must protect the social and economic conditions that make human life and development possible. However, the precise and detailed form that any welfare state takes in our lives is a matter of human choice, design and experiment. Just to take one example, it is one thing to recognise that all human beings have a right to some kind of income; it is another thing to propose that we should organise income security using the particular mixture of benefits and employment rights that we currently use. We do have other options.

For instance, William Temple's arguments for the welfare state, set down in *Christianity and Social Order*, provide a vision for the welfare state that is very different from the welfare state that was established by William Beveridge and his colleagues.[7] Temple's vision was rooted in a Christian starting point: we are all equal and beloved creatures, each with our own unique destiny and value. Building on this fundamental moral reality, Temple saw that the welfare state was the means to ensure every individual could participate in the common life of the community:

> To train citizens in the capacity for freedom and to give them scope for action is the supreme end of all true politics.[8]

In fact Temple's work provides a very useful starting point for understanding how we might rethink the welfare state as a platform for citizenship and as a guarantor of the common good. His vision entails a range of design principles which we might think of as the basis for a more loveable version of the welfare state.

First, Temple recognised clearly that the welfare state needed to be rooted in justice and that its actions should be bound by a web of rights and responsibilities. It was unacceptable that some people should find themselves reliant on what he called the 'blood-money' of charity.[9] Temple fully understood that the indignities of the foodbank were in conflict with true Christian belief. Human rights, converted into meaningful legal rights, are essential to a decent welfare system.

Social justice must also be rooted in a profound commitment to our equality, and this equality allows for no compromise. Each human being is to be valued for their own unique value and the temptation to treat some people as more 'useful' than others must be rejected:

> If each man and woman is a child of God, whom God loves and for whom Christ died, then there is in each a worth absolutely independent of all usefulness to society.[10]

Moreover this value implies a positive, a spiritual destiny, which sees value in our strivings and development. We must live with purpose and with opportunities to extend ourselves:

The first aim of social progress must be to give the fullest
possible scope for the exercise of all powers and qualities
which are distinctively personal.[11]

There is only one way on earth that we can reconcile the demands of
justice, our absolute equality and our diversity as spiritual beings, and
that is to choose to act as citizens. That means we must live according
to a code of honour that demands we each seek to contribute to the
common good, according to our diverse gifts.

The combination of Freedom and Fellowship as principles
of social life issues in the obligation of Service.[12]

This also means that our citizenship must be matched by a respect for
the multiple democratic and community institutions that make active
citizenship possible and meaningful. The state, within the welfare
state, must support the creation of all those small communities we
need in order to thrive:

A democracy which is to be Christian must be a democracy
of persons, not only of individuals. It must not only just
tolerate but encourage minor communities as at the
expression and the arena of personal freedom; and its
structure must be such as to serve this end.[13]

Arguably this marks one of the most important differences between
Temple's vision and the reality of the post-war welfare state. The
failure to respect, sustain and promote these minor communities has
seen the growth of passive individualism, not the promotion of active
citizenship. The very weakness of the welfare state today seems rooted
in its failure to support citizenship and community.

This may also help explain why the decline of the welfare state
seems to have happened more quickly in the UK than elsewhere.
The UK is possibly the most centralised welfare state in the world.
The typical English local authority has a population large enough
to sustain a small country; however, local English government
controls only a tiny fraction of local public spending and it lacks any
significant autonomy over its own policies or priorities.[14] This means
the democratic and constitutional roots required to sustain the welfare
state are particularly shallow in the UK and this makes it relatively
easy for the harm of central policies to spread.

## Twenty-first-century solutions

Temple's Christian vision offers us, then, at least one powerful alternative approach to the welfare state: not as a device for social control or increased utility, but as a platform for equal and active citizenship. In principle there should be no reason to believe that this or other more enlightened versions of the welfare state could not be developed to replace the old model. In particular it is important that we identify approaches which encourage us to stand up against the forces that seek to destroy the common good and our commitment to social justice.

It is important to remember that the welfare state was not an entirely new creation, appearing out of nowhere. For decades before 1945 the Church, trade unions, cooperatives and local municipalities had been developing practical systems of support. The 1945 Labour government did not so much create the welfare state from scratch, rather it nationalised the diverse and patchy array of services that preceded it. Today there are many diverse grass-roots community groups who continue to work on practical solutions to meet needs more effectively and in a spirit of equal citizenship.[15]

Moreover, going further back in history, systems of welfare are found in all societies. Herodotus describes the different health care systems found in very different civilisations, and the Torah is full of measures to achieve social justice, for instance:

> When you reap the harvest of your land, do not reap to the very edges of your field or gather the gleanings of your harvest. Leave them for the poor and the alien. I am the Lord your God.                     (Leviticus 23:22)

Obviously these particular arrangements to safeguard the economic interests of the poor only make sense in an agrarian economy. So, when thinking about the actual design of welfare systems, it is not just about respecting the demands of justice, it is also about understanding the reality of the world in which justice must be honoured. The old welfare state was based on certain assumptions about how the economy and about how families worked. Today these assumptions are out of date and we need to rethink the welfare state in the light of current realities.

We live in a global economy, and while this is troubling for many reasons, it is hard to imagine that this will change. This certainly makes it likely that no set of economic institutions will remain very stable for long. Global competition is also combined with rapid technological development, the increasing use of robots and the replacement of many white-collar jobs with software solutions. It doesn't seem remotely likely that economic security will be provided by any stability in employment arrangements; modern technological developments and market solutions seem to thrive on uncertainty.

We are also putting our planet under increasing strain. Carbon-based fuels are limited and dangerous, nuclear power remains risky, while technologies for sustainable energy production seem increasingly effective. In fact the sources of renewable energy seem more closely aligned with the diversity of our local geographies than with the outputs of powerful international corporations.[16] We may be in line for a significant shift in the politics of our economy when people start to wonder who owns the power of the sun, the rivers, tides and the wind.

Lastly we are increasingly aware that many of our needs simply cannot be met without paying attention to our social lives. Mental and physical welfare, child development and a dignified old age cannot be purchased. It is our capacity to live in constructive fellowship with each other which ensures that our social and development needs are met. Families and communities are critical aspects of the common good and they need to be nurtured rather than exploited.

## Basic income

It is for these kinds of reasons that many thinkers and activists are proposing that we convert our current social security system into a system of basic income.[17] This would mean that every individual would get a basic income, sufficient to live with dignity, and unconditionally, even when they are not working.

Although this idea may seem utopian, it already reflects how parts of our current social security system work. For instance, anyone who has paid attention to UK government policy on pensions will note two things. First, for decades the government has tried to encourage people to put aside more of their personal income for their retirement, but with limited success. Second, the basic state pension has now become the foundation stone of the income security for older people and is now relatively well protected. The reality is that most people are not equipped to plan ahead in the way that governments have hoped. Too many people are already too poor or incapable of long-term planning for their own welfare. So a policy for pensions has evolved, one that accepts the fact that occupational pensions have nearly disappeared and that private pensions will never serve more than a minority.[18] These are all signs of the quiet emergence of a basic income solution.

Basic income is not utopian, it is a highly practical solution to some of today's profound economic problems. If we consider basic income from the perspective of Temple's vision for the welfare state we can see that it has many benefits over the current system.

To begin with, basic income can be based on human rights. We have a right to live and to have the necessary minimum to ensure we can live with dignity. Such human rights are not conditional, they are absolute, and a universal and unconditional right to a basic income is what follows from a real commitment to human rights. To Western ways of thinking, a radical commitment to sharing resources seems counter-intuitive, but societies that share do thrive and, in a world where fewer and fewer people control an increasing share of the world's resources, sharing will be a central principle of any future economy.

The further advantage of basic income is that it clears away one of the most vicious features of the current system: its tendency to stigmatise people who need benefits. Most people who have relied on benefits at some time will feel shame, and this shame is reinforced by intrusive systems of questioning and monitoring. Recently this problem has got much worse. The public now believe that benefit fraud (which is statistically insignificant) is a major problem.[19] The failure to comply with the demands of privatised 'employment' services leads to severe sanctions. Politicians and the media seem to have become increasingly vicious in their pronouncements about disabled people and those on benefits. Isaiah never seemed more relevant:

> They use lies and vicious rhetoric, while dreaming up more schemes to defraud the poor; while all the time the poor just cry out for justice.
>
> (Isaiah 32:7, my translation from the Vulgate)

Although the practical consequences of implementing basic income cannot be fully discovered until it has been tested, it is reasonable to assume that they will bring a range of further benefits. When people have a reasonable level of economic security then they will not stop working, but they will be free to find a better balance between earning, caring and contributing to the wider community. In fact an early version of basic income was established in ancient Athens precisely to ensure that every citizen could play an active role in the democratic process. Basic income could be a first step in moving away from the hyper-elitism of our current electoral system and beginning to develop local forms of participative democracy.

Furthermore, while the precise level of any basic income is likely to remain controversial and subject to some practical testing and variations, one of the great advantages of the system is that it makes the business of defining the lowest basic income a matter of concern to everyone. Just as the NHS is well supported precisely because it is universal, and not subject to charges or means-testing, so basic income gives everyone a real stake in increasing the income of the poorest.[20]

## Other possible reforms

These are some of the reasons why, in my view, basic income is likely to be at the hub of developing a new twenty-first-century welfare system. However, many other aspects of the welfare state could evolve in ways that better respect the common good and our equal citizenship. Here I will briefly consider some of the kinds of potential changes we might consider.

For the health care system, the principle of universal health care, free at the point of use, is one of the most important and effective elements of the current system. It is a principle that will need to be defended as the government continues its drive to privatise the NHS to commercial companies who will inevitably seek to provide enhanced services (at a price) for those with higher incomes.

But while the underlying principle of the NHS should be protected it seems reasonable to question whether every feature of its organisation is fit for the future. Many of the most interesting developments in health and health care internationally build on the importance of equipping people and communities with the skills necessary to avoid health problems.[21] Mental health is significantly improved where people can come together to work to address their own needs. A healthy system is likely to be one where growing professional expertise is combined with increased citizenship and community action.

Free education also remains a critical principle, one that has been eroded in further education and is now threatened at the secondary level. Adult education is disappearing and the university system has tied students and colleges into a debt-ridden system. But above all this, there are serious questions about the degree to which the whole system has been undermined by pointless economic imperatives and by the use of standardised methodologies to replace effective teaching. The current systems feels increasingly industrialised and there is significant doubt that standards of learning and achievement are really being raised.

The paradox of education is that learning, information and skills have never been so well developed and so widely dispersed. However, instead of using the growing educational capacity of the community to improve the teacher–pupil ratio or create other social benefits, the educational system has become increasingly insulated from community life.

Housing is one of the areas that has seen some of the most radical changes in recent years. In the early phase of the welfare state the focus was on building council housing. Over time the focus shifted to a combination of rent subsidy (Housing Benefit) the privatisation of public housing and incentives for social and private landlords. The majority of the population in the UK are insulated from these changes as home ownership levels in the UK have typically been high.

However, during the 1990s, in both the UK and the USA, politicians discovered that lowering the cost of borrowing increased house prices, and that this was a very popular strategy with key electoral groups. Over time this policy has reduced the number of people who can afford to buy a home, while shifting resources towards the better-off. The whole strategy is flawed and will probably require profound changes in the taxation of property before any kind of better balance can be achieved.

The fifth and weakest pillar of the welfare state is social care, although this name is controversial, for, as disabled people make clear, 'care' too easily implies an unhealthy dependency and passivity on the part of the person who is 'cared for'. It makes better sense to recast 'care services' around a right to independent living and to ensure that people have clear and controllable entitlements to additional support or funding for support.

This is another area where there has been significant recent change. In the past the care system was largely institutional – hospitals, homes, centres. But disabled people and families were able to develop new solutions that gave them control over their own care budgets. However, since 2009 severe cuts to local government (who provide these services) have savaged the system. So the central reform of a new system must be to establish a fair and sustainable funding system and to eliminate the severe means-testing which bedevils the current system.[22]

## Conclusion

The term 'welfare reform' is currently misused. It has become code for a series of cuts and changes that are regressive and mean-spirited. But genuine reform is possible, in fact it is necessary. The welfare state was developed rapidly, following years of debate and disagreement. It was forged in the fulcrum of war and revolution, and it was built at a time when there was an excessive faith in the capacity of the state to design, control and manage society by rational and centralised procedures.

Today we need the welfare state just as we did then. None of the insecurities that once made the welfare state necessary have disappeared; in fact technological and environmental change has increased our need to work together to ensure the safety and security of all. However, the spirit of a decent twenty-first-century welfare state will need to change if it is to safeguard the common good and, most importantly, if we wish to inspire people to defend and to improve the welfare state. We will only get the welfare state that we are willing to build and defend; without better advocacy we will watch past achievements be frittered away.

All of this presents an interesting challenge to the Church. The welfare state did, in many ways, replace some of the welfare functions of the faith organisations with those of the state. But, as Temple recognised, this was a positive change, one that the Church needed to support. Today the welfare state is under threat and there is a risk that the Church will step into its old role as the giver of last resort. But this would be unfortunate and regressive, the Church would be conspiring with injustice.

The real challenge is for the Church to be an active leader in re-imagining the welfare state as a positive platform for citizens and communities. On this path, the role of the Church, within local communities, would not be diminished, but its role would be to provide a place for the whole community to come together, to support each other and to act as citizens to safeguard the common good.

## Questions

- Do you believe William Temple's vision for welfare can be reframed for the twenty-first century?
- What role do you think Christians should play in developing this vision?
- Is basic income a good solution to the current difficulties with the benefits system? What are the advantages and disadvantages?
- Should we reform other aspects of the welfare state? Do you agree with the proposals outlined in this chapter?

## Notes

1. It seems that the first use of the term was by William Temple in *Christianity and the State* (London: Macmillan, 1928). Interestingly he never uses this term in his later book *Christianity and Social Order* (Harmondsworth: Penguin, 1942). T. H. Marshall, another great theorist associated with the birth of the welfare state only uses the term once in his classic *Citizenship and Social Class* (London: Pluto Press, 1992).
2. See Bernadette Meaden, 'The shrinking safety net', pp. 56–70 in this publication.
3. Arguably the term is not only increasingly pejorative, it is also used in ways that are imprecise. After all, most states would see themselves as advancing welfare. J. Veit-Wilson 'States of Welfare: A conceptual challenge', *Social Policy and Administration*, Vol. 34, No. 1, March 2000, pp. 1–25.
4. Between 2011 and 2016 much of my own work involved calculating the cumulative impact of government cuts on disabled people and people on low incomes. See Simon Duffy, 'A Fair Society? How the cuts target disabled people', The Centre for Welfare Reform, 2013. In 2016 two UN committees severely criticised the UK government for its policies in this regard (UN Committee on Economic, Social and Cultural Rights (CESCR) (2016) Concluding observations on the sixth periodic report of the United Kingdom of Great Britain and Northern Ireland; UN Committee on the Rights of Persons with Disabilities (CRPD) (2016) Inquiry concerning the United Kingdom of Great Britain and Northern Ireland carried out by the Committee under article 6 of the Optional Protocol to the Convention).

5.   N. Kildal and S. Kuhnle (eds), *Normative Foundations of the Welfare State: The Nordic experience* (Abingdon: Routledge, 2005).

6.   In its original conception the idea of the welfare state referred to all those services or systems that served to advance social welfare for all. However today there is a tendency to only think of the most stigmatised elements of the welfare system as being part of the welfare state. So, while benefit recipients are stigmatised, patients of the NHS are not. This one-eyed approach even extends to employees of the state, who can forget that, being paid by the state, they are certainly also 'recipients of welfare'. The cultural norm at work seems to be an idolisation of 'independence' which encourages people to ignore how deeply dependent we all are on the common structures which sustain our lives and livelihoods.

7.   This whole section draws heavily on Temple's *Christianity and Social Order* and the quotes that follow are all taken from Temple. I have explored his arguments in more detail in Simon Duffy, 'Love and welfare', Centre for Welfare Reform, 2016.

8.   Temple, *Christianity and Social Order*, p. 37.

9.   Ibid. p. 11.

10.  Ibid. p. 37.

11.  Ibid. p. 37.

12.  Ibid. p. 42.

13.  Ibid. p. 40.

14.  It is probably indicative of the fundamental problem that there is a lack of public discussion and of effective analysis of the degree of centralisation in the UK. However, one indicator is that local government in 2014–15 raised £31 billion (4%) of all public spending and controlled spending of £169 billion (23%). Moreover this data includes devolved spending in Northern Ireland, Scotland and Wales; extreme centralisation is even greater in England. Public Expenditure: statistical analyses 2014 HM Treasury London: TSO, 2014.

15.  See for example the Women's Centre in Halifax. Simon Duffy and Clare Hyde, 'Women at the Centre', Centre for Welfare Reform, 2011, or Simon Duffy, 'Peer Power', Centre for Welfare Reform, 2012.

16.  See Ellen Teague, 'The threat of the Anthropocene' and Edward P. Echlin 'Living within our bioregion: sharing plant earth' in this publication, pp. 145–167.

17.  There is a lively international campaign for this idea and a vast literature. Malcolm Torry, *Money for Everyone* (Bristol: Policy Press, 2013); Daniel Raventos Panella, *Basic Income: The material condition of freedom* (London: Pluto Press, 2007).

18.  For example, in 2015 only 39% of working-age adults were contributing to some degree to a private or occupational pension. Pensions Policy Institute, Pension Facts 2016, 2015.

19.  A recent poll showed that the general public believed 24% of all benefits were claimed illegally. The real figure is 0.7%, meaning the public were wrong by a factor of more than 34.

20. Ipsos MORI, 'Perils of Perception: Topline Results Fieldwork', 14–18 June 2013.
21. There is some concern that the basic income approach is insensitive to the differences in income that are required because of diverse costs like housing, or needs, such as disability. However, I have argued elsewhere that flexibility can be built into basic income without losing most of its benefits: Simon Duffy, 'Basic Income Plus', Centre for Welfare Reform, 2016.
22. Nigel Crisp, *Turning the World Upside Down* (London: Royal Society of Medicine Press, 2010).
23. See Virginia Moffatt, 'Rolling back the state', in this publication, pp. 85–98.

# 6. Rolling Back the State

Virginia Moffatt

> Do not merely look out for your own personal interests,
> but also for the interests of others.      (Philippians 2:4)

Paul's exhortation to the community of Philippi was in the context of their need to take care of each other, but it could equally apply to the way we as a society look after each other.

I have spent most of my adult life working in the public and voluntary sector, inspired by my faith and this mission to look after the 'interests of others'. In this chapter, I'll be reflecting the historical changes that have happened over the last seventy years that have latterly made such a task monumentally more difficult. From the post-war consensus, built on a sense of the need to work for the common good, to the neoliberal consensus that tore it down, leading to our current age of austerity, which is threatening to destroy public services for good.

## The post-war consensus

In 1942, William Beveridge produced a groundbreaking report on social insurance and welfare. The document laid out a response to the five social ills of the era: Want, Ignorance, Squalor, Disease and Idleness.[1] The so-called Beveridge Report was to prove hugely influential, and was embraced by politicians on all sides of the political spectrum. Perhaps, because there was a sense of solidarity in a country battered by war, or perhaps, because war had broken down the barriers between classes allowing those with more to understand how those with less lived, or perhaps the experience of war created a kinder national spirit. Whatever the reason, over the next six years, a number of influential acts were passed that increased the state's responsibility in the delivery of public service. As a result, for the first time UK citizens were entitled to free health services and education, increased opportunities for housing, a welfare safety net and social and community services.

The so-called 'post-war consensus' was a remarkable moment in British history, when parties of all political persuasions united to reduce inequality, and provide health, housing and education for all. Despite the inevitable flaws in the legislation, it was a time when 'common good' principles seemed to run through government policy-making. And, as Bernadette Meaden[2] and Simon Duffy[3] have noted, many of those policy developments were deeply influenced by Christian thinkers such as William Temple.

The post-war consensus resulted in a series of important acts between 1944 and 1948 that in turn were drawn from the same concept of building a 'new Jerusalem'[4] that has inspired this book. The first of these was the 1944 Education Act, passed by Churchill's coalition government, which made education a statutory responsibility. After the war, Attlee's Labour government, went further with the 1946 Housing Act, 1946 National Insurance and 1948 National Assistance Act and 1948 NHS Act, all of which increased the role of the state in providing support for its citizens.

The 1944 Education Act increased the statutory role of local government in education, raised the education age to 16 (though this wasn't to be achieved till the 1970s) and established the principle of free education for all. It was an important achievement that arose from the recognition poor families could not sustain the costs associated with free places at grammar school. This paved the way for further acts over the next thirty years which would abolish the selective grammar school system, replacing it with a broader comprehensive system.[5]

The 1946 Housing Act also gave more powers to local government, and resulted in a flurry of housing developments, particularly in inner-city areas that had been subject to bombings, and where many slums had existed. Over the next thirty years, it led to a huge housing boom and a massive increase in the number of council houses, which was supported by all political parties.[6] In fact, although council housing is a policy most associated with Labour, it was Conservative governments, such as the one led by Harold Macmillan, who created the most housing in this era.[7]

It is hard today, with all of us used to free health care, to understand what a huge cultural shift the foundation of the NHS brought to Britain.[8] Before this time, most people could not pay to go to hospital, and could barely afford a GP. In his moving book *Harry's Last Stand*, Harry Leslie Smith documents the miserable death of his sister, in pain, unable to move because his parents simply did not have the means to pay for her cancer treatment,[9] a situation that seems unthinkable now.

Finally, the 1946 National Insurance Act increased the welfare safety net[10] discussed in Chapters 4 and 5, while the 1948 National Assistance Act abolished the hated Poor Laws. It also laid powers on local authorities to fund support to citizens who needed assistance to take care of their physical and emotional needs. This enabled social services departments to provide social care for older people, sick and disabled people and other vulnerable groups.[11]

The cumulative impact of these acts cannot be underestimated. For the first time in British history, everyone had access to health care, education and improved access to housing. The combination of these post-war developments and a growing economy was an improvement in living conditions and a more equal society.[12]

Of course, one of the challenges for government is meeting the needs of the population in ways that don't do inadvertent harm. While there were great benefits from the incursion of the state into these areas, there were also problems. Although the state could ensure there was service provision across the country, rather than piecemeal philanthropy, government agencies could nonetheless be controlling and cruel. An example of the worst excesses of this were detailed in Ken Loach's famous film *Cathy Come Home*, which follows the fortunes of a young mother who loses her home due to a combination of lack of employment and rent increases, and then goes on to lose her children to the state because of lack of compassionate support.[13] Additionally, although the boom in council housing provided better quality homes for tenants, it also resulted in the break-up of some long-term communities.[14] Post-war building materials were also in short supply, leading to some poorly constructed prefabs that were decaying by the 1980s and brutalist housing estates that became rife with crime.[15]

There have been other criticisms of state services. It has been argued that they limit freedoms, for example, the choice of faith schools to set their own agenda.[16] Additional concerns have been that they are too regulated and that regulation is ineffective[17] and that they are not as efficient as private sector organisations.

Despite these criticisms, the post-war consensus resulted in well-funded public services and a sense that successive governments were committed to policies that had wide benefits for the whole of society.

## The neoliberal consensus

As other writers in this book have noted,[18] the 1970s saw a changed reality across the world. Oil crises and problems with industrial relations brought chaos and turmoil, which led to the rise of Ronald Reagan and Margaret Thatcher, the development of free-market ideology and the formation of the neoliberal consensus. Starting cautiously at first, but emboldened by their second (and in Thatcher's case, third) term, these politicians embarked on a major programme to 'roll back the state'. Utility companies and transport were the first areas to be targeted, with major privatisation programmes made attractive by the idea that ordinary people could buy shares and make money.[19]

Another early Thatcherite policy was to provide council tenants with the opportunity to buy their own homes, the so-called 'right to buy' policy. The laudable goal of ensuring every citizen could be a property owner was undermined by the effect it had on council housing. Because councils were not allowed to spend capital receipts on further homes, this resulted in the post-war council housing boom coming to an end. The amount of council stock reduced, putting pressure on local authorities to house individuals and families.[20]

Throughout this period the NHS and local authorities also found their budgets squeezed as central government expenditure fell, forcing cuts in social care, education and community services. Meanwhile, compulsory competitive tendering saw the outsourcing of rubbish collection and other council services in what many felt was a direct attack on unions.[21] And although health and social care were protected from privatisation, the government began the first steps towards marketisation through the introduction of some key policies. In 1988, Sir Roy Griffiths, published a green paper which became known as 'The Griffiths Report'. This influential document led to the 1990 Community Care Act, the foundation of care management teams purchasing packages of care, and the 'mixed economy of care'. The report recommended that social care was provided from a mixture of state, nonprofit and private organisations and this soon ensued.[22] Around the same time, market principles were introduced into the NHS for the first time, resulting in the 1991 purchaser/provider split and leading to the start of an increasingly complex system of health management.[23]

Meanwhile in education, the 1988 Education Reform Act gave schools the power to leave local authority control and manage their own finances, set up the national curriculum and introduced league tables and testing at regular intervals.[24] Education itself was not threatened with privatisation at this time, though setting schools free from local government control would later pave the way for academies. However, the prescriptive nature of the curriculum and frequent testing led many educators to raise concerns that schools have since been restricted in the way they could teach, ensuring children had a less creative and interesting educational experience;[25] and the first steps to make students pay for higher education were taken in 1989 when maintenance grants were replaced with student loans.[26]

By the time Labour took power in 1997, all utility services were fully privatised and the concept of the market was embedded in social and health care and other welfare services. And just as Macmillan's government had pushed forward socialist principles that it had come to accept, Tony Blair's government now furthered this privatisation agenda. His so called 'Third Way' between socialism and capitalism, in fact resulted in a softer form of Thatcherism, made more acceptable because it was couched in the language of meeting social need and came with increased resources. By the end of his first term, one of his chief political allies, Peter Mandelson, was proud to boast, 'We're all Thatcherite now'[27]. A positive impact of the Blair years was a much needed increase in investment in public sector spending, particularly in health, social care and education.[28] There were also some important social policy initiatives at this time that undoubtedly made a difference to people's lives. The 'Valuing People' white paper took up many policies developed at the grass-roots level, by people with learning disabilities and their supporters, turning them into a progressive government agenda. This in turn led to an increase in supported living, employment, health and education programmes across the country.[29] Unfortunately, the white paper was never made into an Act of Parliament, weakening the ability of councils to maintain these changes under the fire of austerity. Another development, Sure Start, saw a programme of preventative support for families rolled out across the country with great success.[30] This too was a policy Labour could be proud of. Nonetheless, it was the commitment to continue the ideas Thatcher started that would prove a longer-lasting legacy. While Blair and Brown might not have been wholesale privatisers, their actions increased private involvement in the public sector, creating the drawbridge over which the ravaging hordes of privatisation would later run once David Cameron came to power.

There were several New Labour policies that created this situation. First, Labour introduced the idea of academies into the education system, giving schools the opportunity to escape from the control of the local education authority and be run as independent companies.[31] Similarly health providers were turned into foundation trusts, so that they could also operate more like businesses,[32] and Private Finance Initiatives were used to fund schools and hospitals, often at a huge expense.[33] Additionally, the costs of higher education increased for individual students with the introduction of tuition fees.[34] Increasing demand for residential care led to pressures on social care budgets, making large companies offering lower prices a more attractive proposition for local authorities. With EU rules loosened on tendering, they also embraced procurement as a means to reduce prices, leading to outsourcing in all areas of provision including social care and community services. At the same time national government contracts were routinely procured with international corporations, such as G4S winning contracts for running services for refugees, and IT company Atos running the now infamous Work Capability Assessment programme.[35] By the time Blair left office in 2007, the relationship between public funders and private providers was well established, though the significance of this change was masked by the fact that public services had sufficient resources for few to question if it mattered who was actually running them.

And then came the bankers crash of 2008, and everything changed.

## The age of austerity

In 2008, at the time of the bankers' crisis, George Osborne, the then Shadow Chancellor, was frequently on the television arguing that the public sector was profligate and the only way to save the economy was to reduce its funding. Though I can find none of these interviews on the internet now, I remember them clearly, and the way he later cleverly translated this into the message that Labour had broken the economy and couldn't be trusted to fix it. In fact, as I used to regularly shout at the television at the time, it wasn't the public sector's fault: the crash was due to overselling and lack of regulation in the banking sector.[36] Furthermore, the Chancellor, Alistair Darling had developed a strategy that seemed to be working. Using a combination of some cuts in public sector expenditure, protection for the banks, and investment, there were signs of the beginnings of economic growth by early 2010.[37]

However, this was an election year, and the Conservatives had been out of power for thirteen years. The Labour Prime Minister, Gordon Brown, was unpopular, and the signs of recovery were tentative to say the least. The opposition leader, David Cameron, was keen to portray himself as a new breed of compassionate Conservative, hoping this would give him a strong chance of winning an election after three bruising defeats. He did not quite achieve his aim. Uncertain times led to an uncertain result; for the first time since the 1970s Britain had a hung Parliament.

With the Conservatives gaining such a small majority, many of us assumed that the Liberal Democrats would form a coalition with Labour. After all, they were the incumbent party and seemed to be more natural allies. However, after several days of negotiations, to everyone's surprise the Liberal Democrats threw in their lot with the Conservatives. Even though part of the deal meant the party accepting Conservative spending plans, the resulting joint press conference in the rose garden at Downing Street was upbeat and light hearted, with David Cameron and Nick Clegg confidently declaring they were building a new form of politics.[38] Within weeks, George Osborne's first budget would demonstrate what that 'new politics' would look like, when he made good on his promise to cut expenditure on public services. Couched in the language of 'we're all in this together' and 'there is no alternative', he proposed a 25 per cent cut from the public sector between 2010 and 2014, a move unions described as 'a declaration of war'.[39]Although the justification for such deep cuts was that the economy could only recover if they were implemented, many interpreted it as an excuse to implement a further rolling back of the state.[40]

This suspicion was furthered by the swiftness with which the coalition went on to raise tuition fees, breaking a key promise in the Liberal Democrat manifesto. Any hopes that the Liberal Democrats might put a brake on Conservative policies were soon dashed with their support for the 2012 Welfare Reform Act, whose harmful impact was outlined in Bernadette Meaden's chapter.[41] Nor did they fight their partners over the 2012 NHS and Social Care Act, despite the fact that it increased opportunities for private companies to bid for NHS contracts, created further complexity of the management of the NHS and was interpreted by many as being the start of full- scale privatisation.[42] Similarly the 2010 Academies Act led to the government accelerating the academisation programme[43] and encouraged the development of free schools run completely outside local government control.[44] This series of acts had as critical an impact as the post-war acts of the 1940s. They tore further into the foundations of the welfare state and indicated that the age of austerity was simply an excuse to bring free-market ideology into every aspect of the public sector.

Although many protested against austerity during the years of coalition government, when it came to the 2015 election, the Conservatives finally managed to gain the majority they had been denied in 2010. It was by no means a decisive victory, but it gave them the power and the confidence to continue with this trend for cuts and privatisation. George Osborne's 2015 Autumn Statement resulted in a further reduction in public spending, bringing the grand total to 33 per cent by 2020, the lowest it has been since before the war.[45] At that point, hundreds of thousands of jobs had already been lost in the public sector, and it was predicted that job losses for the decade 2010–20 would reach 1 million.[46] And though the March 2017 Budget threw a small crumb of comfort with an increase in social care of £2 billion over three years,[47] it is unlikely to have sufficient impact to make last change.

Austerity has resulted in reductions of public services up and down the country. A particularly high-profile area is libraries. The loss of 343 libraries in this period is nothing short of tragic.[48] Not only do libraries enable children who don't have access to books at home the chance to read and educate themselves, but they are often community hubs, providing activities for the elderly, young people and small children, assistance for unemployed people seeking work and shelter for homeless people. Our communities are poorer without them.

But the people who have borne the brunt of the cuts, are those least able to bear it. Sick and disabled people have suffered the double whammy of cuts in social care and benefits, resulting in poverty, stress and deteriorating health.[49] Cuts have also fallen disproportionately on women, people of colour and poor people, while leisure centres, public parks and youth services have all been hit.[50] The great developments of the Labour years have been set back decades, with learning disabled and physically disabled people seeing their dreams of independent living destroyed by lack of resources to support them.[51] Additionally, there has been a massive reduction in Sure Start and other children's centres being closed up and down the country.[52]

If this wasn't bad enough, the nation is also in the grip of a housing crisis, the culmination of poor housing policy over the last forty years, which has been exacerbated by austerity. The buy-to-let policies initiated in the 1980s and the sell-off of council estates in the last decade have reduced the amount of council housing available, resulting in a rise in people living in temporary accommodation or forced to leave the area in which they grew up. Social housing is also contracting, while benefit cuts and the 'bedroom tax' have resulted in many losing their homes. House prices continue to rise, fuelled by buy-to-let policies that favour rich landlords and first-time buyer deals that result in 'affordable' properties being priced at £450,000, while 'generation rent' live in precarious rented accommodation unable to get onto the housing ladder, and the closure of hostels for homeless people has seen an increase in homelessness.[53]

There isn't a single section of society that hasn't been affected by this. Since 2010, we've seen protests from sick and disabled people, students, teachers, lawyers and junior doctors, a sure sign that something is wrong. Even David Cameron's home county of Oxfordshire raised concerns about cuts,[54] while his mother signed a petition against the closure of her local children's centre and his aunt joined local protests over the issue.[55] And yet the argument continues that austerity is the only way to reduce the deficit, something George Osborne promised to deliver by 2015.[56] At the time his approach was disputed by many economists,[57] and they have been proved right. By 2015, the deficit was only halved while public debt had increased.[58] Nevertheless, austerity rolls forward, despite the devastation it has caused.

I started my career in social care in 1984 at the beginning of Margaret Thatcher's second term. Those early years were tough, and spending cuts undoubtedly had an impact on our ability to deliver a good service. Nonetheless, it was an optimistic time. I was surrounded by people who, like me, were committed to ensuring people with learning disabilities had the same opportunities as everyone else. In the years that followed, I was proud to be part of a movement that enabled people to gain greater independence and control over their lives. Together we achieved a great deal. Somewhat naively I believed that things would always be this way and that we would continue to see such improvements. For years I believed that though politicians on Left and Right might disagree about the means, they all accepted the premise that Paul expresses in Philippians, that we should look after the 'interests of others'. Austerity has proved me wrong.

Over the last seven years I have watched in horror as the progress made in all sections of the welfare state has collapsed in the onslaught of funding cuts. In 2014, I finally left my job in social services, because after years of restructuring, increased workload and dwindling budgets, I could no longer bear trying to square the circle of ensuring good quality services with insufficient funding. Since then, through my time as an academy board member, and a few months spent in a GP practice, I have witnessed similar pressures in education and health. Everywhere, good committed people are overburdened and stressed as they try to deliver the service people need, without having enough resources to do so – services that cannot be delivered by a large corporation whose bottom line is profit.

The post-war consensus was not perfect. Nonetheless those of us lucky enough to grow up during that period experienced free university education, affordable housing, free health care and the knowledge that the welfare safety net was there to help us in times of trouble. We grew up believing that whoever was in power, our government recognised they had a responsibility to act in the interest of the common good. The neoliberal consensus has done the opposite, so that as my children prepare to leave home, they face a life saddled with university debt, struggling to pay their rent, threats to free health care and no guarantee of state help if things get tough, whilst austerity policies have wreaked further damage to communities, resulting in the loss of vital public services up and down the country.

It doesn't have to be like this. And we shouldn't let it. And judging by the increased vote for progressive parties in the 2017 election, there is a growing awareness that things need to change. In the next chapter, I will discuss how we might go about this through the re-creation of wealthy communities, rolling back the market and re-imagining the role of the state, so that once more it works for the common good.

## Questions

- What public sector services do you use regularly? How have they changed since 2010?
- Has your local area experienced many funding cuts? Who do you hold responsible for this?
- Have you or your church community responded to local cuts in services? Is this sufficient?
- How do you think we can reverse austerity and the privatisation agenda?

## Notes

1. William Beveridge, 'Social insurance and allied services (The Beveridge Report), HMG, 1942.
2. See Bernadette Meaden, 'The shrinking safety net,' in this publication, pp. 56–70.
3. See Simon Duffy, 'A new vision for welfare', in this publication, pp. 71–84.
4. Tristram Hunt, 'Clement Attlee's progressive pilgrimage', *Prospect*, 15 September 2016.
5. Houses of Parliament website, The Education Act of 1944, http://www.parliament.uk/about/living-heritage/transformingsociety/livinglearning/school/overview/educationact1944/
6. Hansard website, Housing (Financial and Miscellaneous Provisions) Act 1946, http://hansard.millbanksystems.com/acts/housing-financial-and-miscellaneous-provisions-act-1946
7. Larry Elliot, 'A brief history of British housing', *Observer*, 24 May 2014, https://www.theguardian.com/business/2014/may/24/history-british-housing-decade
8. Hansard website, National Health Act 1948, http://hansard.millbanksystems.com/acts/national-health-act-1948
9. Harry Leslie Smith, *Harry's Last Stand: How the world my generation built is falling down and what we can do to save it* (London: Icon Books, 2014).
10. Hansard website, National Insurance Act 1946, http://hansard.millbanksystems.com/acts/national-insurance-act-1946
11. Hansard website, National Assistance Act 1948, http://www.legislation.gov.uk/ukpga/1948/29/pdfs/ukpga_19480029_en.pdf
12. Wikipedia, 'Economic History of the United Kingdom', https://en.wikipedia.org/wiki/Economic_history_of_the_United_Kingdom
13. Jeremy Sandford, *Cathy Comes Home*, Wednesday Play, directed by Ken Loach, produced by Tony Garnett, first shown on BBC1, 16 November 1966.
14. Becky Tunstall (ed.), 'Breaking up communities? The social impact of housing demolition in the late twentieth century', record of a study and information sharing day at the University of York, 2 November 2012,

https://pure.york.ac.uk/portal/en/publications/connected-communities-
-breaking-up-communities(ba80206a-ba8b-4188-90fe-e8e01f18289a).html

15. Andy Beckett, 'The fall and rise of the council estate', *Guardian*, 13 July 2016.

16. Philip Booth, 'Pluralism and the common good in a market economy' in Nicholas Sagovsky and Peter McGrail (eds), *Together for the Common Good: Towards a national conversation* (London: SCM Press, 2015).

17. Simon Duffy, 'Why CQC fails to regulate care properly', *Huffington Post*, 17 January 2017.

18. See John Moffatt, 'Whatever happened to the common good?', Bernadette Meaden, 'The shrinking safety net' and Simon Duffy, 'A new vision for welfare', all in this publication.

19. Alistair Osborne, 'Margaret Thatcher, one policy that led to more than 50 companies being sold or privatised', *Sunday Telegraph*, 5 February 2017.

20. Dawn Foster, 'Right to buy: A history of Margaret Thatcher's controversial policy', *Guardian*, 7 December 2015.

21. Tony Travers, 'Local government. Margaret Thatcher's 11 year war', *Guardian*, 9 April 2013.

22. Sir Roy Griffiths, 'Community care: Agenda for action' ('The Griffiths Report'), Green Paper, HMG, 1988.

23. House of Commons Briefing Paper Number CBP 05607, 'NHS Commissioning before April 2013', 23 September 2016.

24. Education Reform Act 1988.

25. Anthea Lipsett, 'National Curriculum constrains teachers and pupils', *Guardian*, 11 June 2008.

26. Heidi Blake, 'Grants, loans and tuition fees: a timeline of how university funding has evolved', *Daily Telegraph*, 10 November 2010.

27. Matthew Tempest, 'Mandelson: we are all Thatcherites now' *Guardian*, 10 June 2002.

28. Robert Chote *et al.*, 'Public spending under Labour', 2010 Election Briefing Note no. 5, Institute of Fiscal Studies (IFS BN92).

29. Department of Health, 'Valuing People – A new strategy for learning disabilities for the 21st Century', Cmd 5086, 28 March 2001.

30. Rachel Williams, 'The evolution of Sure Start: the challenges and successes', *Guardian*, 19 October 2011.

31. Andrew Eyles and Stephen Machin, 'The introduction of academy schools to England's Education', CEP Discussion Paper no. 1368, Centre for Economic Performance, August 2015.

32. NHS History website, A short guide to NHS Foundation Trusts, http://www.nhshistory.net/foundation.pdf

33. Jonathan Owen, 'Crippling PFI deals leave Britain £222 bn in debt', *Independent*, 11 April 2015, http://www.independent.co.uk/money/loans-credit/crippling-pfi-deals-leave-britain-222bn-in-debt-10170214.html

34. Anoosh Chakelia, 'The story of education fees: from keepy uppy to political football', *New Statesman*, 27 February 2015.

35. See Virginia Moffatt, 'Rolling back the market', in this publication, pp. 99–116.

36. Philip Aldrick, 'Sir Mervyn King admits BoE failed over financial crisis', *Daily Telegraph*, 14 February 2017.

37. Jeremy Smith, 'Austerity deficits and the fiscal balance', Economists for Rational Policy Briefing 2, 23 February 2015.

38. Helene Mulholland *et al.*, 'David Cameron and Nick Clegg hail "historic and seismic shift" in politics', *Guardian*, 12 May 2010.

39. Polly Curtis, 'Budget 2010: Public sector cuts a "declaration of war" say unions', *Guardian*, 22 June 2010.

40. George Eaton, 'Cameron is wrong, the spending cuts are ideological', *New Statesman*, 31 December 2010.

41. See Bernadette Meaden, 'The shrinking safety net', in this publication, pp. 56–70.

42. Kings Fund website, 'The NHS after the Health and Social Care Act', https://www.kingsfund.org.uk/projects/new-nhs

43. Politics website, 'Academies', http://www.politics.co.uk/reference/academies

44. BBC News website, 'What is the rationale behind free schools?', http://www.bbc.co.uk/news/education-13266290

45. Local Government Association website, 'Future funding outlook for councils from 2010/11 to 2019/20, http://www.local.gov.uk/node/7981028

46. David Walker, 'Tories don't know the impact of 500,000 more public sector job cuts', *Guardian*, 15 June 2015.

47. Ekklesia website, 'Key points from the budget', 8 March 2017, http://www.ekklesia.co.uk/node/23813

48. BBC News, 'Libraries lose a quarter of staff as hundreds close', 29 March 2016.

49. Simon Duffy, 'Counting the cuts', Centre for Welfare Reform, 2014.

50. Unison website, 'Cuts to local services', https://www.unison.org.uk/at-work/local-government/key-issues/cuts-to-local-services/

51. Karen McVeigh, 'Benefit cuts threaten independent living for thousands of disabled people', *Guardian*, 15 March 2016.

52. Peter Walker, 'Sure Start closures almost doubled last year, figures show', *Guardian*, 8 December 2016.

53. Andrew Francis (ed.), *Foxes Have Holes: Christian reflections on Britain's housing* need (London: Ekklesia, 2016).

54. George Monbiot, 'David Cameron hasn't the faintest idea how deep his cuts go. This letter proves it', *Guardian*, 11 November 2015.

55. Ashley Cowburn, 'David Cameron's aunt "joined anti-cuts protest at the weekend"', *Independent*, 15 February 2016. http://www.independent.co.uk/news/uk/politics/david-cameron-s-aunt-joins-oxford-anti-cuts-protest-a6875021.html

56. Conservative Home, 'George Osborne confirms intention to eliminate the deficit in first Commons clash with Alan Johnson', 13 October 2010. http://www.conservativehome.com/parliament/2010/10/george-osborne-confirms-intention-to-eliminate-deficit-by-2015-in-first-commons-clash-with-alan-john.html

57.  Paul Krugman, 'The austerity delusion', *New York Times*, 24 March 2011.
58.  Full Fact website, 'Election 2015: Debt and deficit', 30 April 2015.

# 7. Rolling Back the Market

## Virginia Moffatt

At the time of writing, public services are crumbling in every sector. Winter pressures, always a problem in the NHS, have lead to deaths in A&E, with the British Red Cross declaring the situation to be a humanitarian crisis.[1] After six years of cuts, social care services are in such disarray that three different select committees have called for a cross-party investigation.[2] The closure of night shelters has led to city streets being full of homeless people,[3] while affordable housing is a pipe dream for many. Cuts are predicted in education and in the prison system, riots are frequent.[4] Libraries and leisure services are closing, highway services are unable to keep up with potholes, the infrastructure of our country is breaking down, and with it any sense of a society built on common good principles. Not only is this causing specific damage to individuals who need extra support to survive – homeless people, sick and disabled people, families – but it is also damaging society as a whole.

We didn't get here by chance, as I suggested in my previous chapter. This is the result of politicians from Thatcher and Reagan onwards attempting to provide public services according to principles of laissez-faire economics. As John Moffatt notes in Chapter 2[5] such policies claim roots in ideas from Adam Smith's *The Wealth of Nations*. These include the notion that a perfectly free market can sort out the best outcome, and the modern corollary that public spending can and should be reined in. But it is plain to see from the above, designing public policy based on market forces is resulting in the worst outcomes for everyone. Not only has such thinking been destructive to public services and local communities, we have yet to see the benefits. Though economic growth for 2016 was 2.2 per cent, a marked improvement on the 1.5 per cent growth in 2010,[6] it was down from 2014.[7] Furthermore, the same period has seen a rise in the national debt and as I pointed out in the previous chapter, the promise that austerity would eliminate the deficit has not been realised.[8] Rather than pursuing policies to increase the wealth of the nation, which in fact creates inequalities and damages society,[9] we should turn our attention instead to look at ways to increase the wealth of all our communities. And we should consider this not just in economic terms but in human ones. Community wealth isn't just about the income flowing into an area – though that is important – it is also about how that income is spent and on whom, and the non-fiscal contributions each member can make, caring, volunteering, creating art and so on.

There is a strong moral imperative to build communities that consider the needs of others. As Pope Francis recently remarked, 'You cannot be a Christian without practising the Beatitudes. You cannot be a Christian without doing what Jesus teaches us in Matthew 25.'[10]

> For I was hungry and you gave me food, I was thirsty and you gave me drink, I was a stranger and you made me welcome, lacking clothes and you clothed me, sick and you visited me, in prison and you came to see me.
> (Matthew 25:31–46)

A truly wealthy community can only exist when everyone feels they have a stake, and everyone has resources to survive. While most people look to their immediate family, friends and neighbours to flourish, the state has an important part in ensuring the local infrastructure works to make that happen. In particular, public services are necessary to ensure the health and well-being of those who need extra help: women fleeing domestic violence, disabled people, those who are ill, homeless, refugees.

However, it is not just those in need of extra support who benefit from public services. Everybody uses roads and footpaths, and will suffer when they are full of potholes. Even the very healthy require medical treatment from time to time. And we can all be enriched by museums; we can all enjoy parks or get fit at leisure centres. Those of us who are parents want good education for our children, and those who are not still reap the rewards of an educated workforce. When all of these elements of public service are working effectively, our communities can be places where people can work, learn, share art, play, talk and think together. Even if we never used a single public service, we are still affected when they are cut. Without decent health care, sickness levels will rise, resulting in lost productivity in the workforce, which in turn has a negative impact on the economy. Loss of preventative youth and community services coupled with lack of decent educational opportunities can lead to young people having fewer options open to them, which in turn can lead to an increase in crime. The effect of closing night shelters is that more people sleep on the streets, and there is a rise in begging and antisocial behaviour. It is not only morally right to protect public services – it is in all our interests to do so.

When austerity began, following the banker's crash in 2008, politicians on all sides of the House of Commons argued that it was politically necessary. And few disagreed with George Osborne's first austerity budget in 2010. Now that the impacts are being experienced across the UK, this consensus, thankfully, has shifted. Labour, the SNP, the Green Party and Plaid Cymru are all vehemently anti-austerity, while the Liberal Democrats, who helped make it a reality in office, have also shifted their views. UKIP has adopted some positive ideas for public services, and recently even Theresa May has suggested we need to have a 'shared society',[11] although, as Simon Barrow notes in Chapter 3,[12] it remains to be seen whether this is anything more than a political soundbite.

However, if we are to stop public services deteriorating further, we need to encourage politicians to build a post-austerity consensus that ensures they work for the common good. We need to build on the voices that were finally being heard during the 2017 election: the sick and disabled people, teachers, health workers, police, carers, who all cried out for change. To do so we need to increase resources, reassess and roll back the market and re-imagine the role of the state in the provision of public service.

## Increasing resources

'Throwing money at a problem doesn't necessarily solve it' is an oft-repeated mantra in public service and one that is patently true. It is sadly all too easy to think an injection of cash will provide an instant fix to a problem, when there is a more efficient way of doing something, or the issue is actually the competency of the service. However, it is also true that if there is insufficient money in the system, no amount of creativity or restructuring will improve matters. As noted above, when we've reached a place where every section of public service is struggling, it is time for a rethink.

The 2016 Autumn Statement continued the trend of the previous six, confirming that the £3.5 billion savings plan announced in George Osborne's spring budget would continue.[13] As a result, despite the fact that councils can levy an extra 3 per cent in council tax for social care, they face further reductions in spending in 2017/18.[14] Furthermore, that additional tax means citizens are being charged twice for the same service, and even then the funding is insufficient. In addition, it puts an extra burden on councils in poorer areas. And although the March 2017 Budget's commitment to increase social care funding by £2 billion is welcome, it is unlikely to resolve the crisis. The disability charity Leonard Cheshire has pointed out the funding 'falls short of a long term solution',[15] while North East Councils argued that it is 'too little, too late'.[16] We urgently need a massive reinvestment in local government to repair the damage inflicted on our communities by cuts to social care and other public services.

There are some who will still argue that we have not got the money to do this. However, this is a hollow argument when set against the knowledge that the welfare state of the 1940s was built in times of worse austerity.[17] We are a wealthy nation, we always have choices about where we apportion our budget. For a start, we could invest in chasing corporate tax avoiders, who lose EU governments £760 billion per year according to the tax expert Richard Murphy.[18] Additionally, many economists argue, as Jeremy Smith does, that focusing on the deficit is unhelpful; economic growth can be kick-started by investing in public sector services and reducing VAT, as Alistair Darling did in 2008/9.[19] The same author also notes, in a companion paper, that reduced wages means lower tax revenues. He proposes that increasing wages, in addition to increasing public expenditure, as President Obama did in the USA, would improve public services and living conditions as well as leading to growth.[20] Portugal has demonstrated the wisdom of anti-austerity policies, when it recently reduced its deficit, despite concerns that abandoning austerity would be bad for the economy.[21] Finally, we could rethink some of our current choices of expenditure. The Trident nuclear weapons system costs us £35 billion a year, a figure that will rise to £40 billion by 2020/21.[22] The arms industry is heavily subsidised by government despite only contributing to 1 per cent of GDP and 0.6 per cent of employment.[23]

If we want truly wealthy communities wouldn't it better to invest that money in services for the common good?

## Reducing the burden on individuals

One of the key arguments of austerity has been that it was necessary to prevent our children inheriting debt. Not only is this patently false, as the deficit has not been eliminated, and the national debt has risen, but austerity has actually made things worse for the next generation. Today's young people will spend the rest of their lives repaying the cost of education, struggling to make rent, and possibly in the future having to fund health care too. The only way we can ensure better prospects for everyone is if the government re-establishes the principle of free health, education and social care for all and develops strategies to ensure that the costs of housing are no more than a third of an individual's wage.

## Reassessing the role of the market

As John Moffatt noted in Chapter 2,[24] the idea that the state can provide everything is as unhelpful as the idea that the state should do nothing. The trend of the last forty years has been the assumption that the market knows best and the last decade has seen a massive growth in privatisation of public services and outsourcing of in-house provision, even though opinion poll after opinion poll has demonstrated that there is a strong desire to re-nationalise utilities and concern about privatisation of welfare services such as the NHS.[25]

Private companies now have large stakes in the public sector, often controversially so. G4S, for example, has a range of contracts to manage detention centres, refugee services and children's services.[26] These remain in place, even though there have been many allegations of abuse and poor performance over the years.[27] Recent concerns have also been raised that refugees have been stigmatised by a decision by G4S to paint the doors of their homes, red marking them out from other houses in the street.[28] Meanwhile, companies such as Atos Healthcare, Maximus and Capita have been much criticised for their role in Work Capability Assessment, and Personal Independence Payments assessments.[29] In addition, Capita has been challenged by MPs over the poor performance of its contract for GP support services.[30]

The NHS has also increased outsourcing and privatisation in the last five years. Since the 2012 NHS Act forced local Clinical Commissioning Groups (CCGs) to increase opportunities for private suppliers when awarding contracts, there has been a marked growth of non-NHS provision, resulting in an interest from overseas investors.[31] In the spring of 2017, the Prime Minister's visit to the United States gave rise to speculation that NHS contracts will be given over to US providers. Meanwhile councils have seen a rise in privatisation during the same period.[32] And both NHS and local government outsourcing is subject to as much controversy as central government. A recent report noted that CCGs are failing to monitor out-sourced contracts due to the fact that although they are the funders, they are not responsible for managing the competitive procurement processes to select providers. These are run by separate entities called Contract Support Units who are outside CCG control. This is likely to get worse when CSUs themselves are privatised.[33]

This increase in privatisation has already seen some high-profile failures, such as Circle pulling out of Hinchbrooke hospital following an inadequate Care Quality Commission report,[34] Virgin Care's poor quality 111 service in Croydon,[35] and the collapse of a contract given to an in-house consortium due to lack of financial sustainability.[36] Similar problems have arisen in a multitude of local authorities, where contract failures have led to costly disputes and rising costs,[37] while the collapse of Southern Cross has highlighted the risks of private finance in the social care sector.[38] Additionally, Southampton's recent decision to outsource care plan reviews to Capita has led to accusations that social workers are being given bonuses to cut care packages.[39] And since the very process of procurement is complex and time-consuming it is likely to cost as much as it saves. In fact, one local authority, Sevenoaks District Council, has ditched outsourcing altogether stating that in-house provision is more cost-effective.[40]

A final concern about outsourcing public sector services to private providers is that there is a clash of values inherent in such transactions. Services whose core purpose is to meet health, social or community need do not fit easily into a business model that is about making profits for shareholders. As the Southern Cross fiasco shows, when finances are buoyant, private companies can afford to meet standards. But, faced with tightening economic conditions, unscrupulous organisations will cut corners, and the result will be disastrous for people who rely on their support.

In sum, giving public services over to the market has resulted in inefficiencies, rising costs and failure to deliver high quality. And we are all poorer for it. It is time we scrapped the marketisation of public services and re-imagined the role of the state.

## Rolling back the market

As noted above, we have become trapped between two sterile arguments that government has to do everything or that government must do nothing. Simon Duffy has argued that even framing it this way is unhelpful. He suggests that this narrow view of the market misses the point and that we should instead think of the marketplace as being like the Roman agora. This public place was separated from the private space, and allowed citizens to meet and learn, government officers to do their work, philosophers to discuss ideas, and people to worship in the temple. The institutions of state, justice and religion were situated on the hill above, allowing citizens to flourish in a messy community below.[41] I agree that this is a more creative view of what the market could be, but would also argue that the state institutions he describes had a role in enabling the agora to flourish. So for the purposes of this chapter, I will confine my discussion to the narrower definition and discuss the role that the state and the private sector should play in the delivery of public service. Given the failures of both, perhaps it is time to reframe this into thinking, who does what best and how can it be facilitated so that we have the services we deserve?

It is possible, as Brian Griffiths suggests,[42] that the market can operate for the common good. However, the evidence is clear that it fails to do so when applied to public services. In fact, the marketising of health, education and social care has been disastrous. We must therefore withdraw private involvement in the public sector as much as we can and create a new framework for service delivery.

This is easier said than done, particularly because we are subject to international and European trade deals that foster competition and open our markets to other countries. We are currently bound by EU procurement law, so that public sector tenders must follow EU directives. If we remain in the single market after Brexit we will still be subject to these,[43] but if we don't, it is likely we will be seeking new trading partners such as America, India and China. Furthermore, although President Trump has, for now, rejected the Transatlantic

Trade and Investment Partnership (TTIP)[44] which threatens to increase the power of international organisations over national governments, such ideas will probably resurface in the future. And indeed, the EU Parliament has recently voted to approve the Comprehensive Economic Trade Agreement (CETA),[45] which has similar problems, including giving undemocratic legal protections to companies who cause harm to communities.[46]

A number of strategies will therefore be required to reduce the role of the market in public services.

### 1. Campaigning

Both the TTIP and CETA deals have already been subject to mass protests. Now CETA is to be put before European parliaments for approval, there is an opportunity to take part in campaigns to ensure the UK government rejects it. If TTIP resurfaces under a future, less isolationist American President, there will also be the opportunity to campaign there. In addition, we need to have a campaign calling for a change in EU procurement law that exempts any service whose primary purpose is for the common good. This would include welfare, arts, community, transport and utility provision. When we leave the European Union we need to be prepared to challenge our government if it seeks trading relationships that promote the market influence over the public sector.

### 2. Reverse existing privatisation

Wherever possible, the government should re-nationalise privatised services that fit into the category above. On a national level, this cannot be done all at once, as there are so many contracts in private hands it would be too costly to buy them all back. However, the government could pass legislation that approved nationalisation of these services and set a timetable to do it as contracts come up for renewal. Similar legislation is required to repeal the 2012 NHS and Social Care Act and the same approach will need to be taken to bring existing contracts back into the NHS. On a local level, councils could follow the example of Sevenoaks District Council and begin the same process.

We should also consider using our power as constituents and voters to support parties who are partially or fully pro-nationalisation and against harmful international trade deals. At present these include Labour, the SNP, the Green Party and Plaid Cymru.[47] We should continue to challenge the parties who favour privatisation, the Liberal Democrats, Conservatives and UKIP, to move their position on these issues. And we should make it clear to politicians who have shares in companies benefiting from privatisation that we do not support their agenda.

### 3. Find loopholes

The above two suggestions will take extensive lobbying and campaigning and are long-term goals. In the meantime, we remain subject to EU Procurement Directives that require national and local government and the NHS to follow a particular set of rules to ensure competitive markets. There can be a tendency among public sector managers to assume that these have to be followed wholesale, but careful reading shows that there may be loopholes that can be used to protect certain services. For example, directive 5 of the 2014 EU Directives, states that public authorities do not have to outsource all services, while directive 118 states that 'certain health, social and related services' might be subject to a light touch regime.[48]

### 4. Promote ethical purchasing

There is also a tendency in the public sector to think of procurement as a blunt commercial tool that promotes the private sector. It doesn't need to be like this, however. The 2014 European Directives also emphasise the importance of involving people who use services in tenders, and frequently state that purchasers need to consider issues such as environmental impacts, labour laws and social responsibility,[49] whilst the Chartered Institute of Procurement and Supply has developed training resources on ethical purchasing for professionals working in this area.[50] All of this is helpful for ensuring that public sector procurement is carried out in a manner that promotes the common good.

### 5. Make the market unpalatable for the private sector

When I was working for Oxfordshire County Council, we found standard procurement processes hampered our ability to ensure we chose the best quality, most innovative and value-based providers. We were fortunate to have a creative procurement team who were open to suggestions for a redesign of the process. As a result we devised selection criteria that included consideration of finance, quality and value as well as ensuring service users and carers had a strong say in the decision. This proved to have a deterring effect on one provider who chose to withdraw their bid when it was clear that our contract conditions might be costly for them.

A well-thought-out procurement process can eliminate potential bidders by ensuring the invitation to tender is unattractive to any organisation whose sole interest is profit. For example, it can set conditions that all employees must be paid the real living wage and above; have vetting procedures that exclude organisations that are polluters or have a record of human rights abuses anywhere in the world; design the brief so that it needs a detailed working knowledge of the local area; make it clear that the contract will be well regulated and monitored. This will add costs to the contract and minimise the amount of money a company can make, which might be off-putting to a provider whose main motive is profit. If an unsuitable bidder rises to these challenges, ensuring they are subject to rigorous scrutiny in the selection process, and that people using the service are part of the tender panel, will help ensure they don't progress further. If, after all this, the wrong organisation still wins, having break clauses and high levels of monitoring will ensure that if things go wrong the contract can easily be terminated.

It will probably take a combination of all of the above to ensure we roll back the market from the provision of public sector services. As we do so, we need to consider how they should be managed instead and what else the state can do to develop wealthy communities

## Re-imagining the state

As I stated in the previous chapter,[51] there are undoubtedly problems with state provision in the public sector. Furthermore the argument that the state should provide everything or nothing is not a helpful one. A better approach is to recognise that national and local government have a variety of roles in ensuring public sector services work for the common good. And using such approaches will enable wealthy communities to flourish in the agora that Simon Duffy imagines.

### 1. The state as provider

The strength of state organisations is that their large size means they have the resources to manage services across national, regional or local areas. This in turn lends itself on a national level to the management of services such as infrastructure, utilities, the NHS and transport, and a local level to the management of highways, parks, museums, leisure centres and libraries. Where it makes sense for the state to provide services it should do so.

## 2. The state as funder

However, there are many sectors where the state isn't the best organisation to provide the service, for example social care, advocacy, community projects. Here the state should confine its role to being a funding body. Under current procurement laws, this role forces the state to undertake competitive tenders to select service providers. In the short term, the harmful impacts of this can be minimised in the ways I describe above. Over time, as we change the national and international rules on the market, we can begin to consider more helpful ways that state funders can work with providers.

Where organisations have had long-term contracts, they should be reviewed by the funder in partnership with people using the service (and their families if appropriate) to ensure their provision continues to be ethical, person centred, efficient, cost-effective and of the highest quality. They should then be offered a new funding arrangement for five years to ensure stability and quality. However, within that arrangement there should be opportunities to review and break the agreement if the provider fails to meet any of the above criteria. Once these arrangements are agreed the funder should set up a collaborative local network with providers and people using services and their families, that will decide who has the capacity to take on a new development, or pilot an innovative initiative. This will also allow for people using social care services who want to use personal budgets or individual service funds to manage their own services to select from a range of high-quality providers if they wish.

## 3. The state as supporter

Education has been greatly damaged by the rush to academisation which has resulted in the loss of local authority departments that once provided schools financial, health and safety and human resources support. If we returned this responsibility to local authorities and extended it to all provider organisations in education, social care and community services this would offer an economy of scale that would make such support cost-effective. This would enable those organisations to focus their energies more effectively on service delivery. It would also help service users purchasing their care directly via direct payments to make the most effective use of their individual budget.

### 4. The state as regulator

While Brian Griffiths[52] is right to warn of the dangers of regulation, nonetheless some regulation is necessary to ensure that provider organisations are delivering a quality service. For example, requiring social care providers to train their staff in manual handling or have effective safeguarding policies helps keep service users and staff safe. Expecting a fire service to carry out regular safety checks of their equipment or a hospital to have good infection controls reduces risks to the public. The most effective regulatory systems are ones that focus on the experience for the user of the service and involve people using the services and their families in monitoring. They should be light touch initially, but have triggers to increase monitoring if there are causes for concern. In addition, they must have teeth, so that serious failures of delivery have immediate and appropriate consequences, such as financial penalties or termination of funding agreements.

### 5. The state as facilitator

Government is best placed to develop national and local strategies based on demographic information and analysis of need. This means supporting and enabling the development of services that arise to meet that need, fostering existing provision, and creating an environment where new and innovative projects can thrive by offering seed funding and funding for long-term growth. This role is particularly important for housing where, as Andrew Francis points out in his essay collection on housing,[53] a national ten-year programme is needed to tackle the housing crisis.

In addition local authorities can support community development by facilitating opportunities for asset mapping across their area, identifying faith groups, volunteers, civil societies, unions and other projects that provide benefit and can be supported in their work, as well as discovering places which are asset poor and need further assistance.

Local and national governments can also encourage economic growth through developing public transport projects, house building, and offering subsidies to innovative start-ups, or tax relief to small businesses. Furthermore, local authorities can support the development of businesses that can enrich a community such as craft shops, bookshops and food stores and use bye-laws to ensure they have affordable rents. And they can play a part in piloting innovative new economic models, including the development of local currencies(54) and supporting the transition towns movement.(55) These in turn can build healthy, wealthy and resilient communities. And of course, when public services are well funded, they create a workforce that pays taxes and consumes goods locally and nationally.

## Creating wealthy communities

As noted in this chapter and the previous one,[56] the experience of the austerity years has been devastating for communities up and down the country. However, it doesn't need to be like this. We are one of the wealthiest countries in the world,[57] we have a choice as to how we use that wealth for the good of all.

So what does a wealthy community look like?

A wealthy community is one where each citizen has access to an affordable safe home, education and health. In a wealthy community, there are accessible parks, museums, leisure centres and libraries where everyone is welcome. A wealthy community ensures that every disabled person is supported to live independently in their own home, every homeless person has assistance to find permanent housing, every child in care has the opportunity to find a safe home and new family. In a wealthy community everyone has a place, and an opportunity to participate.

At the time of writing, March 2017, it feels as if we are a long way from realising this vision, and yet I do not believe it is impossible to achieve. Many Christians are involved both in projects to mitigate the impacts of austerity (such as foodbanks) and in critical reflection to challenge its basis.[58] I firmly believe that just as William Temple helped influence the development of public services in the 1940s, now is the time for Christians to work with people of all faiths and none to challenge politicians and policymakers to reverse austerity, roll back the market and build better services for the future. The past few years have been hugely damaging for all of us, but the recent election shows this is no longer acceptable to large numbers of people. Now is an opportune time to begin building the new Jerusalem Simon Woodman discusses in the final chapter.[59]

> Then I saw 'a new heaven and a new earth,' for the first heaven and the first earth had passed away, and there was no longer any sea. I saw the Holy City, the new Jerusalem, coming down out of heaven from God, prepared as a bride beautifully dressed for her husband. And I heard a loud voice from the throne saying, "Look! God's dwelling place is now among the people, and he will dwell with them. They will be his people, and God himself will be with them and be their God.    (Revelation 21:1–4)

We have the power to respond to this vision. Together we can make it happen.

## Questions

- What would an injection of resources mean for your local community? Where would you invest it?
- Do you think there should be restrictions on privatisation of public services? How can we contribute to mitigating its effects?
- What assets does your community have? How can you ensure they flourish?
- What role, if any, should Christians play in re-imagining the state?

## Notes

1. Dennis Campbell, Steven Morris, Sarah Marsh, 'NHS faces "humanitarian crisis" as demand rises British Red Cross warns', *Guardian*, 6 January 2017.
2. Laura Donnelly, 'MPs plead for cross party review of health and social care as sector reaches "breaking point"', *Daily Telegraph*, 6 January 2017.
3. Crisis Briefing, 'About homelessness', January 2017, http://www.crisis.org.uk/data/files/Homelessness_briefing_2017_EXTERNAL.pdf
4. Sky News website, 'Tales from Jail. Why UK prisoners are rioting and why there will be more', 24 December 2016, http://news.sky.com/story/tales-from-jail-why-uk-prisoners-are-rioting-and-why-there-will-be-more-10706368
5. John Moffatt, 'Whatever happened to the common good?', in this publication, pages 30 - 42.

6. The Guardian Data Blog 2013, UK GDP since 1955, https://www. theguardian.com/news/datablog/2009/nov/25/gdp-uk-1948-growth-economy

7. Trading Economics website, United Kingdom Annual GDP Growth Rate, December 2016, http://www.tradingeconomics.com/united-kingdom/gdp-growth-annual

8. Office of National Statistics Digital, Trends in the UK Economy, 27 February 2015, http://visual.ons.gov.uk/uk-perspectives-trends-in-the-uk-economy/

9. Era Dabla-Norris *et al.*, 'Causes and consequences of income inequality: A global perspective', IMF 2015.

10. Cindy Wooden, 'Pope Francis: You can't defend Christianity by opposing refugees and other religions', *Crux*, 13 October 2016. https://cruxnow.com/cns/2016/10/13/christians-reject-refugees-hypocrites-pope-says/

11. Theresa May, 'The shared society', *Sunday Telegraph*, 8 January 2017.

12. See Simon Barrow, 'The uncommon good', in this publication, pp. 43–55.

13. Rhiannon Bury, 'Autumn statement. Summary', *Daily Telegraph*, 23 November 2016.

14. Anushka Asthana, 'Council funding freeze means cuts to many essential council services', *Guardian*, 21 February 2017.

15. Leonard Cheshire website, 'Budget 2017: response to social care funding', 8 March 2017, https://www.leonardcheshire.org/support-and-information/latest-news/press-releases/budget-2017-response-social-care-funding.

16. ITV website, 'North east councils say extra social care funding is "too little too late"', 8 March 2017, http://www.itv.com/news/tyne-tees/2017-03-08/north-east-councils-say-extra-social-care-funding-is-too-little-too-late/

17. See John Moffatt, 'Whatever happened to the common good?' in this publication, pp. 30–42.

18. Richard Murphy, 'Tackling corporate tax avoidance is an alternative to EU austerity', *Guardian*, 15 December 2015.

19. Jeremy Smith, 'Austerity, deficits and the "fiscal" balance', Economists for Rational Economic Policy Briefing 2, 23 February 2015.

20. Jeremy Smith, 'Public debt and deficits. Back to basics!' Economists for Rational Economic Policy Briefing 3, 23 February 2015.

21. Associated Press, 'Portugal cuts budget deficit to lowest level in four decades', *Salon*, 15 February 2017, http://www.salon.com/2017/02/15/portugal-cuts-budget-deficit-to-lowest-level-in-4-decades/

22. Full Facts website, 'How much does Trident cost?' 2016, https://fullfact.org/economy/trident-nuclear-cost/

23. Sam Perlo-Freeman, 'Special treatment. UK Government support for the arms industry and trade', November 2016, SIPRI, Campaign Against Arms Trade.

24. See John Moffatt, 'Whatever happened to the common good?' in this publication.

25. Will Dahlgreen, 'Renationalise energy and rail services says the public', You Gov, 4 November 2013, https://yougov.co.uk/news/2013/11/04/nationalise-energy-and-rail-companies-say-public/

26. G4S website, 'Care and justice services', http://www.g4s.uk.com/en-GB/What%20we%20do/Services/Care%20and%20justice%20services/

27. Wikipedia 'Controversies surrounding G4S', https://en.wikipedia.org/wiki/Controversies_surrounding_G4S

28. Dan Bloom, 'Private firm G4S "shouldn't be allowed to profit from refugees" over red doors scandal', *Daily Mirror*, 20 January 2016.

29. John Prings, 'Atos, Maximus and Capita forced to admit assessment failures', Disability News Service, 4 February 2016, http://www.disabilitynewsservice.com/atos-maximus-and-capita-forced-to-admit-assessment-failures/

30. Sofia Lind, 'MPs to debate Capita's GP support failures in Parliament', *Pulse*, 2 November 2016.

31. Carter Schwartz, 'NHS outsourcing attracting wave of investors from across the pond', 10 February 2016, http://carterschwartz.co.uk/nhs-outsourcing-attracting-wave-of-health-investors-from-across-the-pond/

32. Rene Millman, 'Local government spending outsourcing spending increases by nearly a quarter', Public Technology.net, 11 February 2016, https://www.publictechnology.net/articles/news/local-government-outsourcing-spending-increases-nearly-quarter

33. National Health Executive website, 'CCGs failing to monitor and enforce contracts for outsourced services', 21 April 2015, http://www.nationalhealthexecutive.com/News/ccgs-failing-in-duty-to-monitor-and-enforce-contracts-to-outsource-services-says-report

34. Nicholas Watt, Denis Campbell and Randeep Ramesh, 'Circle pulls on hospital deal and sparks storm over private firms in the NHS', *Guardian*, 9 January 2015.

35. Dennis Campbell, 'NHS watchdog says Virgin Care run clinic put patients at risk', *Guardian*, 4 February 2014.

36. Gill Plimmer, 'Collapse of £1.2bn NHS contract raises tendering questions', *Financial Times*, 4 December 2015.

37. Alan White and Kate Belgrave, 'Nine spectacular council outsourcing failures', *New Statesman*, 29 August 2013.

38. Richard Wachman, 'Southern Cross's incurably flawed business model let down the vulnerable', *Observer*, 16 July 2011.

39. John Prings, '"Immoral" Capita offered £200 bonuses to social workers to slash care packages', *Disability News Service*, 2 February 2017, http://www.disabilitynewsservice.com/immoral-capita-offered-200-bonuses-to-social-workers-to-slash-care-packages/

40. Saba Salman, 'Guardian Public Services Award 2016 overall winner: Sevenoaks District Council', 30 November 2016.

41. Simon Duffy, 'Ideal markets or real markets', 28 March 2014, http://simonduffy.blogspot.co.uk/2014/03/ideal-markets-or-real-markets.html

42. Brian Griffiths, 'Markets and the Common Good', in *Together for the Common Good: Towards a national conversation* (London: SCM Press, 2015).

43. Eversheds Sutherland website, 'The effects of Brexit on UK public procurement legislation and the application of EU state aid rules in the

UK', http://www.eversheds-sutherland.com/global/en/what/articles/index.page?ArticleID=en/Public_Procurement/UK-public-procurement-legislation

44. Lee Williams, 'What is TTIP? And the six reasons why it should scare you', *Independent*, 6 October 2015, http://www.independent.co.uk/voices/comment/what-is-ttip-and-six-reasons-why-the-answer-should-scare-you-9779688.html

45. War on Want website, 'What is CETA?' http://www.waronwant.org/what-ceta

46. European Parliament News, 'CETA: MEPS back EU-Canada trade agreement', 15 February 2017, http://www.europarl.europa.eu/news/en/news-room/20170209IPR61728/ceta-meps-back-eu-canada-trade-agreement

47. War on Want website, 'TTIP and the 2015 Election: Where do the parties stand?' 18 April 2015, http://www.waronwant.org/media/ttip-and-2015-election-where-do-parties-stand. I note that UKIP also has an anti-TTIP position but cannot endorse supporting them as a political party due to their unethical views on immigration.

48. European Commission website, Directive 2014/24 EU of the European Parliament and Council of 26 February 2014, http://eur-lex.europa.eu/legal-content/EN/TXT/?uri=CELEX:02014L0024-20160101

49. Ibid.

50. Chartered Institute of Procurement and Supply website, 'Ethical Procurement and Supply', https://www.cips.org/en-GB/training-courses/Ethical-Procurement-and-Supply-/

51. See Virginia Moffatt, 'Rolling back the state', in this publication, pp. 85–98.

52. Griffiths, 'Markets and the Common Good'.

53. Andrew Francis (ed.), *Foxes Have Holes: Christian reflections on Britain's housing need* (London: Ekklesia, 2016).

54. Dan Atkinson and Vicki Owen, 'From Brixton to the Bristol pound how towns have turned to printing their own money to beat the High Street crisis', This is Money website, 22 September 2012, http://www.thisismoney.co.uk/money/saving/article-2207119/From-Brixton-Bristol-Pounds-towns-print-money.html

55. John-Paul Flintoff, 'Local, self sufficient, optimistic: Are Transition Towns the way forward?' *Guardian*, 15 June 2013.

56. See Moffatt, 'Rolling back the state', pages 85 - 98 in this publication.

57. City AM, 'World wealth: Britain crowned fifth richest country in the world behind the US, China, Japan and Germany', 3 November 2015, http://www.cityam.com/227917/world-wealth-britain-crowned-fifth-richest-country-in-the-world-behind-us-china-japan-and-germany

58. Hilary Russell, *A Faithful Presence. Working Together for the Common Good* (London: SCM Press, 2015).

59. See Simon Woodman, 'The new Jerusalem: building a vision for the common good', in this publication, pp. 191–204.

# PART 3

# PEOPLE AND PLANET

# 8. Migration and the Common Good

Vaughan Jones

There are few areas of social policy where as many mistakes have been made than in the field of immigration, despite the movement of people being a constant throughout human history and a driving force of social change. The issue is charged with emotions and conflicts. For some it is a shared memory of nationhood. For others it evokes a sense of threat and danger and the disintegration of common-held values and identity.

While considering the common good, we might ask why the gains of migration are experienced by some and not by others. Does the downside outweigh the upside, or vice versa? In an ethical discussion, we should also consider what might transform the experience of migration into something demonstrably advantageous for all.

Migration in the modern world takes many forms. Most migration is from the developed world to the developed world[1] – 119 million fall into this category, with 25 million forcibly displaced. Migration is associated with employment, trade, study and, for the lucky ones, romance.

Globalisation has created a new category of global citizen. Corporate companies depend upon the mobility of their staff. Rarely are these people called migrants. Even if their stay lasts for more than the twelve months needed to be officially designated a migrant they would rarely be identified as such. Living in gated communities close to city centres, they are unlikely to absorb local culture save at the chic bars and restaurants they frequent.

International study is a global business. The business model of universities, and not only the Ivy League, Russell Group prestigious institutions, is centred on attracting overseas students who pay large fees. Universities recruit researchers and teaching staff who will enhance their reputation and will not limit themselves to in-country nationals.

Young people now have the opportunity and capacity to travel, for a gap year or two or three. People in their middle and even later years are willing and able to spend a time in another country, working with an international non-governmental organisation or for retirement. Travel is affordable and instant communications mean that there is little disruption to personal relationships.

Freedom of movement in the European Union has given tremendous opportunities for EU citizens to work in other countries. Around 1.2 million British citizens are working in other EU countries, with Spain being the most popular. Many have chosen to settle in their retirement in climates more conducive, and with better food! Others will be working, or developing their language skills. Over 3 million EU citizens are living and working in the UK.[2]

One of the major economic gains from freedom of movement has been the movement of people working for lower wages. Often this is referred to as low-skilled work but that is not always a good description of the work itself or of the people who do the work.

The world is also experiencing a high level of what is termed 'forced migration'. Those with limited options are moving away from: the impact of climate change; local or country-wide conflict, communal violence, civil war; or income inequality. The majority of forcibly displaced people leave their homes for other parts of their country. They are known as Internally Displaced Persons (IDPs). Others are located in official refugee camps run by the United Nations High Commission for Refugees (UNHCR) or the Red Cross/Crescent. Many international non-governmental organisations, such as Médecins Sans Frontières and Save the Children make a vital contribution in these situations. Less well known are the many informal settlements which have emerged in countries which neighbour conflict zones.

As we are now very familiar from news bulletins, many people who are forcibly displaced make the journey to a safer country independently. These journeys are dangerous and fraught with difficulties. The crossings over the Arizona desert and the

Mediterranean, or the Pacific from South-East Asia to Australia are high risk and result in tens of thousands of deaths.

When people come to a country looking for asylum or a temporary respite, their vulnerability continues. They must navigate a new language, access affordable accommodation, face limitations on entitlements to work, attain legal status within immigration and asylum rules and regulations. These are enormous challenges. This may include reuniting families where one member moves to establish a new life with the intention of bringing the rest of the family once all the necessary arrangements can be made. This could include earning the money to pay for travel, finding suitable accommodation and acheiving legal status.

One dimension of forced displacement is the phenomenon of modern slavery. Some are coerced or deceived into forced work without recompense and under duress. They are treated as property or commodities. Estimates of the number of slaves in the world today vary enormously and figures between 21 and 46 million are cited.[3] Not all by any means will have crossed borders but many will and are part of the clandestine, hidden migrant population.

Migration is multi-faceted but the discourse is framed from colonial, class, gender and race perspectives. Concerned (and not-so-concerned) reporting of migration tends to identify migrants as poor, Muslim, less well educated, hostile to their new country and taking advantage. More dispassionate discourse on migration focuses on numbers and treats the people who migrate as economic units – commodities. Migrants, to some, are worthy of humanitarian pity, and to others are a hostile force intent on causing harm.

There are now over 21 million people recognised as refugees by the UNHCR, a figure which is higher than 60 million when IDPs are included.[4] While there were also 60 million refugees during the Second World War, today economies are stronger and the overall population much larger (2.5 billion in 1945 and 7.4 billion[5] today). The large-scale movement of people is not new. Transatlantic slavery moved between 9 and 11 million people from Africa to the Americas.[6] In the first decade of the twentieth century 1 million people a year emigrated from Europe to the United States.[7] Migration is part of all our family stories. Many have maintained an ethnic and cultural identity on a transnational basis. We only need think of Ismaili Muslims or the Jewish community or the widespread Celtic diasporas.

Thomas Niall in his book *The Figure of the Migrant*[8] outlines four archetypes which have identified migrants throughout history. They are: the Nomad, the Barbarian, the Vagabond; and the Proletariat. All of these are derived from history and they are all prevalent in contemporary discourse. The Nomad is the wanderer who disturbs the order of settled communities – the immigrant newcomer. The Barbarian is the enemy at the gate reflected in the contemporary debates linking migration with terrorism. The Vagabond is the wandering beggar, the 'health tourist' or the people who come here for our benefit system. The Proletariat is the migrant worker, low paid, low skilled debasing wages.

The interrelationship between migration and work is important. Arguments for and against migration frequently focus on an economic argument. Migration works for the economy, especially for a developed one. There are some real gains. Migrants tend to be entrepreneurial, a product of their survival needs. Therefore many new businesses are set up. Migration creates new employment. At the same time, a ready supply of labour, often over-skilled for the available roles, is good for any business.

There is an argument that migration lowers wages and reduces the employment opportunities available to people born in the country. There is some evidence[9] that there is a slight depression of wages for the lowest-paid jobs. But we need to take a helicopter view of this. We are living in a country in which labour market regulation is weak. Guy Standing[10] has talked of a growing 'precariat', i.e. people whose employment rights have been weakened and are vulnerable to lower wages, weak enforcement of health and safety standards, limited or no pension entitlement, cuts in the social wage. Competition in industries such as food production depresses wages. These are the factors which drive down living standards and migrants are victims of the system rather than the cause.

Migration cannot be separated from overall labour market concerns and regulation. Education, training and increased productivity are more likely to raise indigenous living standards. Some developing countries, for example Bangladesh or the Philippines, structure labour exports into their economic planning. Their expatriate citizens work across the globe and send back much needed tax revenue and money to family. It is calculated that remittances to developing countries outweigh the whole of the international aid budget.[11] Migrants overall produce 9.4 per cent of the global total GDP despite the migrant community representing just 3.4 per cent of the world's population.[12]

Migration is also about demography. Western countries have declining birth rates and rising life expectancy. Social care has been privatised and limited government spending and competitive price wars restrict wages for those who work in social care. This is an opening for migrant workers. NHS workforce planning has failed to produce the number of highly skilled staff needed for advanced health-care techniques. It is cost-effective to recruit staff already trained.

The world's population is increasing rapidly. The sheer number of people in some parts of the world, for example where climate change is having an impact, means that some national economies are unable to sustain their populations. Migration begins with choices that are made by individuals and families. The decision to move will not be made easily. The call to adventure and optimistic expectation of a safer, more prosperous life is too hard to resist. Where the local situation is fraught with danger or offers little hope, the decision to move is a matter of necessity. People make their choices and we should not belittle the agency of the migrant and their family.

We are witnessing massive shifts in global demography. To someone living in an area unused to incoming migrants, this can be disconcerting. However, only 3.2 per cent of the world population are migrants. This means that any issues from rapid demographic churn ought to be manageable within the framework of national policies, provided that there is political leadership. Having said that, there has been a large-scale displacement of people in recent years resulting in large numbers of refugees coming to Europe. Again a sense of proportion is needed. Had the countries of the European Union, wealthy countries like the USA, Australia, Japan and Canada agreed to responsible sharing, the resettlement of people could have been handled with not particularly large numbers arriving in each country. However, the international community has proved to be singularly inadequate. The blame is passed to the migrant.

A national politician is caught in a trap. On the one hand, migration cannot be stopped and it is needed to address an ageing population and for a dynamic economy in the globalised capitalist order. On the other, local populations resist the social and cultural changes which migration brings and less scrupulous politicians of both the Left and the Right exploit concerns or make unachievable promises for short-term electoral gain.

How can migration be controlled? Many millions of euros, dollars and pounds are spent on controlling migration. At its worst, it is the politics of death. The wall between Mexico and the United States has gaps. There are places where you can sneak through the fence into the 'promised land'. But they take you into the Arizona desert where over 2,000 have died this century.[13] Death rates in the Mediterranean have reached 1,000 per week.[14] Were the money spent patrolling the Mediterranean with the intention of turning migrants back – the rescue and return policy – to be spent on processing people on arrival then the migrants could pay the small amount for a ferry. Instead, the business of control has opened up a lucrative trade in people smuggling.

The balance scales of humanitarian protection and securitisation move up and down. The debate is rarely about the lives of migrants in trouble, but about reaction to events. Tragic or dramatic footage appears in the media and there is a movement towards humanitarian approaches. Then a terrorist incident, unrelated to migration, results in a backlash and more demands to heighten security. The migrant becomes the focus, which can serve to deflect from the underlying, and real, security questions. The causes of insecurity are not dissimilar from the causes of forced displacement – war, civil unrest, deep-seated grievances and the exploitation of people by extreme political forces.

It makes enormous sense for a national territory to have knowledge of who is living there at any given time. Authorities need to determine whether or not someone receives the benefits which are afforded to its citizens or not. Entry into full citizenship should be managed through an equitable and efficient process. Controls are in place but are not as efficient as they might be for the most vulnerable.

Turning to the question of the common good, we can ask who benefits from migration. We can query whether the advantages and disadvantages are equally shared. We can also ask whether or not current theological responses are 'fit for purpose', to employ a phrase once levelled at the Home Office.

The Bible provides us with some key, and over-used, texts. The parable of the sheep and the goats –' I was a stranger and you made me welcome' – and the flight into Egypt – 'Our Lord was a refugee once' – are the most commonly quoted references. Identifying the refugee as the suffering Christ makes us feel better about caring for them. We need to ask the hard question of whether our theological analysis has the effect of 'othering' the migrant.

There are a number of avenues for exploration. The first is anthropological. Who are refugees and migrants and how can the fundamentals for human dignity and value be upheld in the migration process? The second is sociological. How can society become open, flexible and integrative in periods of rapid demographic change? The third is political. What is the responsibility of the nation state to those who enter its territory and those who wish to enter its territory? How do these interrelated questions contribute to a theological position, coherent with tradition, Scripture and the Christian nonconformist conscience? Do they lead to a fourth strand which is ecclesiological? What are the implications for a transnational institution called church when so many of its members settle in other countries along with their cultural heritage?

Beginning with the anthropological question – we have noted already that the overwhelming majority of migrants are not needy people, but people who have made an active choice to move. They are agents of their own destiny, demonstrating a remarkable resilience and capacity to adapt. It is a denial of their basic humanity to say that people have no choice. Even if that choice is not particularly palatable.

If we focus on migrants then we see there are as many stories of migration as there are individuals. If we think about the common good, then the drive, energy and entrepreneurial spirit of migrants is a source of wealth, innovation and exchange from which all can benefit.

If we also focus, as we must, on those forcibly displaced, then we must also acknowledge resilience. They display tremendous courage and bravery in making difficult journeys. We should not overlook how resilience leads to mutual help and aid. Diaspora communities self-organise through clan relationships, community organisations, political affiliations and faith communities. Churches, temples and mosques are the source of help and advice for newcomers.

Human rights should take precedent over citizens' rights. While a state may withdraw rights and entitlements including the right of residency, it cannot withdraw fundamental human rights. So the right to family life, the right not to be subjected to torture or degrading treatment are vital where removal from a country is under consideration. The right to education, health, shelter are essential in the treatment of an individual who is seeking to live in another country. Around the world today, 50 million children have migrated across borders or been forcibly displaced within their own countries, with 28 million having been uprooted by horrific conflicts.[15] The United Nations Convention on the Rights of a Child is vital legal protection for them.

The common good has to be enshrined in statute as well as in the goodwill of a faith community or a society. Human rights are the international benchmarks for the proper treatment of migrants. They are constantly under threat not only from despotic regimes but increasingly from wealthier, developed countries. International law is a vital protection for vulnerable migrants.

Our faith is rooted in the fundamental dignity of the human person as revealed in the incarnation. Jesus of Nazareth was a human being with a new understanding both of humanity and divinity. His life was set in a place and a time. His responses to the community, culture, heritage and faith of his day were specific to that time and place. The faith that grew up following his death projected outward from the specifics of temporality and location to a set of beliefs which have been re-contextualised again and again over two millennia. Jesus' understanding of the relationship between the One he called 'Abba' – 'our Father who is in heaven' – and humanity is intimate and present. So we can affirm Jesus as alive – as he moves from being a person in time and space to become our access to a divine presence. Jesus sanctifies our humanity. We are who we are because of the creative source of life in the universe, and Jesus brings that energy and defines it as love.

In so doing, he determines that humanity is a manifestation of the divine source of life, and that each individual has value. They are especially valued when their dignity and fundamental humanity is being denied. This is a crucial understanding which undergirds the more legalistic concept of universal human rights. So Jesus determines that the poor are blessed – as are the landless peasants, those who mourn for loved ones and lost lands, language and faith, and those who are persecuted and rejected. The radical message of the Christian Gospel is that God has taken sides. There is no common good in which some are left out in the cold. The challenge for believers is to stop seeing Christ as the other in need of charity but to hear Christ's call for true equality and justice.

Looking now at the sociological questions – there are undoubtedly significant social policy issues. It is churlish to deny that migration creates problems as well as opportunities. The emergence of new communities in towns, cities and villages can be disturbing. Many are open about their appreciation of the opportunities for inter-cultural exchange and learning. Not all negative responses to migration are racist. There are pressures on public services. If there is an ensuing pressure on health and education provision then all will suffer. The impact on housing can be acute. In some areas it will put up the cost of private sector housing. These are matters of planning and governmental responses.

In the popular discourse, migrants fail to integrate. They refuse to learn the indigenous language and only socialise within their own communities. Much of this is grossly unfair. Integration must be about exchange rather than an expectation that one side must assimilate the culture of the other. In any country a lingua franca is essential for governance and communication. This should not inhibit the use of other languages.

Integration is the responsibility of all of us and not just migrant communities. The government of the UK have adopted a policy of creating a 'hostile environment' for new migrants and refugees. In such a circumstance, we should not be surprised if new communities are isolationist, nervous of authorities and the systems which manage migration. A hostile environment is matched by a welcoming environment. There has been an explosion of goodwill towards the newcomer from community and faith organisations. Significant within this has been the activism of young people.

A stand-off between community and government cannot be called a quest for the common good. A new compact is needed between government and community. Legislation and resources are required from government, and both migrant and established communities must take responsibility to engage in creating good, harmonious relationships within communities.

If we are committed, together, for the common good then government's responsibility is first and foremost to make the process of arrival fair and efficient, especially for those seeking asylum. Current processes can thwart those needing sanctuary from attaining it. If the international community were governed by the principles of justice and human rights then humanitarian protection would be assured for those who need it. We are not in that situation at present and the world leadership as it is currently configured is not conducive to the action needed.

For local and regional government, the issues of housing, education, health, language learning all need to be addressed. Engaging civil society in this provision helps the newcomer to build relationships with established members of the community.

Integration into the world of work is crucial but this requires government actions which will benefit all and not just newcomers. Skills development, labour market regulation, anti-discrimination legislation, and the enforcement of health and safety standards all matter as much for the wider community as for new entrants into the labour market. Many newcomers enter the labour market at a level below their skillset. However, talent should be recognised without an automatic assumption that they should stay at that level.

Policing is another area of concern. Refugees and new migrants are vulnerable to crime and exploitation. Immigration raids induce fear in communities. Requirements for schools, health centres, private landlords to be part of the infrastructure of control create a constant sense of 'us and them' and separate rather than include the newcomer.

Much is made of the role of the media in stoking an atmosphere of hostility. There is a daily barrage of negative coverage of migrants in the popular press. A criminal act by a migrant is told in a way which implies that all migrants are criminal. Whereas the 'quality' press limit their coverage to abstract stories of migration policies. Research at the London School of Economics[16] indicated that very rarely is the gender, age, name, professional qualifications of a migrant mentioned. Neither do the quality press quote migrants themselves. It is government agencies and NGOs who speak for them.

One of the most surprising statistics from the polling agency Ipsos MORI is that 55 per cent of people believe that immigration has had a negative impact on the NHS and 42 per cent on Britain as a whole.[17] However, only one in five of the population believe that immigration has had a bad effect on them personally. This means that the rhetoric of the press and the political class is having an effect, which brings us to the question of leadership.

Government has a responsibility for the common good. Uncontrolled, clandestine migration has a negative impact on the well-being of communities. It creates a breeding ground for organised crime and exploitation and puts unpredictable strain on public services. Governments have a responsibility to ensure that a country is prosperous and that its prosperity is shared.

Christians with an international and justice orientation must ask whether a nation state can operate in isolation. The common good of one state is not necessarily the common good for those who need its protection or wish to share in its future. The central theological question is who owns the state. Psalm 24 begins, 'The earth is the Lord's and all that is in it, the world, and those who live in it.' That is incredibly radical in the context of the modern state. The Bible times knew a different political order. Territory was shared between clans, both settled and nomadic, with imperial rulers exacting tribute and taxation from them through force of arms. The modern state defines a territory as belonging to a complex order of government, commerce and people. National identity is a construct which becomes very important to some citizens, but is of less importance to others. The European Union and the United States of America and the United Kingdom are examples of how the nation state can operate between differing cultural and territorial boundaries. However, there is a strong instinct to 'control' borders. There is no underlying theological conception behind the nation state. The notion of a 'state church', such as the Church of England, is a very odd construction.

The major political challenge then is the notion of the modern state and the nature of the international political order. National identity will guide political choices and rightly so. It will certainly guide electoral outcomes within democracies. This is the fundamental challenge, and possibly an insurmountable obstacle for those of us who believe that there should be greater ability for people to move freely from country to country for mutual prosperity and safety. Open borders may be a dream but not a viable political option.

This leads us to the ecclesiological question. The Church is a transnational organisation not a national institution. In the days of universal Catholicism, that was easy to maintain. Following the schisms of Orthodoxy, Protestantism, Roman Catholicism, Pentecostalism, we should perhaps re-imagine the Church as a diaspora of diasporas. The Church has undergone a radical transformation in the latter part of the twentieth and the beginning of the twenty-first centuries. The shift of gravity from the North to the South is well documented, as is the growth of African-, Asian- and Latin American- initiated churches. This is an era of massive expansion and the explosion of faith in the Southern continents is being felt in metropolitan places in Western countries. It is not just a one-way street. Some of the negative conservative dogma prevalent in the United States in particular is also informing a growing social conservatism in the developing world. It is a dynamic situation. However we view what is happening to the Church, it is happening because of migration. Ideas, people, churches are on the move.

In our urban context a European-initiated Protestant church may well be pleased with a congregation of 20–30 people. Some of our churches keep the doors open with less than 10 people attending. At the same time, there are thousands in church communities such as the Ethiopian Orthodox and Pentecostal congregations. Roman Catholic churches too are being revitalised by migrants. This calls for a radical rethinking of ecumenical relationships and the fundamental question of ownership of space and the historic legacy of resources.

To summarise our theological reflection – migration is normal and part and parcel of the human experience but our modern global economy and the impact of climate change, income inequalities and violence are creating particular and real challenges. Through media pressure, the need for counter-terrorism and political leadership with short-term electoral considerations, governments have tended towards securitisation and have limited their humanitarian instincts. While refugees and low-paid migrants are experiencing hostility, they themselves are self-organising and surviving. All in all migration is a positive, enriching – both culturally and economically – influence on modern times. The Church is one of the major beneficiaries of migration.

Our theology can over-emphasise mercy while framing the migrant as a needy person. However, this interpretation of the context and of Scripture may not be helpful. The nation state is at the root of the migration dilemma. In drawing lines over the map of the earth we create artificial constructions of identity, which include a people with common histories but exclude others. When we realise that the earth and the territory within those artificial lines do not belong to us but to God, then we have an impasse between the politics of modernity and the theology of the Bible. Some have reconciled this by creating a national church and others by valuing our transnational nature. However, the migration of human beings from one place to another, be it the missionaries of the nineteenth and twentieth centuries going from North to South or the reverse pattern in late twentieth and early twenty-first centuries means that the Church is living a transnational, diasporic reality. Christians are in deep conflict and there are massive injustices within the Church. In some places, it amounts to an unrecognised apartheid. The Church mirrors the divided world and fails to be an eschatological sign of how the world could be.

The common good must replace the construction of the migrant and native with our common humanity. Government, civil society and citizens must understand the mutuality and dependencies which exist between mobile and static communities. The land is not ours to possess just as the biblical Israel was never the possession of its inhabitants but a generous gift from God. There was always space for others. The abomination was not the foreigner but the worship of a false god. Our false gods are locked in the complex structures, which drive migration. Our vision should be of a world in which people are no longer forced to move but can do so freely for mutual enrichment. There is a lot of work to be done. That work is practical within our communities; political in the construction of a new international order based on human rights; cultural in reconstructing identity beyond the idea of nation; economic in facilitating mutuality of exchange; missiological and ecclesiological in re-imagining church not as a national or international body but as an exiled community on a journey to the city whose founder and architect is God; and theological in discovering what it means for ourselves, our possessions and our land to belong to God.

## Questions

- Do you think our theological approaches acknowledge the agency of migrants themselves or do they contribute to 'othering' them?
- What opportunities can you find to build bridges between communities?
- Where do you see the 'dividing walls of hostility' in our society, and what will break them down?
- How can you tell the positive story of migration within the Church and beyond?

## Notes

1. McKinsey Global Institute Report, 'People on the Move: Global Migration's Impact and Opportunity' 2016, http://www.mckinsey.com/global-themes/employment-and-growth/global-migrations-impact-and-opportunity

2.  Migration Watch UK website, 'The British in Europe and vice versa European Union MW 354', https://www.migrationwatchuk.org/briefing-paper/354
3.  The United Nations estimates that roughly 27 to 30 million individuals are currently caught in the slave trade industry. See also http://www.globalslaveryindex.org/ which estimates there are 45.8 million.
4.  UNHCR website, 'Figures at a glance', 'Global trends 2015', 'Statistical Yearbooks', http://www.unhcr.org/uk/figures-at-a-glance.html
5.  infoplease website, 'Population Statistics. Total population of the world by decade 1950–2050', http://www.worldometers.info/world-population/
6.  The Gilder Lehrman Institute of American History website, 'Facts about the slave trade and slavery', https://www.gilderlehrman.org/history-by-era/slavery-and-anti-slavery/resources/facts-about-slave-trade-and-slavery
7.  Spartacus Educational, 'Immigration to the US: 1900–1920, http://spartacus-educational.com/USAE1900.htm
8.  Thomas Niall, *The Figure of the Migrant* (Redwood City, CA: Stanford University Press, 2015).
9.  Migration Observatory, 'The labour market effects of immigration', Migration Observatory Briefing, http://www.migrationobservatory.ox.ac.uk/resources/briefings/the-labour-market-effects-of- immigration/
10. Guy Standing, *The Precariat: The new dangerous class* (London: Bloomsbury 2011).
11. World Bank Global, 'Migration and remittances fact book 2016', https://siteresources.worldbank.org/INTPROSPECTS/Resources/334934-1199807908806/4549025-1450455807487/Factbookpart1.pdf
12. McKinsey Global Institute Report, 'People on the Move: Global Migration's Impact and Opportunity', 2016, http://www.mckinsey.com/global-themes/employment-and-growth/global-migrations-impact-and-opportunity
13. Tara Brian and Frank Laczko (eds), 'Fatal Journeys: Tracking Lives Lost during Migration International Organization for Migration' (IOM Publications, 2014), https://publications.iom.int/system/files/pdf/fataljourneys_countingtheuncounted.pdf
14. Source  IoM,  https://www.theguardian.com/world/2016/may/31/mediterranean-death-toll-880-last-week-unhcr-migration
15. UNHCR Uprooted – the growing crisis for refugee and migrant children 2016, https://www.unicef.org/videoaudio/PDFs/Uprooted.pdf
16. LSE Research, 'Migration and the media', http://www.lse.ac.uk/media@lse/research/Migration-and-the-media.aspx
17. Ipsos MORI Base: 1,257 GB adults, aged 18+, interviewed by telephone, 11–14 June 2016.

# 9. Crossing Borders, Overcoming Barriers

Savitri Hensman

Perhaps at this moment, in an NHS emergency department, a health care team is intent on saving the life of a critically ill patient. There is a sense of urgency but not panic because the staff trust one another's skill and commitment. Though she was born here and they originate from various parts of the world, they are united in their dedicated focus; and afterwards, when her heartbeat and breathing are stable again, there will be a moment of collective rejoicing.

A few miles away, maybe, preparation is underway for a wedding, with the usual last-minute flurry of activity. The couple are from different ethnic groups and, as their love has deepened, they have grown to appreciate each other's cultural heritage and learn about experiences previously unknown to them. Several friends and relatives still live abroad or have emigrated from the UK, so a few of those invited will be flying in for the ceremony or have sent greetings from overseas. When all are gathered and the vows are exchanged, those present will join in pledging their support to the spouses in their life together.

As Vaughan Jones[1] made clear in the previous chapter, immigration is often thought of in terms of problems, especially for the 'host' country. However, even today, amidst divisions and inequalities, there are instances when it brings practical, emotional and spiritual benefits across differences of origin and culture. Indeed, at best, it may anticipate a peaceful and just world in which barriers are broken down, hurts healed and all are, and feel, cherished and appreciated.

Without glossing over the difficulties which can arise, it is possible to develop a vision of the future which gives priority to human flourishing, both among those who arrive and those already settled in the UK. Immigration policy and practice need not be dominated by fear or the desire to exploit but instead serve the common good.

## Migration, seeking refuge and the common good

The concept of the common good is not always easy to apply in concrete situations, as the opening chapters demonstrate. It can be misinterpreted as being about avoiding conflict, which may mean that existing power structures and dominant ideas go unchallenged. This may result in the maintenance of the status quo. It can even be misused to deepen inequalities, especially if the community whose good is sought is restrictively defined and assumptions are made about what will bring overall benefits.

For instance it is sometimes assumed that the shortage of social housing for people already in the UK would be eased if migrants and refugees were not moving in. There should indeed be greater support from central government for areas where sizeable numbers of people are being settled. However, without tackling housing policies which have drastically reduced the stock of affordable accommodation (see chapter 6)[2], while offering lavish profits to the most prosperous private landlords and property companies, any property freed up might well end up being knocked down or sold off, as has happened to much of the housing formerly owned by councils or housing associations.

Indeed campaigns which bring together white majority ethnic and minority ethnic (often foreign-born) people to resist the further loss of such housing have had some success. Sometimes measures which might appear to benefit 'ordinary' UK residents, at the expense of 'foreigners' who are even needier, may harm both, whereas solidarity may be mutually beneficial.

Theologians such as Anna Rowlands[3] have thoughtfully addressed the question of what the 'common good' might involve in relation to immigration, drawing on Catholic Social Thought. It may be helpful here to examine possible ways in which the Bible (read in the context of tradition, reason and experience) might contribute to a nuanced view of how this concept might be usefully applied, a matter also touched on in the previous chapter[4].

To begin with, the scriptural tradition on which Jesus builds in the Gospels, and his own teaching and witness, do not lend themselves to the idea that avoiding conflict is necessarily virtuous, even within the faith or national community. Nor does it avoid the possibility that those who are most comfortable and prosperous may lose some of their wealth and status so that others may have the basics of life such as safety, food and shelter.

The psalmist proclaims, 'How very good and pleasant it is when kindred live together in unity' (Psalm 133:1) and, in John's Gospel, Jesus prays that his followers 'may be one, as we are one' (John 17:11). But, significantly, he then asks the Father to 'Sanctify them in the truth' and 'that the love with which you have loved me may be in them, and I in them': superficial harmony within the group which sidelines truth and love is inadequate.

He places himself within the prophetic tradition, which involves confrontation of injustice and corruption even if this brings to the surface divisions within the community. When he enters the temple and overturns the tables of the money-changers, he quotes Jeremiah, accusing them of turning it into a 'den of thieves' (Matthew 21:12).

In this passage (Jeremiah 7:1–11) the prophet proclaims that 'if you truly amend your ways and your doings, if you truly act justly one with another, if you do not oppress the alien, the orphan, and the widow, or shed innocent blood in this place, and if you do not go after other gods to your own hurt', God will 'dwell with you in this place.'

This reflects a faith tradition in which justice and mercy are vitally important and which builds on, and nurtures, empathy: 'You shall not oppress a resident alien; you know the heart of an alien, for you were aliens in the land of Egypt' (Exodus 23:9). Jesus takes this a step further in Matthew 25: whatever is done, or not done, to the hungry, thirsty, naked, sick and stranger is done, or not done, to the King by whom the nations shall be judged. Individuals and countries who mistreat the most vulnerable foreigners and residents are courting disaster.

There are xenophobic aspects to biblical tradition but these are challenged from within, by an overall emphasis on love and justice.

The theme of outsiders as bringers of blessing also runs through the Bible. In Luke's Gospel, Jesus is almost killed after challenging his listeners' complacent assumption of national superiority and disdain for foreigners; he refers to the account in the Hebrew Bible of Elijah's stay in Sidon (Luke 4:22–9). In this the prophet, on the run from the authorities at home, ends up relying on the hospitality of a poverty-stricken foreign widow and, in turn, enables the household to eat and brings her dead son back to life.

Indeed in the opening chapter of the New Testament (Matthew 1), readers are informed of Jesus' descent from Ruth, the Moabite who had married an economic migrant and whose faithful love for her Jewish mother-in-law Naomi led Ruth, in turn, to migrate. Her pledge 'whither thou goest, I will go' (Ruth 1:6, Authorised Version) has inspired musicians as well as writers on theology and spirituality, and echoes God's own covenant (Genesis 28:15).

Moreover Joseph, who acts as Jesus' earthly father, is named after a character in the book of Genesis who is sold into slavery in Egypt, only to rise to high rank and save the people of that land from famine, as well as his own estranged family. In the following chapter, Jesus, his mother Mary and Joseph must themselves flee tyranny and seek refuge in Egypt.

This is not to say that the problems of leaving the country of one's birth, especially as a result of violence, are downplayed. The lament of exiles in the pages of the Bible has since been drawn on by those who feel desolate and far from home. Yet even when the experience of migrants and refugees is the result of injustice and disempowerment, unexpected good can sometimes arise.

The New Testament further develops the theme of the Church as a community which crosses national boundaries, bringing people into a relationship of kinship even if they are of different ethnicity and geographical origin. Barriers are broken down, the hope of a new way of life based on love and forgiveness embraced (Colossians 3:1–3, 11–15). This offers a foretaste of God's wonderful realm (or commonwealth), when all are at peace with one another and the Divine.

Hence coming to an understanding of the common good on this matter may involve a willingness to handle, rather than shy away from, controversy, confront prejudice and acknowledge complexity. It is all too easy to be guided by what is seen as benefiting 'the nation', as perceived through the lens of those with power and influence. However, it may be fruitful to focus (as the Bible does, and church tradition at its best) on the experience of the impoverished, oppressed and rejected and of others at their most vulnerable, for instance infants and the dying, as well as on overcoming divisions at a profound, rather than superficial, level.

Biblical authors frequently indicate that those who settle in a foreign country because of persecution, war or lack of economic opportunity deserve to be treated justly and mercifully; and that the stability and security of the 'host' nation, as well as the spiritual health of its people, may be imperilled if this does not happen. Empathy can play an important part in this, as encounter with 'the other' brings to the fore one's own experiences of alienation, powerlessness and loss as well as the capacity to share the good things one has been given.

The outsider may also be the bringer of unexpected gifts, including care, friendship and practical and spiritual wisdom. And people and circumstances shift: the destitute refugee saves the lives of those who shelter him, the widowed immigrant returns to the land of her birth and, out of love, another person accompanies her and ends up far from home.

Moreover millennia later, far-off peoples may claim famous migrants and refugees such as Abraham, Moses and Jesus as spiritual ancestors and play songs at weddings based on the words of Ruth (or watch musicals about Joseph and his coat of many colours!).

The quest for the common good reflects the fact that, at a deep level, people are interconnected despite all differences, including those arising from geographical origin, culture or citizenship. A truly peaceful and sustainable world cannot be achieved until everyone is valued and no section of humankind marginalised.

There can also be a deep joy and fulfilment in discovering a shared humanity while appreciating what is distinctive, giving as well as receiving and cooperating towards common goals which serve communities at local, national and international level. And the spiritual good of all is based on promoting virtue, which for Christians reflects the belief that humans were made through Divine love and called to love one another.

## A better future from the perspective of immigrants and their families

A better future with regard to immigration would involve addressing the needs and feelings both of current and prospective immigrants and their families and of people settled in the UK, paying particular attention to the poor, frightened and insecure.

How the common good would be manifested in this concrete situation would probably become apparent in the course of work at grass roots and wider levels, to build on what is good and combat what is wrong. Christians and other people of goodwill are already engaged in such efforts and maybe more space is required to allow those involved – refugees and migrants as well as longstanding UK residents – to reflect on what they have learnt and might want to develop.

However, I will outline what I think are likely to be some aspects, focusing firstly on the experience of immigrants and then of others in the UK, though in some ways this is an artificial distinction. Many families and friendship networks contain a mixture of UK-born and overseas-born members; and, after a while, some of those who arrived may identify as 'British' while those born here might at times feel 'foreign'.

Asylum seekers would be offered refuge, in accordance with international law, and provided with practical and psychological support. This would include the opportunity to resume as 'normal' a life as possible after traumatic experiences, with the possibility of working if they are able to do so, or resuming school or college if they are young. Tackling the culture of disbelief with which so many are confronted, whether by immigration officials, neighbours or the media, would be essential to this.

Offering security, showing respect for their human rights and recreating some measure of stability would help them to rebuild their lives after often terrible experiences. There would still be loss and sorrow but the conditions for healing would be developed.

This in turn would free them to draw on their skills, knowledge and enthusiasm to contribute to wider society. Already many of those who put time and effort into the well-being of their neighbourhoods, or are especially creative or caring, are (or have parents or grandparents who were) refugees. But all too often, how people are treated when they arrive not only perpetuates their suffering but also gets in the way of allowing them to fulfil their potential and thus benefit others.

I do not intend to idealise refugees or indeed migrants who arrive for other reasons. Like UK-born people, some are selfish or narrow-minded: having to leave one's country of birth does not necessarily mean that one is particularly virtuous. And a few would be so damaged by what they have undergone that they would be able to give very little.

But many would be able to realise their capabilities more fully in a positive climate, benefiting others as well as themselves. Some would offer inspiration through their struggles for justice, often against heavy odds. And, through wider insight into their experience, more people in the UK would be alert to the early warning signs when society is at risk of taking a dangerous turn.

In addition family reunion would be enabled for immigrants of all kinds who are already settled here, again in accordance with international human rights norms. Also the further rupture of family bonds would be avoided by an end to threats, and indeed attempts, to deport those with strong connections in the UK. Children born here should no longer have to worry that their mother or father might be taken away in a plane, or not allowed to join them. This too would free up much energy which could be used beneficially: constant anxiety can be hugely draining.

Migrant workers would be treated justly and, throughout society, discrimination against overseas-born and other minority ethnic people would become less respectable. This would reinforce general norms of justice, including stronger protection of workers' rights, and mutual respect across differences of various kinds. It should be remembered that people's identities are multi-faceted so that, for instance, many immigrants are women, disabled, from religious minorities and/or lesbian, gay, bisexual or transgender. Particular attention would be paid to those in those sectors of the economy which have tended to be especially low paid or insecure and the dignity of those who work there secured.

Appropriate health, leisure and educational facilities would be provided to promote people's well-being and the building of positive relationships across communities. All too often public services in areas with high numbers of immigrants have been especially badly hit by cuts; however, even when the funding situation was better, these sometimes tended to exclude minorities. Many voluntary organisations too are struggling. While strict rationing or tight eligibility criteria might appear to save money, there are often greater longer-term costs, and hard-to-quantify damage to people and communities.

In contrast, if people of all ethnicities are adequately cared for when sick or injured but also encouraged to stay healthy, and given opportunities to relax, socialise and expand their horizons, there would be broad benefits. The wide availability of free or low-cost

English classes, with childcare provided where required, would help more people – especially relatively isolated women – to play a fuller part in their neighbourhoods.

While some recreational activities tend to appeal to particular groups, those which bring together diverse people would be adequately resourced and promoted. Support for the arts at community level would not only allow those from different backgrounds to feel that their heritage is valued but also foster a deeper understanding of others' feelings and experiences. Attentive listening and friendship cannot be forced on people but the conditions can be created in which connections can more readily be made and deepened.

Politicians, media proprietors and other power-seekers who tried to stir up hostility, often through untruthful claims, would be robustly challenged. Within migrant communities too, those who tried to bully others into conformity, often making it harder to socialise across differences of various kinds, would find their dominance called into question.

Greater awareness would also be promoted among young people and adults of all ethnicities of the social and psychological factors which can fuel prejudice, including the impulse to scapegoat and the tendency of the powerful to deflect attention from their own shortcomings by blaming vulnerable groups. This would strengthen the bonds within local communities and enable any tensions which arise to be more skilfully and perceptively handled.

At the same time, in the interests of the common good, it would be important to tackle the causes which drive so many out of their own countries at great cost to them and their families. Leaving the country of one's birth often brings a deep sense of loss, especially if it means parting from loved ones.

It may also mean that one's original community loses one's skills and energy, which can cause particular problems in fields such as health care. If emigrating as the result of a catastrophe, possibly while suffering the effects of mental and sometimes physical trauma, the suffering may be even greater.

This would include achieving greater peace and stability internationally (see Chapters 12 and 13[5]). The movement of large numbers worldwide as a result of persecution and violence is a humanitarian calamity and, behind the statistics, are personal tragedies.

Environmental catastrophe would also need to be addressed (see Chapters 10 and 11[6]). This could otherwise become an increasing cause of mass migration by people who have often experienced grave losses.

Extreme poverty as a result of global and national imbalances of wealth and power would also be more effectively tackled, in the quest for the common good. This too would involve challenging the way the world is, which some would find disruptive, but which could help to overcome the barrier to authentic relationships among humans, and between humankind and other living creatures, indeed the earth itself.

In the longer term this might mean that fewer immigrants arrive, not because of harsh measures but because they are able to stay more easily if they so wish, without risking their own or their loved ones' well-being.

## Addressing the concerns of those born in the UK

Many people who were born in the UK, and lived all their lives here, including those who are majority ethnic, have extended families, some of whom are immigrants. (I define families broadly in this instance, to include friendship networks involving an expectation of mutual support.) Hence some of the previous section is applicable to people who are UK-born and white but who would benefit directly from more welcoming and just treatment of those who have moved to the UK.

An approach focused on the common good would however also take account of the fears of those who believe that immigration may be detrimental to them. In many instances, these arise from other factors which should be tackled directly.

This would involve ensuring decent pay and working conditions, with greater security of employment and fewer obstacles to trade unions protecting workplace rights. There would also be an adequate supply of affordable housing and transport, which would be desirable in itself and also reduce the disincentives for local people to engage with parts of the labour market. At present much work is insecure, low-paid and in areas where few families can afford to live if they wish to avoid substandard housing. This in turn may mean that migrants living in severely overcrowded conditions and being badly exploited may end up getting most of the jobs. Such sectors would change dramatically, becoming more safe and pleasant places to work, and it would be possible to buy or rent a home without being wealthy.

Public services would also be better funded and respected, so that there would be less of a sense of cut-throat competition for scarce resources. This would also make the statutory sector more appealing to workers who are UK-born. At present in parts of the health service, for instance, conditions have been made so unpleasant that UK-born workers are emigrating, sometimes halfway across the globe, leaving vacancies to be filled by migrants.

It would also be important to attend to emotional and societal factors that can fuel a sense of insecurity at a time of rapid change, which may be channelled into resentment and antagonism to 'outsiders' and the yearning for an imaginary 'pure' UK. This would include affirming positive aspects of local and regional culture, including supporting the arts and acknowledging communities' history, often involving creativity, compassion and resistance to injustice.

Support should also be provided to those who might be drawn to extremist anti-immigrant movements because of past humiliation or current feelings of isolation or powerlessness. This would involve offering adequate care and acknowledgement to survivors of violence in childhood or adulthood or major bereavement or relationship breakdown which has destabilised them, including those who turn to drink or drugs. Of course many people whose personal circumstances have involved intense suffering are keen defenders of the rights of migrants, refugees and others at risk of injustice. However, some may be drawn to dubious movements which exploit them, especially if these offer a sense of family.

## Overcoming enmity and estrangement, strengthening community

Christians, alongside other people of goodwill, have an important part to play in building a better future for immigrants and their UK-born neighbours. Many are already working towards this, sometimes with considerable courage when this involves confronting the powers-that-be or violently racist and xenophobic movements. This may also involve, for those who are members of ethnic minorities, a resolve not to become embittered or despairing but rather to persist, in hope.

In the course of this, Christians in particular may deepen their sense of having an allegiance which goes beyond nation and ethnicity and a hope beyond death itself. They may become increasingly aware that, in their tradition, they are called to move beyond seeing themselves as 'insiders' within a particular nation, accepting the norms around them and being wary of those who are 'different'. A New Testament writer describes followers of Christ as 'aliens and exiles' (1 Peter 2:9–12), while reinforcing the biblical tradition of being rooted in particular communities and seeking the good of one's neighbours whatever their ethnic origin (Jeremiah 29:7). Non-Christians with a deep longing for peace and justice, and dream of a world not yet realised, may have a similar experience even if this may be harder to articulate.

When barriers are overcome, there can also be a sense of joy which perhaps prefigures a future based on fellowship and mutual care, not fear and mistrust. Creating such a future will not be easy but there will be profound practical, emotional and, above all, spiritual benefits.

## Questions

- Can you think of a time when you had a conversation, or shared in an activity, with someone born in a different country from you, in which you gained something important? What allowed this to happen? How could it be made easier for other people to have similar experiences or reflect on these more?
- Are there projects in your neighbourhood, or place of work or study, which involve solidarity between UK-born people and migrants or refugees? What benefits do they bring to both?
- How easy or difficult is it, in your view, to develop a shared sense of a 'common good' for both immigrants and those born in the UK? How can this be encouraged?
- How could existing activities or networks in which you (or your friends) are involved be built on to work towards a future where barriers among people based on birthplace or ethnicity are overcome?

## Notes

1. See Vaughan Jones, 'Migration and the common good', in this publication, pp. 119–132.
2. See Virginia Moffatt, 'Rolling back the state', in this publication, pp. 85–98.

3.  Anna Rowlands, 'The language of the common good', in Nicholas Sagovsky and Peter McGrail (eds), *Together for the Common Good: Towards a national conversation* (London: SCM Press, 2015, pp. 3–15).

4.  See Vaughan Jones, 'Migration and the common good', pages 119 - 32 in this publication.

5.  See Henrietta Cullinan, 'Without peace and security', and Susan Clarkson, 'For ashes, a garland: embracing the vision of a world without war', in this publication, pp. 168–78 and 179–87.

6.  See Ellen Teague, 'The threat of the Anthropocene', and Edward P. Echlin, 'Living within our bioregion: sharing planet earth', in this publication, pp. 145–57 and 158–67.

# 10. The Threat of the Anthropocene

## Ellen Teague

In June 2011 the Vatican released a document prompting journalists to look up the word 'Anthropocene'. The Vatican's Pontifical Academy of Sciences had produced *Fate of Mountain Glaciers in the Anthropocene*. There was some bemusement about Vatican interest in glaciers, but even more puzzlement that a term that is more commonly used by scientists was now in the heading of a Vatican document. This was two years before the papacy of Pope Francis and four years before *Laudato Si'*, his environmental encyclical.

The journalists found that 'Anthropocene' is a somewhat controversial name for the 'man-made' geologic era in which we are now living. The report's authors judged that we are now experiencing a period in which human activity is the dominant influence on earth's climate and environment.

The report was not authored by the Pontifical Academy itself, rather, the Vatican convened a group of scientists with relevant expertise. The strongly worded document on global climate change, particularly its impact on glaciers, urged humans to act decisively to avert a coming crisis. 'We call on all people and nations to recognise the serious and potentially reversible impacts of global warming caused by the anthropogenic emissions of greenhouse gases and other pollutants,' says the report. It called for the risks to be addressed and reduced. The report suggested that action is necessary as a matter of social justice, especially for the poor. It also tied action to the biblical idea of 'stewardship' for the earth, described as 'a planet blessed with the gift of life'. It linked the conclusions to the line in the Lord's Prayer about 'daily bread', asking that 'all inhabitants of this planet receive their daily bread, fresh air to breathe and clean water to drink'.[1]

The authors of the report were not alone in surmising that we are living in the Anthropocene era. Since industrialisation, the mainstream media has documented growing human-induced environmental threats. Some of the technologies which have emerged during the past 200 years are doing enormous damage to the planet and to other creatures that share the planet with us. We are not only changing the chemical composition of the atmosphere, we are polluting the water in our rivers and oceans and causing the extinction of fellow creatures. Linked to this is growing inequality and poverty, and poor communities are often forced to use the natural world unsustainably in order to survive. Over 140 million people have been forced to migrate in recent years because of climate change disasters: droughts, harvest failures and devastating storms.[2]

The negative impact on the planet caused by human behaviour has now reached crisis proportions. Cities across Asia, for example, regularly experience toxic smog.What is really important at this time is that we humans are challenged to see ourselves as an integral part of the world. We all depend on the earth for the air we breathe, the water we drink, the food we eat and the places we live. This planet is the only one we have. It makes sense to take care of it and to ensure that it will continue to support us in the years to come. However, in order to do so we need to recognise and respond to the threats posed by the Anthropocene era.

## Climate change

Climate change is one of the most serious concerns of our age. Global temperatures have been rising for over a century, speeding up in the last few years. This causes negative impacts such as the melting of Arctic sea-ice and glaciers, prolonged heatwaves, rising sea-levels and extreme weather. The chief cause is the release of carbon dioxide into the atmosphere by burning fossil fuels for energy, industrial farming, and destroying forests. Greenhouse gas emissions are causing the greenhouse effect, trapping heat and making the earth warmer. We need to cut man-made greenhouse gas emissions drastically, phase out fossil fuels and move to renewable energy. We also need to use less energy and be more efficient in the energy that we use.

To give one example of the need for action: in 2015 the government of Bolivia, a landlocked country in the heart of South America, was forced to declare a state of emergency as it faced its worst drought for at least 25 years. Much of the water supply to La Paz, the highest capital city in the world, and the neighbouring El Alto, Bolivia's second largest city, which has historically come from glaciers in the surrounding Andean mountains, has diminished because of rapidly shrinking glaciers.[3]

## Impact of extractive industries

Climate change is not the only threat to the environment. Decades of irresponsible mining and oil and gas exploration have produced devastating effects in many countries rich in natural resources, particularly on local environments and communities, and on the climate. Gas flares in Nigeria, Russia, the Middle East, Kazakhstan and other areas of oil extraction burn constantly, emitting thousands of tonnes of toxic emissions. This results in high levels of atmospheric pollution, which damages crops, and causes severe health problems. Oil and gas pipeline construction damages the environment and exhausts scarce resources, such as land, fishing grounds or forests, which are critical for the livelihood of local populations.[4]

Meanwhile author and environmental campaigner Naomi Klein has documented similar problems in her popular book and film, *This Changes Everything*.[5] In it she notes that thousands of hectares of Canadian forest are being cut down to allow for tar sands exploration in Alberta. The process of oil refining from tar sands produces three to five times more greenhouse gases than conventional oil. And in the USA, the process of extracting shale gas, known as hydraulic fracking, has led to groundwater contamination with toxic chemicals, as well as high levels of radioactivity.[6]

### Forests

Forests are home to well over half the world's land-based species of plants and animal. More than a billion people depend on them for their livelihoods and around 300 million people actually live in forests. They are crucial in the fight against global warming, by absorbing carbon from the air, but if forests are cleared that carbon is released as carbon dioxide and other greenhouse gases. Our forests are in crisis.

The world has lost half its natural forests – and only a tenth of what is left is protected.[7]

The world's huge demand for wood, paper and agricultural products has led to some shocking and unsustainable management of forests. The biggest threats to forests are the expansion of agricultural land, infrastructure developments, mining and fire. Illegal logging is one of the most serious threats. It has driven some wildlife towards extinction and deprived forest communities of vital resources. Multinational corporations carry a huge responsibility for converting forested areas to grow crops like soya (for farm animal feed) or palm oil (for food and cosmetics). Palm oil production is particularly destructive and has led to threats to Indonesia's forests and peatlands, including orangutan areas.

### Biodiversity and ecosystem loss

Biodiversity is essential for the well-being of the planet as increased variety of species means an increased range of food sources, and more resilient and sustainable ecosystems. It is a huge concern that the impact of humans on biodiversity is greater in the past 50 years than at any time before in human history. Between 10 and 15 million species share planet earth with humans but the rate of extinction has been accelerating. The main reason so many species are dying off or risking extinction is the loss of their habitats as a result of agriculture, deforestation, forest fragmentation by roads, urban growth and global warming. Some 75 per cent of major marine fish species are either depleted or dwindling fast due to overfishing. Some 50 per cent of the world's coastal mangroves – vital nursery grounds for countless species – are gone. Nearly one in four mammal species is threatened with extinction. One in eight bird species is at risk.[8]

Since the new millennium, bees have been dying in large numbers in the United States, Australia, Canada, Brazil, China and Europe. Pollinators, especially bees, are what pioneering environmentalist Rachel Carson called keystone species, at the very centre of the entire food web. Remove a keystone and our food system is in trouble. Habitat loss, the intensification of agriculture and the routine use of agro-chemicals are playing havoc with bee populations and opening the door to disease. Bees pollinate around 80 per cent of the flowering crops which provide our food and are essential in the production of at least 90 commercially grown foods. Apples, pears, apricots, melons, broccoli, garlic, onions, peppers, tomatoes and coffee – all rely on bees for pollination. Their loss will exacerbate food problems in a world where, already, 800 million people go hungry every day.[9]

## Food and water

Humanity is also in danger of exhausting key natural resources that we think of as renewable – chief among them our food and fresh water. Soil, for example, is the matrix of most plant and insect life and therefore the food of life itself. As a direct result of soil erosion, possibly 30 per cent of the world's arable land has become unproductive in just 40 years, leading to severe declines in bird and animal life. In one country after another, soil is being allowed to wash or blow away. History shows that civilisations founder when farm productivity declines – usually as a result of soil mismanagement. In order to avoid this, it is essential that soil is conserved.[10]

Additionally, increased meat-eating harms the environment. When land is used to raise animals instead of crops, precious water and soil are lost; trees are cut down to make land for grazing or factory-farm sheds, and untreated animal waste pollutes rivers and streams. According to the Worldwatch Institute, a staggering 51 per cent *or more* of global greenhouse gas emissions are caused by animal agriculture.[11]

Water is our most vital resource. The growing demands made by an increasing number of people adopting urban lifestyles and Western diets, coupled with a changing and less predictable climate, are putting pressure on the planet's freshwater supply as never before. By 2025, 4 billion people may be living in conditions of water stress, and increasing conflict looms. And, even where water is plentiful, the poor are unlikely to have ready access to a safe, cheap supply. Water is being commodified and privatised in every continent.[12]

## Oceans

Oceans cover an incredible amount of our planet. In fact more than 70 per cent of planet earth is covered by ocean, a habitat for a rich diversity of life. But only a tiny fraction of that (around 4 per cent) is designated as protected. But destructive fishing, pollution and climate change are damaging them on a vast scale. Species are being driven towards extinction because of overfishing and habitat destruction. Plastic pollution in the oceans has intensified in recent decades, and this too causes harm to sea creatures.

## Nuclear weapons and the nuclear industry

Another threat comes from the weapons of mass destruction that are held by nine countries. Research into the potential repercussions of a nuclear conflict has shown that aside from the initial human death toll, the use of nuclear weapons could have devastating and long-lasting effects on the earth's environment.[13]

In addition to the potential damage of a nuclear weapon explosion, there is also the issue of existing environmental harm caused by weapon production. This process generates large quantities of waste that oftentimes ends up in oceans, rivers and soil. Despite having spent tens of billions of dollars on waste management and environmental clean-up programmes, the US Department of Energy is still faced with huge waste problems at its nuclear weapons plants. Some of these plants are above major sources of drinking water and it is therefore likely that this waste is reaching and affecting humans despite clean-up projects.[14]

## Consumerism

Over the past three decades we have seen a rapid increase in the consumption of natural resources. Over-exploitation and rising consumption means that the earth's resources are becoming scarcer. The growth in consumption is staggering. It includes a six-fold increase between 1960 and 2008 and per capita consumption has tripled, helped by sophisticated advertising by transnational corporations. Rapid increases in consumer spending involves opening more mines, building more factories, roads, railways and shopping outlets. Increased consumption leads to more waste. It also means expanding agriculture often into crucial ecosystems such as the Amazon and the tropical forests of South East Asia. Corporations bear a heavy responsibility. Corporate power means that they set the world's technological and economic direction, govern trade and industry, the burning of fossil fuels, and the sale and distribution of much of what we eat and grow.[15]

In 2015, the Sustainable Development Goals were adopted by 193 member states of the UN. They set out clear targets and provide a basis for countries to eliminate extreme poverty, develop a sustainable economy and stop degrading the planet's natural resources.[16] This is welcome progress, but if we are to prevent the Anthropocene threats from being realised, they will need to be implemented.

## Creation-centred theology

Thankfully the human community – including people of faith – is beginning to realise that we must make radical changes in the way we treat earth if future generations are to inherit a planet that is healthy, beautiful and fruitful. Achieving this goal of living in a sustainable way will define the nature of Christian mission in the future.

The Catholic Church and other Christian churches have often articulated their theologies of creation exclusively in biblical terms. However, modern science and the theology challenges us to move from an exclusively anthropocentric view of creation to a theocentric and biocentric one. Modern biology, for example, focuses on that segment of the creation story which began with the emergence of life 3.8 billion years ago.

Pierre Teilhard de Chardin SJ (1881–1955) was a theologian who helped move religious thinking into the modern age. He was a French Jesuit priest who trained as a palaeontologist, and helped many religious people understand and appreciate that the theory of evolution did not undermine Christian belief in God's creative activity in the world. Fr Thomas Berry CP (1914–2009), an eco-theologian and geologian (as student of the earth's story embedded within the story of the universe), has spent decades trying to encourage religious people to embrace this new cosmology and also to realise the harmful impact of modern technology on the natural world. Sean McDonagh is a Columban priest and eco-theologian, who worked with indigenous peoples in the Philippines for two decades, and who calls for a new appreciation for the sacredness of the earth.

These creation theologians drew some inspiration from the Bible. In Psalm 104 we see that God cares for all creation, not merely human beings. In paragraph 11 of the Wisdom of Solomon we learn that God lives in and loves all creatures. The Bible also demonstrates that many forces work against life in the world. In the Noah story God threatens to chastise humankind because of their sinfulness. 'The earth is full of the violence of man's making, and I will efface them from the earth' (Genesis 1:13) and therefore God considers sending a flood which will 'destroy from under heaven all flesh in which is the breath of life' (Genesis 6:17). The story of Noah and the Flood sees God instructing Noah how to save himself and his family, and also other species as well. All the creatures of the Earth are party to the covenant which God makes with Noah after the Flood. Prophets such as Joel warned of the dangers of oppressing the poor and destroying the earth (Joel 1:4). Isaiah warned that those who lived extravagant lifestyles, while so many live in poverty and squalor, would be called to justice (Isaiah 5:8–10).

In the New Testament, Jesus as the Word and Wisdom of God is active before the dawn of time in bringing creation to birth out of the chaos. Through him the universe, the earth, and all life was created (John 1:3–5). All the rich unfolding of the universe – from the initial glow of the fireball – through the shaping of the stars and the earth as the only known green planet of the universe, right up to the emergence of life and finally humans with their varied cultures and histories are all centred on Jesus (Colossians 1:16–17). The incarnation – God assuming a created human form – is an extraordinary affirmation of the goodness and intrinsic value of all creation.

The early Christian Church also had a strong theme of care for creation. Irish monks such as St Columban in the seventh century had profound awareness of God's presence in creation. He said, 'those who wish to know the great deep God must first study the natural world'. Benedictine monasteries practised gratitude for the gifts of the natural world and respect for natural systems. In the twelfth century Hildegard of Bingen contributed enormously to the Western Christian's appreciation of the natural world. Her approach to the earth delights in its 'greening'. In her writings she celebrates the uniquely feminine experience of the most intimate processes of the natural world, including the fertility dimension. In the thirteenth century St Francis of Assisi encouraged his friars to have no possessions and to live lightly on the earth. In his 'Canticle of the Creatures', Francis showed a kinship with, and deep respect for, the life in creation. He inspired Pope Francis who took his name upon his election in 2013 because, in his words, 'Francis was a man of peace, a man of poverty, a man who loved and protected creation.'[17]

Despite this tradition, in more recent times, churches that upheld human rights and promoted social justice, were not always as strong when it came to challenging human activity that plundered the planet. However, this changed in the 1980s. The World Council of Churches (WCC) was a trailblazer in helping churches integrate justice, peace and the integrity of creation into the ministry of the churches.

More recently successive popes have begun to discuss these issues. In his 1990 Peace Message,[18] Pope John Paul II called attention to the moral and religious dimension of the environmental crisis. In 2001 he called for an 'ecological conversion' to avert a global ecological disaster, and made the same plea jointly in 2002 with the Ecumenical Patriarch of the Orthodox Church, Bartholomew I. On 1 January 2010, Pope Benedict XVI's Peace Message, asked, 'Can we remain indifferent before the problems associated with such realities as: climate change, desertification, the deterioration and loss of productivity in vast agricultural areas, the pollution of rivers and aquifers, the loss of biodiversity, the increase of natural catastrophes and the deforestation of equatorial and tropical regions?'[19] He urged an examination of modern lifestyles in the industrial world.

Pope Francis's message on the UN World Environment Day, 5 June 2013, stated: 'Consumerism and a culture of waste have led some of us to tolerate the waste of precious resources, including food, while others are literally wasting away from hunger. I ask all of you to reflect on this grave ethical problem in a spirit of solidarity grounded in our common responsibility for the Earth and for all our brothers and sisters in the human family.'[20] Pope Francis's concern is rooted in his experience in Latin America. He chaired the committee which drew up the final recommendations from the Fifth General Conference of the Council of Latin American Bishops at Aparecida, Brazil, in 2007. The document speaks of the pain of Mother Earth and criticises extractive industries (mining and logging) and agribusiness corporations for failing to respect the economic, social and environmental rights of local people, especially the indigenous people.

*Laudato Si'*, released in June 2015, is Francis's first major encyclical and is known as the environmental encyclical, concerned about 'our common home'.[21] Pope Francis is deeply concerned about the unprecedented transformation of the earth's ecology and urges all people of goodwill to act urgently on behalf of earth, on behalf of future generations, and especially on behalf of justice for poor and marginalised people who are most impacted by the destructive power of climate change and environmental devastation. He says, 'I urgently appeal, then, for a new dialogue about how we are shaping the future of our planet.'[22] The encyclical will be studied for many years to come, and serve as a manual on how to engage our spiritual and material selves in this essential transformation.

## Christian witness for the environment

The Christian churches are now speaking the truth about global environmental destruction in a much more forthright way, linking with and supporting global campaigns to make the necessary transition to a more sustainable future. And the world has seen Christian environmental martyrs in recent decades. In the Amazon rainforest, for example, Sr Dorothy Stang SND was murdered in 2005 because of her outspoken defence of the poor and the environment.

In the lead-up to the UN Climate Change Conference (COP21) in Paris in December 2015 church people supported the 'Global Climate march', with over 785,000 people participating in 2,300 events in 175 countries. And at the talks themselves an all-faiths petition calling for climate action contained nearly 2 million signatures. There was widespread acknowledgement that Pope Francis's support for climate action boosted the spirits of negotiators, scientists and climate campaigners. The encyclical *Laudato Si'* called global warming a moral issue and energised not only the faith community but secular environmentalists. Christiana Figueres, the executive secretary of the UN Framework Convention on Climate Change, said the faith lobby empowered those working on the COP21 agreement to be bold. The Global Catholic Climate Movement continues to pull together Catholic groups with the same mission and its website has become a common source for campaigning and resources.

Not only is there was a feeling that climate change is finally on nearly everybody's agenda, but a global renewable energy revolution is also under way. The Fossil Free movement grew exponentially in 2016, which has meant a quarter of UK universities moving to divest from fossil fuels. In North America, indigenous activists led the campaign to halt construction of the North Dakota Access Pipeline, saying they wanted to protect water sources from pollution by oil. Alongside this, clean and renewable energy is now increasingly outpacing fossil fuels, when it comes to cost. As UN Secretary General Ban Ki-moon left office in December 2016, he said, 'The transition to a clean energy future is inevitable, beneficial and well underway, and investors have a key role to play.'[23] This has influenced church moves to disinvest from fossil fuels and shareholder action on extractive industries. Together with Pope Francis's call for an energy transition from fossil fuels, these have all been credited by financial sector experts for helping move them in the direction of sustainable development.

The 'Bright Now' Campaign of Operation Noah particularly works towards fossil-free churches. On 4 October 2016, seven Catholic groups based in five continents announced intentions to divest their financial interests from fossil fuels, the largest and broadest joint declaration to date within the Church and the second such effort that year.

In the meantime, church development agencies (such as CAFOD and Christian Aid) are offering support to small farmers, using traditional knowledge for developing resilient food systems in the context of an increasingly unstable climate. They also support water conservation initiatives.

Alongside advocacy and projects for sustainable development, the churches are now involved in education work, lifestyle initiatives and worship that incorporates ecological realities. The ecumenical group Green Christian has been a leading player for three decades. Examples abound globally of Christian communities working to gradually transition to renewable energy sources, to reduce, reuse or recycle, and to care for God's earth. Catholic parishes in the English city of Reading, California's Chula Vista and Port Pirie Diocese in South Australia are among those internationally which have installed solar panels. More than 20 Catholic parishes in England and Wales have earned Live Simply awards for their commitment to build a sustainable future, act in solidarity with the poor and live as simply as possible. Ecumenically, hundreds of parishes are now eco-congregations and schools eco-schools. More parishes than ever are marking the Season of Creation from 1 September to 4 October and Pope Francis has designated 1 September as a special Day of Prayer for Creation.

Ecological conversion involves acknowledging the Anthropocene reality and supporting ecologically sustainable patterns of production and consumption. It involves advocacy for economic, commercial and political choices that support the well-being of the whole community of life on our planet that includes other species and habitats. So much comes back to challenging consumerism and consumption beyond earth's finite resources, challenging the commodification of life, alongside practical initiatives to get back to working with life systems and not against them. It is a commitment to hand on to future generations of human beings the beauty and abundance that is God's gift to us.

In the next chapter, 'Living within our bioregion', eco-theologian and gardener Edward Echlin looks at how human society can reclaim the common good for humanity and for all of earth's community of species.[24]

## Questions

- What aspects of the Anthropocene concern you most?
- What can you do to address them?
- How can we focus more on care of creation in our churches?
- How does our faith give us hope?

## Notes

1.  The Vatican Pontifical Academy of Science, 'The Fate of Mountain Glaciers in the Anthropocene', June 2011.
2.  International Displacement Monitoring Centre, Global Estimates 2012, http://www.internal-displacement.org/assets/publications/2013/2012-global-estimates-corporate-en.pdf
3.  European Geosciences Union, October 2016.
4.  W. Corbett Dabbs, 'Oil Production and Environmental Damage', Research Paper No. 15, 1996, http://www1.american.edu/ted/projects/tedcross/xoilpr15.htm
5.  Naomi Klein, *This Changes Everything: Capitalism versus the climate* (New York: Simon and Schuster, 2015).
6.  Gayathri Vaidyanathan, 'Fracking Can Contaminate Drinking Water', *Scientific American*, 4 April 2016, https://www.scientificamerican.com/article/fracking-can-contaminate-drinking-water/
7.  World Wildlife Fund website, 'Tackling forest loss and damage', https://www.wwf.org.uk/what-we-do/area-of-work/tackling-forest-loss-and-damage
8.  Endangered Species World Wildlife Fund website, http://wwf.panda.org/what_we_do/endangered_species/
9.  UN Food and Agriculture Organisation, 2016.
10. FAO Corporate Document Repository, 'Keeping the land alive. Soil erosion: its causes and cures', http://www.fao.org/docrep/t0389e/t0389e02.htm
11. Robert Goodland and Jeff Anhang, 'Livestock and climate change', Worldwatch Institute, http://www.worldwatch.org/node/6294
12. Daniel Jaffeend and Soren Newman, 'A Bottle Half Empty: Bottled water, commodification, and contestation', *Organisation and Environment* 26 (3), pp. 318–35 (London: Sage, 2012).
13. Nuclear Files website, 'Effects on the Environment', http://www.nuclearfiles.org/menu/key-issues/nuclear-weapons/issues/effects/environment.htm
14. *New York Times*, 'By products of the bomb, pollution and the weapon factories', 7 December 1988.

15. Farm Aid blog, 'Corporate power and the food we eat', 18 March 2016, https://www.farmaid.org/blog/corporate-power-and-the-food-we-eat/

16. Sustainable Development Knowledge Platform, Department of Social and Economic Affairs, United Nations website, https://sustainabledevelopment.un.org/?menu=1300

17. Catholic News Service, 'Pope Francis explains why he chose St Francis of Assisi's name', 17 March 2013, http://www.catholicnews.com/services/englishnews/2013/pope-francis-explains-why-he-chose-st-francis-of-assisi-s-name.cfm

18. Pope John Paul II, 'Peace with God the creator, peace with all creation', Peace Message, 1 January 1990.

19. Pope Benedict XVI, 'If you want to cultivate peace protect Creation', Peace Message, 1 January 2010.

20. Vatican Radio News Service, 'Pope at audience: counter a culture of waste with solidarity', 5 June 2013.

21. Pope Francis, *Laudate Si'*, Papal Encyclical, June 2015.

22. Ibid.

23. Damian Carrington, 'Fossil fuel divestment funds double to $5tn in a year', *Guardian*, 12 December 2016.

24. See Edward P. Echlin, 'Living within our bioregion: sharing planet earth', in this publication, pp. 158–67.

# 11. Living within our Bioregion: Sharing Planet Earth

## Edward P. Echlin

Sharing the common good and living in community go together like topsoil and sweet rain. They share the familiar Latin word from which their description comes – *communis*. Early in life a child discovers that it has special needs and, eventually, responsibilities. We are never just a me, we are within a we, and an us. Others around us also share needs and responsibilities similar to our own. A healthy community includes the wider earth community within which we live together and upon which we depend. A healthy human community consists of persons who care not just for themselves but for our fellow earth creatures. Neglect or disdain of fellow earth creatures is at the heart of the ecological crisis, including human-induced climate change, the reality of which no responsible person would call a 'hoax'.

We are all members of a limited biosystem, the biodiverse cooperative community of living and also non-living beings within a limited *place*. We depend on the cooperation of the biodiverse community of creatures around us and interdependent with us. The late prophet of partial self-sufficiency, John Seymour, described a living biosystem as a 'soil community' which is what we and our fellow earth creatures are.[1] We humans are especially responsible for cooperating with the other soil creatures who together share and contribute to the wider earth or soil community within which we are interdependent members. A biosphere therefore is an interdependent variety of living and non-living beings in a place. A *bioregion*, as its name denotes, is literally a life place, a unique region with natural, and not just human-designated, boundaries. A bioregion, such as the European, is geomorphic, climate dependent, water inclusive, capable of being a human-inclusive living community. However, as Ellen Teague argues, we are now an Anthropocene community, we humans control our planet.[2]

We who share the European continent share a bioregion. The EU includes people with different histories and millions of other species with whom we share in our European earth community. The thought of parts of the bioregion under human control withdrawing from Europe – the so-called Brexit fallacy – is not only impossible, it is foolish and selfish. For we can never sever our bioregional connections. Scientists estimate there are 80 million species sharing planet earth, many of them in our fertile European bioregion. An estimated 5.5 trillion insects and butterflies fly above the southern UK annually. Our own species is endowed with gifts of intelligence and reason as well as technical skills for which, and with which, we are responsible to God for caring for the European bioregion. I have lived nearly half my life in a different bioregion, North America, which like Europe is gifted with myriad species. In former ages it was cared for by indigenous people including the Sioux of the Dakotas and the Iroquois and Huron of my native Michigan. Today these responsibilities are shared with myriad descendants from other world bioregions.

Earth scientists describe a bioregion as an area literally grounded in various soils and stones within which we cultivate food and erect buildings. It includes the sources of the water which we drink, different kinds of weeds, and millions of insects, birds, mammals, plants and trees. Within a natural climate the cycles of the seasons provide appropriate times to plant and harvest, feed and nurture the various soils in succeeding growing seasons. A bioregion provides unique resources for ourselves and fellow creatures including the carrying capacity of diverse habitats and waters and the places where we can live and flourish in rural areas, towns and cities. A bioregion includes myriad treasures which it both holds and withholds.

Bioregions engender cultures of people native to a land – we think of course of native American peoples of mountains, prairies, and deserts who have lived sustainably in these inherited territories. Within a bioregion there develop essential social and economic arrangements shaped by generations of inhabitants and adapted to the inherent geomorphic attributes of both rural and urban environments. All this is, in essence, bioregionalism.

## Climate change

Within human-dominated bioregions there exists the widely recognised killer of the biotic, life itself, in what Al Gore brilliantly described as 'an inconvenient truth' – climate change. Climate change is inconvenient because it damages the living earth for which we are responsible, and also because it demands a change of lifestyles and economies from climate damaging to sustainable. Comfortable people living unsustainably do not want to admit their economies are climate damaging. Some go so far as to call climate change 'a hoax'. Throughout the earth people depend on appropriate climate for food, water, clothing, building materials, and most of life's necessities. Agriculture and food production depend on reliable and symbiotic weather which in turn depends on a reliable climate. People can and sometimes do nurture a sustainable climate. They can also damage and change it, which is what our species, including its ever growing population, is now doing. Climate change is the challenge, the crisis of the present. In our time climate change means earth heating or global warming. We damage climate primarily by burning fossil fuels, and by generation of methane gases. The result is 'greenhouse gases' which infiltrate the atmosphere, change the climate and disrupt the customary cycles of our bioregion. Climate change is a lethal tragedy. Fortunately people, including especially those in industrialised bioregions, can, by modifying lifestyle and becoming climate friendly, restore healthy climate. But change includes sacrifice, less pursuit of 'wealth' and luxuries. Hence the 'inconvenient truth'.

The primary change we must make is to reduce the mining and burning of fossil fuels. A future sustainable world must have left most of our fossil fuel reserves safely in the ground. We can, if we have the salutary will, live comfortably and sustainably depending less on oil, coal and gas and increase our use of alternative energies including solar and wind, while insulating our buildings and developing methods of storing energy for use when it is not being generated. I was so satisfied with my fourteen solar PV panels on my south roof that I installed seven more on my smaller west-facing roof. We also enjoy two solar thermal panels for heating water. Much of the electricity and warm water we use is generated by our own panels. We now need methods of storing heat during bright days for long nights. In the meantime we sell what we don't use to the national grid, so our own little energy generation is not wasted.

There are also what is called, often confusedly, positive (bad) and negative (good) feedback accompanying climate change, to which we can often contribute. A prime example of positive – or bad – damaging feedback to climate change is the melting of the Arctic glaciers and sea ice. These are called our 'white canaries' – the whiteness of the ice reflecting back into the skies the warmth of climate change thereby helping to stabilise the weather. With global warming, however, the northern oceans melt and become positive (bad) feedback as their now dark-coloured ice-free waters absorb and store warmth and contribute to earth heating.

## A flourishing biodiversity

As the dominant species within our bioregion we can assist life to flourish. This does not mean we must always be 'doers', 'hands on', interferers. Rather, the best service we contribute to the health and biodiversity of our bioregion is simply 'letting be', encouraging life to flourish. There is no greater beauty than biodiverse spectacles of our planet 'fully alive'. Television has discovered this 'free' or natural spectacle and increasingly films our fellow creatures flourishing within their biosystem without our interference, including television specials called 'The Planet' and similar titles. These specials, with or without commentators such as David Attenborough or Tim Peake, are often inspiring to behold. They encourage and reward our solidarity and community with other living beings, not least our fellow humans living in diverse habitats. They also inspire what scholastic philosophy called 'the principle of subsidiarity', meaning that this larger and stronger part of a community need not always make the big decisions and do the big deeds, but 'let's be', encouraging the local and smaller communities to do what they know to be best.

Solidarity among people and subsidiarity are essential to a flourishing common good. People, in the description of earth scientists, are the dominant species. We live in the Anthropocene, human-controlled earth, as our era is sometimes called. This is consistent with science and good eco-theology. Of pressing importance, however, is that humans under God recognise the needs of other creatures. For future flourishing we must reverse the decline in worldwide wildlife populations that have fallen by 58 per cent since 1970. As God's image we do not exercise an arrogant 'dominion'.

Despite the contemporary obsession with 'the market economy', the importance of food to the common good in developed and poorer countries cannot be over-stated. Food depends on much of the biodiversity of a bioregion. The need for food brings people together and fosters community sharing. Community sharing is a key principle of the Common Agricultural Policy (CAP). As its title suggests, the CAP works for a fair distribution of food to human communities and the flourishing of a bioregion with its biodiversity, which produces food. The CAP tries to remedy human-induced climate change. The policy tries to avoid crippling food markets of developing societies and to avoid 'dumping' of subsidised food products on local growers who cannot compete successfully. Here again we recall the useful principle of subsidiarity as applied to small farmers and growers. Large industrial agriculture often has a tendency to sweep aside and supersede small farmers and growers. There is an abiding irony here because small-scale and family farmers sustainably produce food of a quality that large growers cannot always match.

Anyone who attends local farmers markets' appreciates the treasures which local farms and local wisdom are. Students of the Bible know the importance of shared meals to the Israelites and to Jesus. The feeding of the 5,000 is but one example (Matthew 14:13–21). The Last Supper and the many other meals shared by Jesus illustrate the importance of food and meals and, as has been recently noticed, the importance of tables around which people shared meals.[3]

Individual participation in producing and enjoying food is important for the common good. Not only must we support small farmers. It is also helpful, to ourselves and the community, to grow some ourselves, preferably with concomitant teaching of children. The scarcity of allotments because the 'brown' land they occupy is needed for housing painfully illustrates the problems associated with over-population, including from migrations. Local food growing, including allotments and even balconies, churchyards and front gardens, demonstrates the satisfaction, sustainability and even assistance of local partial self-sufficiency. I am fortunate in growing in my back garden the only local apple in the national collection at Brogdale of over 2,000 varieties. I also gave one to a local school with adequate grounds and an interested caretaker. The variety, raised by a local horticulturist near the local hospital, is called 'Lady Hopetown', recalling the time when there were literally dozens of local schools, and Bexhill was a genuine town of hope. Including my own 'Lady

Hopetown' apple there are now at least five of that local apple, including one at St Peter and Paul school and three in the national collection.

It is sensible to cherish – and even promote – the gifts, even treasures, of one's own bioregion, including not just food but also clothes and various materials. We marvel at annual harvest time in our fruit-growing bioregion to behold local growers – and cooks – who at least in certain indigenous fruit varieties are self-sufficient. It is thrilling in autumn harvest to visit orchards which offer, in addition to their beauty, fresh fruit, derivative juices and cider. Local residents discover recipes which produce local preserves including varied chutneys, jellies and juices, and sweet and dried fruit. Here we witness the local – as well as wider when exported – 'common good' in practice. What is true of apples, often with local cattle or sheep grazing beneath the trees, is true of other fruits including pears, plums, grapes and berries. To demolish and replace whole traditional orchards for other uses while importing foreign-produced fruit is potentially dangerous or risky and less nourishing and tasty.

## Migrations

Even in structured bioregions such as Europe, we experience individual or small-group migrations without an agreed response to either migrants or the countries they enter with the intention to settle and seek employment. In these pages Vaughan Jones demonstrates well the goodness in migrations for both the migrants and those in adopted communities.[4] It is often argued that migration is a natural way of living for most migrants. I believe, however, that for most people a settled family life and employment in a familiar country represents the most natural way to live for individuals and the common good. There are, however, people who must migrate for various reasons. We must assist and welcome them. Our common good includes both migrants and natives who share the land and a common humanity.

The common good includes a humane and sensitive way of treating refugees and other migrants. Some migrants, for a variety of reasons, find it difficult or even impossible to root themselves with jobs in a settled community. We can recall the so-called Calais Jungle which was once the home of thousands of rootless people of different ages and abilities. Calais was succeeded by other scattered migrant bases. People-smuggling continues with 'going prices' for different countries of origin. Afghanistan, for example, was until recently more expensive than Iran.

There are a few general principles we can follow as migrations persist. The first and most important one – which most but not all people accept – is that settled family life, with employment, within one's native bioregion, is natural for humans and whenever possible is the most comfortable and fulfilling way for people to live. There will always be persistent 'wandering', but family life within a home community remains desirable for the majority of people. For refugees, migration may seem desirable, especially when returning to a former home base is impossible or even dangerous. Increasingly within Europe and at its borders there continues to be a significant minority, mostly but not exclusively young men, engaged in a travelling and searching way of life. Groups and individuals such as Citizens UK and Lambeth Citizens and many church groups and other religions try to assist migrants and refugees to integrate in the UK or elsewhere and build communities, in the words of Citizens UK, 'in the world as it should be'. All of us should assist unsettled persons to find or rebuild a family or community life and, when practical, to return to their national homes. One has only to talk to some migrants, including people 'sleeping rough', to realise that helping migrants to rebuild lives is challenging. For Christians, however, it is a way to 'love thy neighbour' and 'feed the hungry', all of whom are included in the outreach of Jesus' incarnation. We must endeavour to build a fairer way of life in which all share, in the words of Green Christian's 'Joy in Enough'.[5] We remind ourselves that a fairer UK and 'Joy in Enough' mean that everyone has a fair share of the bioregion's gifts but no one has a superfluity of wealth such as now admittedly exits. To the Bible's teaching and the Christian tradition of 'Joy in Enough' we now turn.

## The Christian way

The Bible, cherished by several monotheistic world religions, teaches respect for the earth's biodiversity, especially the bioregion where the Jewish people and Jesus lived. The Bible's first words describe God's appreciation of all earth creatures and human responsibility under God to care for them. In the Bible's opening words we read that God created all the earth's people, 'male and female' he created them. In an often misunderstood sentence God creates them in his 'image' with 'dominion' over all earth creatures (Genesis 1:28). These important words must be read and understood in their context.[6] To be God's 'image' means that humans are like priestly kings or rulers under God to whom they are responsible for the welfare of earth's bioregion. God's 'image' does not mean that humans are gods, but are like a responsible democratised kingship including all humanity. The 'dominion' humans share does not mean domination but is like a gentle stewardship or responsibility for the earth under God. In the second and older creation story people are pictured wholly within the earth, earthlings from the soil. Adam is a soil creature, from the soil (*adamah*), and Eve is also *adamah* because she is created from Adam's rib. Together they are given responsibility for the birds of the air, the fish of the sea, plants of the soil, in brief 'earth's' bioregions. This beautiful imaginative picture is reflected throughout the Bible, including the psalms. In the flood story, people are included with other earth creatures in a cosmic covenant with God, with special responsibility for earth care or ecology.[7]

God pledges a fruitful climate, 'as long as earth remains seedtime and harvest, cold and heat, summer and winter, day and night shall not cease' (Genesis 8:22). God pledges a regular climate. Similar pictures of God as Creator shine throughout the Bible, including several beautiful psalms, as for example, 'For the Lord is a great God and we are the people of his pasture, and the sheep of his hand' (Psalm 95:11f.; cf Psalm 98; 104).

As a boy and young man in his Nazareth years Jesus learned the importance of earth creatures and especially of food and the soil itself which he worked with his elders. Jesus in his ministry taught in his actions the importance of food and of shared meals, including the familiar prayer, 'Give us this day our daily bread'. In his beautiful *Laudato Si'* Pope Francis praises the practice of grace before and after meals:

> I ask all believers to return to this beautiful and meaningful custom. That moment of blessing, however brief, reminds us of our dependence on God for life; it strengthens our feeling of gratitude for the gifts of creation; it acknowledges those who by their labours provide us with these goods; and it reaffirms our solidarity with those in greatest need.[8]

In his early years at Nazareth Jesus learned about and rejoiced in all the Nazareth creatures which share with us and contribute to the common good. He knew the fig trees, which in Nazareth old town still grow and produce figs from the stone walls. He delighted in the olive tree and its fruit and shade. He knew the insects flying around and about the plants and the birds who sang. He appreciated forever hungry dogs, the fox that travelled through self-made holes in the wall, and the sheep who both ate and fertilised the grass. Later at Capernaum and the Lake he learned about the tilapia fish that fed his contemporaries.[9]

We now recognise that in becoming man in Jesus, God entered what is now called 'the Deep Incarnation'. All earth's creatures are interconnected, including those insects that fly above southern England. In becoming flesh in Jesus, God is in relationship with all earth's bioregions. The resurrection assures us that the whole earth creation shares 'the common good' of eternal life together in our living God.

## Questions

- How does awareness of the bioregion help make us better understand our obligations to the planet? How does an understanding of Christian eco-theology assist with this?
- What can we do to personally ameliorate climate change? What can we do politically (e.g. joining groups, challenging politicians)?
- How can we influence the media in a more green sustainable direction and to cover more environmental stories?
- Why is 'saying grace' before meals important? Do you agree with the Pope's suggestions on this?

## Notes

1. John Seymour, *The Ultimate Heresy* (Bideford: GreenBooks, 1989), p. 123.
2. See Ellen Teague, 'The threat of the Anthropocene' in this publication, pp. 145–157.
3. Thomas O'Loughlin, *The Eucharist: Origins and contemporary understandings* (London, Bloomsbury T&T Clark, 2015), pp. 61–94.
4. See Vaughan Jones, 'Migration and the common good' in this publication, pp. 119–132.
5. Joy in Enough, Green Christian website, www.greenchristian.org.uk/joy-in-enough

6.   Robert Murray, *The Cosmic Covenant* (London: Sheed & Ward 1992), pp. 98–9.
7.   Richard Bauckham, *Living with other Creatures: Green exegesis and the Bible* (Milton Keynes: Paternoster, 2012), pp. 2–7, 20–62.
8.   Pope Francis, *Laudate Si'*, p. 227.
9.   Bauckham, *Living with other Creatures*, pp. 66–7.

# 12. Without Peace and Security

## Henrietta Cullinan

For commons to be 'good' they need to be life-giving for everyone, not just a chosen few, not just one nation state. Peace and security is necessary for life, for people to be able to pursue their livelihoods and look after their families. In that we are born free, and we have a choice, we must 'choose life' as Deuteronomy tells us in chapter 30, verse 9, to enjoy the blessings and mercies promised by God. Or in the song of Zechariah: 'He swore to our forefather Abraham that free from fear, and saved from the hands of our foe we might serve him in holiness and justice, all the days of our life in his presence' (Luke 1: 73; 5).

Early Christians were forbidden to bear arms. As Walter Wink explains in *Engaging the Powers*,[1] Christians opposed serving in the Roman Army, of which idolatry was an integral part. Even the flags, uniforms, camp boundaries were sacred: 'Worship of the war machine of androcracy's current representative, Rome, was the acute manifestation of the religion of violence.'

When the Roman Empire became Christian, Augustine was the one to come up with just war theory. Just war theory provides a set of seven criteria by which to judge when it is just for Christians to go to war. One is that the use of force should be the last resort and another that force should be proportional. There are also other criteria to judge actions taken during war and afterwards. For example, Christians in the UK considered the Second World War was a just war. They believed that the decision to go to war fulfilled most of the criteria of just war theory. However, the Roman Catholic Church was already moving away from just war theory as official teaching. Pope Benedict XV used his first encyclical to deplore the horror of modern weapons just before the First World War. He saw just war theory as merely excusing war and as unable to deal with the present-day reality of war.[2]

According to Wink, no Christians have ever waged a war that could be described as just, or that obeyed just war principles. He divides recent wars into three types: holy war that seeks to completely destroy the enemy, war of national interests and war of *machismo*, where neither side will back down, such as the Falklands War.

Discussed like this, war is an abstract concept, and has been used in this way, most famously by Bush when he coined the term 'War on Terror'. The suffering caused by any wars is all too real and it is imperative that we consider whether, as I discuss later in my experience of Afghanistan, it's ever going to be good for anyone.

In 1948 the United Nations International Declaration of Human Rights came into being and, supported by many laws, ensures that people have a right to a life 'free from fear and want'. Writing after the end of the Second World War, on the situation for the Jews in Germany, Hannah Arendt wrote in *Origins of Totalitarianism*[3] that it was only then becoming clear, with the destruction of a state, that when people are excluded from the state, they lose their rights. Nowhere is this more cruelly apparent than for the citizens of contemporary war zones, and now in the situation for refugees and migrants in Europe. Having been forced to flee war and oppression in their own countries, Eritrea, South Sudan, Afghanistan, Syria, they face loss of rights again in Europe. This is particularly apparent for victims of the War on Terror, the prisoners at Guantanamo and targets of extra-judicial killings by drone. It is as if the War on Terror itself has created statelessness, and therefore loss of human rights. The question for this essay is inevitably how far peace and security for common good has become only for 'our' common good and no one else's, the common good upheld for one country, ours, but not another. Just war theory was intended to reduce the violence in war, but when used as an excuse to permit war, it promotes an inevitable inequality and racism, hatred towards the other. It creates a distinction between 'the deserving and undeserving poor' of Dorothy Day, referred to by Simon Barrow in Chapter 3.[4] In relation to peace and security, S. Brian Willson, the US peace activist who lost both his legs blockading arms shipments bound for Central America, wrote: 'We are not worth more. They are not worth less'.[5]

These words for me are the essence of pacifism. In the light of these two quotes, I will now look at three aspects of our nation's security, the ongoing war in Afghanistan, drones and nuclear weapons, how they are against our faith, do nothing to keep us safe, and represent a failure of our governments to act for the common good.

## The war in Afghanistan

On a recent visit to Kabul I was privileged to listen to the voices of poor women, young people and refugees. To witness, even in a small way, how difficult daily life is in a city that is still a conflict zone, which successive powers have turned into a testing ground for new military apparatus, should outlaw any idea that a war could be just or even permissible. War tramples on human rights, the right to be free from fear and want, the right to make your voice heard, the right to health-care and education. Afghanistan, described by Kabul residents as a 'cow that everyone wants to milk', a cash cow for security and building firms, has been turned into a perpetual battleground where there is no security. It is now rated, after Syria, as the second most dangerous country in the world.

For a UK citizen, Afghanistan has important lessons and reflections. Our forces have been stationed there for over fifteen years, since the USA invaded Afghanistan after 9/11 with the aim of forcing the Taliban to hand over Osama Bin Laden. Even though many troops have been withdrawn and we are no longer at war, Defence Secretary Michael Fallon has committed troops for other roles, for the foreseeable future.

To visit Afghanistan is to be vividly aware of the long journey many refugees make all the way to Turkey, Europe. I met young people who saw this as their only option, to support their family and to escape the unpredictable violence. Many of the freedoms and privileges, that we thought were commonplace and that we can now see as fragile, have long been denied the Afghan people. As a result of war, they have been hampered in their work towards any kind of commons, especially the provision of a safe infrastructure.

The Kabul river, that flows from the surrounding mountains, is an opaque, thick grey trickle. Cascades of plastic and rags sweep through open sewers into the river bed. The city's water supply comes from underground aquifers that are refilled each year by melting snow, accessed by a deep well in each domestic courtyard. Population expansion has meant that some wells have dried up. Climate change has meant that snows have failed, and that the water is no longer 'sweet'. There are worries that a new Chinese copper mine at Mes Aynak will create a toxic crater and pollute Kabul's water supply.

Whole blocks of the city still lie flattened by US airstrikes and roads remain unsurfaced. I met women, now middle aged, whose injuries from Russian airstrikes in the 1980s make it hard to work. Young people have lost friends and relatives in airstrikes, drone strikes, and now in Taliban and IS attacks. The United Nations Assistance Mission in Afghanistan's report[6] for 2016 lists 3,498 civilians killed in conflict-related violence. Of these, 923 are children. At the same time Europe now deports Afghan refugees back to Kabul, where they often have no family or support. There are already 1.5 million refugees and internally displaced people in Afghanistan.

For the poor, basic foods, such as potatoes and beans, are expensive. Women I met in a Kabul refugee camp tell me sometimes they live on bread and tea. Sometimes they can't even afford tea and have to buy water. For those with a bit of money there are lavish beauty parlours, private hospitals and even a water park. Countless new Saudi-style apartment blocks, clad in mirror glass or coloured plastic tiles, are springing up despite the lack of infrastructure. Three-storey-high blast barriers come as standard in the grander blocks, to protect inhabitants against suicide attacks and car bombs. Even modest households have put up concrete walls and sentry posts to protect themselves. War carries on for the poor, refugees, street children, while the rich can access freedom through private security, protection of personal property and greater mobility.

The long years of war have resulted in untold damage to civil society and prevented the civic participation that would provide the chances for people to even consider their own common good. For a group of seamstresses I spoke to, the only way of making their voice heard, without education, was to go on a demonstration, which they said their husbands wouldn't like and which is also dangerous. Lack of civil society means that government is not held to account. Banks, the judiciary and police are vulnerable to corruption. The women told me that they believe aid money goes straight into lining pockets instead of being used to help the poor.

The discussions with Afghan women, their difficulties in bringing their government to account, encouraged me reflect on current political engagement in the UK. For our own security we need to be able to make our voices heard.

## Drones

As well as being an example of the aftermath of successive wars, Afghanistan is where the UK first used armed drones in a battlefield in 2005.

A drone is the name given to any unmanned vehicle, but particularly aircraft, which can vary in size from a miniature surveillance drone to the size of a very small jet. The RAF uses MQ9 Reaper drones, equipped with a camera, linked to targeting equipment, and armed with two 500lb laser-guided bombs and four Hellfire missiles. Images from the drone's cameras are sent via satellite back to the operator, who can then also fire the missiles remotely. The UK's drones are now being used to conduct airstrikes in Syria and Iraq, alongside Typhoon and fighter jets, but it is not known where they are stationed.[7]

When I first started keeping vigil outside the City of London office of General Atomic, the manufacturers of the Reaper, many passers-by had never heard of drones. If they had, usually the men, they often tried explaining things like, 'You can't halt technology,' and, 'You've got to get the bad guy!' These two comments are so interesting. The first one is a reminder that it is the new technology itself that forces us to ask new questions, ethical and political. The second one points back to a public lack of moral engagement with any kind of use of force, as if there were no Geneva conventions and the drone programme could be judge, jury and executioner.

As well as the interesting technical details of new drones, there are complex ethical, legal, economic, political discussions around their use. The fact that drones are unmanned means that many of the normal checks and balances of combat cannot apply. Only now are lawmakers deciding what limits there should be to the level of violence unleashed.

There are as many mistaken preconceptions and myths about drones as there are ways of talking about them. One unhelpful claim is that a drone is just like any other aircraft and a drone strike is just like any other airstrike. Another mistaken claim is that they are a humane weapon, that saves the lives of both soldiers and civilians, since they are a 'precision' weapon, able to locate dynamic targets, by which the military mean living human beings, with 'pinpoint accuracy'. There are many ways in which this is not true. Drones have been responsible for a disproportionate number of civilian deaths. A 2014 report by Reprieve[8] found 1,147 civilians have been killed in covert attempts to kill 41 targets in Yemen and Pakistan. In *Sudden Justice*, Chris Woods[9] provides evidence that because drone cameras cannot identify targets accurately, and because enemy targets have learnt how to protect themselves by not using phones, drone operators have to rely on human intelligence, which puts the lives of the huge numbers of informants in grave danger. He also suggests that because the drone is out of reach of the enemy combatants' weapons, terrorists have turned to soft targets, for instance the British tourists on the beach in Tunisia. Drones have created more terrorists and put us all in danger.

Drone attacks have been blamed for preventing gatherings, such as weddings, funerals or the 'jirga', the traditional meetings in Afghanistan where conflict resolution and disputes are resolved. Drones destroy community, just when it is needed most, as the threat of an attack prevents people from leaving their homes. The constant whine of the drone's engines over a village means children are afraid to go to school or play outside.

Drone attacks contravene many of the conventions around ethical conduct in war and just war theory. It is not possible to surrender to a drone. A drone operator cannot take prisoners. There have been reports of Hellfire missiles fired at 'first responders', weddings and even funerals.

In *Drone Theory*, a book on the political, technological and ethical aspects of drone warfare, Chamayou considers whether drone operators are truly combatants.[10] He uses Emilio Lussu's story of a sniper who, seeing an enemy soldier having a bath, decides not to shoot. He turns to his companion saying, 'Look here – I'm not going to fire on a man alone like that. Will you?' The opportunity to make this individual decision, to refuse to shoot, is not necessarily about rights or morals but what the soldier chooses to do. Chamayou sees this as the beginning of a peace movement, when we can decide collectively we are not a nation of killers. The opportunity for a personal decision is removed by drone warfare.

Opponents argue that the use of drones actually increases the likelihood of war, since traditional barriers to using force – such as putting the lives of troops at risk – are removed. Instead of being a last resort, the case for war is brought forward. When soldiers' lives are not put at risk, when operations are secretive, no decisions have to be taken in Parliament, there is the increased likelihood of political leaders deciding to use force.

The complexity of the US drone programme, and the UK's involvement in it, seems purposefully designed to make sure the public can't protest against it. Drone engines are made by the same company that provides in-flight entertainment on commercial flights and that makes domestic electric heaters. Drones are leading to what several writers such as Rosa Brooks and Mark Danner are now calling 'forever war'. There is no specific battlefield but a collection of 'kill boxes' that follow individual 'dynamic targets' across time zones and sovereign states. Calling political leaders to account is hard when there is no official war to protest against, when so few people even know where or when drones operate.

## Trident

Contributing to perpetual war in a different way is the UK's continuous nuclear deterrent, Trident, comprising four Vanguard submarines, loaded with Trident ballistic missiles armed with nuclear warheads. The UK currently has 215 nuclear warheads, each one eight times as destructive as the bomb detonated at Hiroshima. The UK has had a nuclear bomb since 1952 and a continuous deterrent since 1969. Some believe that having an 'independent' nuclear deterrent earns us a place at the table, an example of Walter Wink's machismo argument, but Britain hasn't had an independent deterrent since 1960.

In the summer of 2016, Parliament voted to replace Trident to the condemnation of many church leaders. Campaign for Nuclear Disarmament (CND) estimates that this will cost £205 billion, although estimates vary, with the Ministry of Defence estimating £167 billion over thirty years. The fact that we are still developing the Trident nuclear weapons system and its replacement, in spite of the fact that it will soon become technologically obsolete, shows that many politicians would still put their faith in a weapon of mass destruction.

A nuclear weapon is designed to annihilate the enemy and the enemy's country. A nuclear engagement would be, according to Wink's classifications, a holy war. Whether a nuclear attack could be a 'last resort' becomes an existential question. To initiate or respond to a nuclear attack – either way would lead to annihilation. This was the logic behind the 'mutually assured destruction' of the Cold War, in which neither side could launch a nuclear attack against the other without being totally destroyed by the ensuing counter attack.

To use nuclear weapons as a deterrent is threatening and planning the murder of many innocent people. Timmon Wallis compares this with the threat of a suicide bomber, a comparison taken up by the recent guerrilla poster campaign by Darren Cullen from 'Spelling Mistakes Cost Lives'. Wallis asks if it is acceptable to be making such a threat when attempted murder carries the same sentence as actual murder in a British court.[11]

When I was working in a Further Education college, I had encounters with scores of disadvantaged young people as they made tentative steps towards improving their future. In this context, however trying, the thought that other, usually older, people were planning and designing a weapon that would result in destruction of the earth was shameful and heart-breaking. International Campaign to Abolish Nuclear Weapons (ICAN)[12] argues that nuclear weapons cannot distinguish between military and civilian targets, making them the most unsafe weapon for civilians; they would also put neighbouring countries not involved in conflict in grave danger. A nuclear attack would cause an environmental disaster, contaminating water and food supplies.

We don't have armoured cars patrolling the high street. Instead we have nuclear warheads hidden away in a loch. And yet according to a poll by Bristol University only 3 per cent of people feel safer because of Trident. As reported by CND in February 2017, Trident is useless against the threats we do face: terrorism and climate change. In itself Trident is vulnerable to cyber attack. The submarines thought to be protected by their cloak of underwater invisibility can now be detected by underwater drones.

For Christians or anyone of faith the political and economic arguments for or against Trident must surely be subsumed under the humanitarian and environmental considerations.[13] The way in which our nation clings to nuclear weapons is idolatrous, similar to the way the Roman Army made their vanguard into a legionary god.

Even if I oppose the UK's attachment to nuclear weapons, I am still a citizen and thus attached to Trident – what to do! I cannot refuse to join the Roman Army. I cannot refuse to bear arms, as the arms are borne on my behalf. The question for all of us is how far can we go in our refusal to support Trident for the common good?

## Creating peace and security for all

In Kabul , along with everyone else, I was affected physically by the air pollution, created by all the wood and coal fires and diesel fumes. I had never thought that much about pollution in London until I returned from Kabul, when all of a sudden I could smell that same diesel particle smell everywhere. Pollution is just as present in London, but heavily disguised. It occurred to me I could say the same about security.

At home I am free to roam, ride my bike, hop on and off buses. I am free to join a demonstration without fear of being caught in a suicide bombing, or being attacked by the police. Go on any demonstration and the police will tell you they are there to ensure your own safety, to uphold your right to protest peacefully. But then if you're protesting outside something like an arms factory or an arms fair their role is first to protect a lawful business. For the common good, we need people to be free to express their opinions, but increasingly crowd-control tactics are such that many people are afraid. They might be kettled, have CS gas thrown at them, be squashed into barriers. But our two most controversial and expensive, morally hazardous, security systems are invisible and avoid public scrutiny. Nuclear weapons are hidden underwater and the drones – not many get to see one or know where they are.

Peace and security, the right to be free from fear and harm are essential commons, not just for our family or our country but all people. But as Simone Weil wrote in 1930, 'the most defective method' would be to examine the way we maintain security 'in terms of the end pursued and not by the nature of the means employed'. We need to reclaim and re-examine the methods our governments use. Our preferred security methods – an increasingly militarised police force, border controls, nuclear weapons, armed drones – do little to make us safer and are a moral hazard to ourselves. The threats we face will not be mitigated by resorting to violence, hugely expensive weapons or small cheap ones. The greatest threats we face are terrorism, but also global inequality, lack of water and food, climate change. These threats are very real for many people and soon will be affecting us in the West. For our own safety we should be turning our resources to these. We should put our trust in the transformative power of human relations, in working together, and not in the empty idols of weapons and secrecy.

On the criteria of last resort Wink quotes Niall O'Brien, an Irish Columban missionary in the Philippines: 'having no last resort human beings come up with alternatives from the depths of their creativity.'[14] In April 2016 a group of lay people, theologians and clergy met in the Vatican to make a stand for just such a creative approach, calling for 'active nonviolence'. One of the final statements of the conference was to no longer teach just war theory, to end all war and ban nuclear weapons.

Amongst the resources, publicised by the Catholic Nonviolence Initiative, are examples where active nonviolence has been successful in resolving longstanding conflicts in countries such as South Sudan, where Bishop Paride Taban founded the Holy Trinity Peace Village. In the next chapter, Susan Clarkson gives another example, the Borderfree Centre in Kabul, a project of the Afghan Peace Volunteers, as she explores the possibilities for a world without war.

## Questions

- Read S. Brian Willson's quote: 'We are not worth more. They are not worth less.' What does this mean for you in your own situation? What does this mean for drones? For Trident?
- How far would you go to resist Trident?
- What does forever war look like for you? Think about the signs in your own situation.
- The nation state: how far do you think the nation state is the cause of loss of basic human rights for some and not others?

## Notes

1. Walter Wink, *Engaging the Powers: Discernment and resistance in a world of domination* (Minneapolis: Fortress Press, 1992).
2. Louisa Cahill, 'Official Catholic Social Thought on Gospel Nonviolence', background paper to Conference on Nonviolence and Just Peace, Rome, 2016.
3. Hannah Arendt, *Origins of Totalitarianism* (New York: Houghton Mifflin Harcourt Publishing, 1951), p. 296: 'We became aware of the existence of a right to have rights (and that means to live in a framework where one is judged by one's actions and opinions) and a right to belong to some kind of organised community, only when millions of people emerged who had lost and could not regain these rights because of the new global political situation. The trouble is that this calamity arose not from any lack of civilization, backwardness, or mere tyranny, but on the contrary, that it

could not be repaired, because there was no longer any "uncivilised" spot on earth, because whether we like it or not we have really started to live in One World. Only with a completely organised humanity could the loss of home and political status become identical with expulsion from humanity all together.'

4. See Simon Barrow, 'The uncommon good', in this publication, pp. 43–55.

5. David Hartsough, *Waging Peace: Global adventures of a lifelong activist* (Oakland, CA: PM Press, 2014).

6. UNAMA website, Press Release, 'UN calls on parties to take urgent measures to halt civilian casualties as numbers for 2016 reach record high', 6 February 2017, https://unama.unmissions.org/sites/default/files/6_february_2017_press_release_civilian_casualties_annual_report_english_0.pdf

7. Drone Wars website, 'About drones', https://dronewars.net/aboutdrone/

8. Reprieve, http://www.reprieve.org.uk/press/uk-bases-used-targeting-secret-us-drone-war-documents-indicate/

9. Chris Woods, *Sudden Justice: America's secret drone wars* (London: Hurst and Company, 2015).

10. Gregoire Chamayou, *Drone Theory*, translated by Janet Lloyd (London: Penguin Books, 2015).

11. Timmon Wallis, 'Nuclear Weapons: Frequently asked questions', pamphlet from Quaker Peace and Social Witness.

12. ICAN, http://www.icanw.org

13. Ellen Teague discusses this further in 'The threat of the Anthropocene' in this publication, pp. 145–57. See also Timmon Wallis, 'Nuclear Weapons', p. 1: 'Recent studies by the scientific community have suggested that major climate effects for the whole northern hemisphere could result from just one Trident submarine attack, leading to death by starvation alone of up to two billion people.'

14. Simone Weil, *Formative Writings* (New York: Routledge, 1999) p. 173.

15. Wink, *Engaging the Powers*.

# 13. For Ashes, a Garland: Embracing the Vision of a World without War

## Susan Clarkson

The prophecy of Isaiah in the Hebrew Scriptures has long been a source of inspiration for those who embrace the way of nonviolent love and have the courage to work wholeheartedly for a world without war. Indeed, the prophecy in Isaiah 2:4, 'They shall hammer their swords into ploughshares and their spears into sickles', has given a whole movement of nonviolent direct action its name; the Ploughshares Movement.

For this essay, however, I'd like to take as a starting point aspects of Isaiah 61:2–3:

> The spirit of Lord Yahweh is on me
> for Yahweh has anointed me,
> He has sent me to bring good news to the afflicted,
> to soothe the broken hearted,
> to proclaim liberty to captives,
> release to those in prison …
> to comfort all who mourn …
> to give them for ashes a garland.

This passage is echoed and fulfilled in Luke 4:16–21 when Jesus not only makes it his own but invites us to join him on the path of nonviolent love. This path, incidentally, leads to crucifixion but also to resurrection. Of course neither a desire for a world without war, nor the courage to work for it, is confined to Christians, as we shall see later in this essay, but there are many aspects of Jesus' words and actions which resonate with many who do not identify as Christian. The common ground for Christians and others is a belief in the basic goodness of all humanity. We respect that of God in everyone, and act accordingly.

At the beginning of 2017 we see in its stark tragedy the effects of war across our world. The suffering of millions of displaced people, innocent victims of war and other atrocities, bears witness to the utter failure of world governments and leaders to care for the most vulnerable in society. To a great extent we, as citizens of the world, often collude with our governments and so humanity is caught up in a downward spiral of despair. A major challenge for those who work for peace is to look unflinchingly at this collusion and see ways in which it can be counteracted.

At this time, too, Western democracy is deep in crisis as we contemplate the future for Britain preparing, not very thoughtfully, for so-called Brexit. The future for the United States and the world as Donald Trump assumes the presidency is no less uncertain. Both in Britain and the USA, as well as in Russia, France, Germany and other countries, there is a worrying and menacing growth of nationalism masquerading as patriotism. Our leaders are using their speeches to whip up this nationalism. Both the British Prime Minister and the American President pretend that this is what 'ordinary' people want. Nationalism breeds racism and bigotry as well as violence and militarism.

Our culture tends to support the false message that nations can only progress if they have a strong military industrial complex and sustain their position in the world by force. One of the most dangerous and debilitating beliefs among us today is that there is such a thing as 'good' violence; that violence perpetrated by 'good' people on 'bad' people is justified. Nationalism thrives on this myth, the Myth of Redemptive Violence. Walter Wink, the noted theologian and biblical scholar, examines and explores this in much of his writing.[1] This myth seeps into our culture on so many levels.

For example it is interesting and instructive to look at which films and television series are the most popular. Note how many films at the cinema or on streaming websites are perpetuating the myth of the 'good guys' beating the bad. It is also interesting and somewhat disturbing to look at a list of BBC documentaries available currently and in the BBC archive which deal with the military history of Britain.

In order to counteract and challenge the pervasiveness of nationalism and militarism in our lives and culture, and to withstand the myth of redemptive violence, we need to allow our hearts to become strong and compassionate and to nurture a willingness to look inside our hearts to see if the Gospel message of nonviolent love is alive and active there. This requires a genuine openness and it requires time, but it is well worth it. Sometimes if we try to work for peace without recognising our own need for inner peace, we run the risk of burning out. This does not mean we have to have a perfect inner life to bring peace to the world, but it does mean that we are willing to continue our own spiritual journey with its unexpected twists and turns, while busily working with others on the same road.

It is important to state here that this essay is written from the point of view of privilege. I am a white woman, a senior citizen, living in security in Britain. The following reflections are influenced by this and present some ways in which others who are also living in comparative privilege can both envisage and enflesh the vision of a world without war. The majority of children, women and men in the world do not live in security and comfort and most are struggling to survive from day to day, hour to hour. As people of privilege we can look at our world and ask ourselves, 'How can we improve the lives of our brothers and sisters and how can we best live our lives so that our actions do not make their lives less secure?' We are all children of God and the foundation for creating a world where all are free from fear or harm is not only a belief in this truth but a willingness to act on this belief. If we believe that all are equal in God's sight, or indeed that all are equal in our sight, we can hardly collude with either the myth of redemptive violence nor its companion, the just war theory.

There are many signs of hope in our society today which serve to strengthen the quavering heart. These signs may take the form of individual initiatives, campaign groups and groups that engage at grass-roots level in work for justice and a world without war. In this essay I shall take only three examples. First, a message from Pope Francis, an extremely influential individual who has taken an initiative to embrace nonviolent love. Second, I shall look at two communities who, in different countries and cultures, not only live the vision of a nonviolent world but also give us models for our own search. There are, I know, many other examples of groups and communities who share the same vision and who also inspire others to embrace and enflesh their own vision. These are not mentioned here but readers will be able to name many such communities. The two I have chosen I have included simply because I have some personal experience of their work.

In his message for the World Day of Peace 2017,[2] Pope Francis took as his theme, 'Nonviolence: a style of politics for peace'. In this message, as well as stressing the importance of peace beginning in the heart, the home and the community, Pope Francis highlighted teachings from his predecessors about peace. He also spoke about the work for peace done by prophets such as Gandhi and Martin Luther King and others both within and outside the Catholic Church. His message is moving and practical and members of the Roman Catholic Church can be justifiably proud of such a leader. By the tone and content of the message Pope Francis presents an alternative to the just war theory long held by Christians as a justification for war. If Catholics and others study and reflect on this document and its call to action it could bring about a new spirit and renewal within Catholicism not seen since the Second Vatican Council.

There is a movement which has its roots in Catholicism but which has attracted people from other faiths and none because of its vision and practice. This is the Catholic Worker Movement, founded in 1933 in New York by Dorothy Day and Peter Maurin.[3] There are Catholic Worker communities all over the USA as well as communities in Canada, Mexico, England, Scotland, Germany, the Netherlands, France and Australia, at the time of writing. There is a wealth of documentation available about the aims and history of the Catholic Worker, much of it written by Dorothy Day herself, but for our purposes here it is interesting to look at the fundamentals of this movement, one of the greatest gifts given to the world by the United States, and at what we can learn from these fundamentals to put into practice ourselves.

Catholic Worker communities live alongside and offer hospitality to vulnerable people; for example in Britain the communities have always focused on offering hospitality to asylum seekers. There are also Catholic Worker communities in rural areas where the members live lives of simplicity and sustainability as well as offering hospitality and resistance.

The Catholic Worker Movement has always been, and still is, committed to nonviolence. This caused much consternation during the Spanish Civil War and the Second World War among Catholics in the USA who supported the just war theory. Community members, as well as offering hospitality, campaign for a more just and peaceful world. This has often led to Catholic Workers engaging in nonviolent direct action to resist the war machine. Many have appeared in court and spent time in prison for these actions and have inspired many others to follow suit.

At its best, the Catholic Worker community in a city or rural area forms a hub around which volunteers gather for the work and the witness. This extended community is important as not everyone can live in community nor be free to risk arrest for direct action. In many cases a core community may have a high turnover of members but often the wider circle of volunteers may spend years carrying out the work inspired by Dorothy Day and Peter Maurin.

Those of us who live in a place where there is no Catholic Worker community can still take inspiration from the writings of Dorothy Day, Peter Maurin and others. Neither of the co-founders envisaged that the communities would be 'elite' groups but hoped that parishes and churches would provide space for the living out of the Catholic Worker vision. This vision was originally, and still is, expressed through the Catholic Worker newspaper.

Dorothy Day and Peter Maurin embraced the philosophy of Personalism. For them the work of hospitality and resistance to war and war-making sprang from a belief that we have the power to take responsibility for situations and do not place our faith in state systems. Christian Personalism is anarchism at its best and encourages all of us to see how we are all responsible for the creation of a new nonviolent world where love permeates all actions. If we accept that we are responsible for the flourishing of nonviolent love, we won't spend time and energy complaining about what 'they' should do. Of course our personal responsibility may, and often does, urge us to call our government to account over unjust legislation and too great a dependence on military might. When confronting a government action, either through a campaign, a demonstration or direct action, it is a helpful practice to do, at the same time, an anonymous act of kindness for someone, to keep alive the realisation that we are all responsible for the state of the world. Prayer is also a nourishing practice for us when embarking on confronting the powers and can never be underestimated.

So, what can we do, where we are, to perform the Works of Mercy, resist war and live sustainable lives? This is where reflection and acknowledgement of our limitations comes in. We are all capable of looking around our environment, finding groups which offer practical help to society's most vulnerable and volunteering. We can also join a group working for the abolition of war and war-making. In Britain there is the Movement for the Abolition of War,[4] Campaign Against Arms Trade,[5] the Campaign for Nuclear Disarmament,[6] Drone Campaign Network[7] and many others.

There are many people who are already actively working in the peace movement. Sometimes we overstretch ourselves, join too many groups and live with unnecessary stress. One way to alleviate this is to choose one or two issues only and to focus on them. We often feel there is so much to do and not enough people to do it. Trust in others on the same path is helpful. If we can trust others to do what we cannot we'll save ourselves much stress and anxiety. A habit of reflection and examination of our lifestyle can really help us to pace ourselves so that the peace we seek is within us. It doesn't stay there, however, and if we are aware that we try to live peacefully and nonviolently with those around us, we will be better equipped to join the campaign for a world without war.

So far I have written about peacemaking in Britain and in the United States. The strength of the Catholic Worker and other peace communities in the developed world is that they can show a way to peace from deep within our capitalist society, from the belly of the whale if you like. I want to present to you now a group of people who live lives of hospitality and resistance to war in the heart of their war-torn country: Afghanistan.

It was Kathy Kelly of Voices for Creative Nonviolence[8] who first met the Afghan Peace Volunteers on a visit to Bamyan Province, Afghanistan, several years ago. Their history can be found on their website[9] and it is truly inspiring. It is a story of courage in the face of adversity and a determination to live according to the principles of nonviolent love in the midst of a deeply violent and dangerous society.

The Afghan Peace Volunteers (APV) live in Kabul. In the beginning they were only young Hazara men and their aim was to form community with representatives from the different ethnic groups found in Afghanistan. Their inspiration comes from Gandhi and Martin Luther King as well as other prophets of nonviolence. There is now a community of women also and both communities work together on a variety of projects, notably a school for street children. Another project they facilitate is the duvet project, which gives work to local women who make duvets which are then distributed by the

APVs to local families in the winter. The community also runs a centre for peace where local people can study ways of living nonviolently and campaigns can be planned and carried out.

On the 21st of each month the APV connect to supporters and friends around the world on a Global Day of Listening.[10] In these sessions the APVs give news of their lives and others give news from around the world about various peacemaking initiatives. Of late there has been much input about sustainability and environmental issues.

Voices for Creative Nonviolence and Voices for Creative Nonviolence UK[11] continue to support the APV by fundraising and by visits of solidarity when appropriate. As has already been pointed out, the APV work against a background of violence and threat. They carry out their work for peace both locally and globally amidst street explosions and suicide bombings. Even more remarkable is the fact that their country has been ravaged by war for decades and its people traumatised, yet they carry on building peace and helping to heal broken lives. Their example is a powerful inspiration to all who work for peace and spurs us all on to do what we can in the safety of our own society. The very fact that we are, in the main, safe and secure, urges us to use the freedom we have to make our voices heard.

In conclusion, let us return to the passage from Isaiah with which we began. Listening to the leaders of our governments at this point in time we hear no compassion, no desire to bring good news to anyone, nothing to heal the broken-hearted nor to free captives. We know what we hear and it chills the heart. We are presented with a challenge today not only to rekindle the fire of nonviolent love in our own hearts and keep the fire burning, but to reach out and give love and comfort to others so that they too can feel the warmth of love in their lives.

We learn from others who share our desire for a world without war, whoever they are and from whatever country and culture. The first lesson is to begin with nourishing the spirit of nonviolent love in our own hearts and within our immediate community, family, friends, workmates, church, and all the other groups in which we find ourselves. This we do by prayer, taking care of ourselves and not taking on too much but by doing what we do do, well.

Quaker Advices and Queries no. 28 has some wise words on this:

> Every stage of our lives offers fresh opportunities.
> Responding to divine guidance, try to discern the right
> time to undertake or relinquish responsibilities without

undue pride or guilt. *Attend to what love requires of you which may not be great busyness.* (my italics)

We learn from communities like the Catholic Worker Movement, the Afghan Peace Volunteers and many others, that our resistance to war always includes some form of work with people more vulnerable than ourselves. This we can do within our own surroundings. As Wordsworth tells us, the best portion of our lives are the 'little, nameless, unremembered acts of kindness and of love'.[12]

We cannot all live in a community setting but we are all part of small communities and community life thrives on the generous mutual sharing of gifts. The words of Margaret Meade, the cultural anthropologist, are often used as an encouragement to us to persevere in our own sphere, working with others, sharing our strengths and weaknesses and believing in nonviolent love and the real possibility of a world without war: 'Never doubt that a small group of thoughtful, committed citizens can change the world; indeed, it's the only thing that ever has.'

So, thoughtful, committed, courageous, hard-working and, above all, compassionate, we can indeed give our suffering world, suffocating in the ashes of despair, a garland of hope, light, warmth and nonviolent love.

## Questions

- What signs of hope do you see around you? Name individuals, groups, communities, movements and initiatives that inspire you.
- What aspects of the vision of the groups named above do you think are most needed in the world today?
- What do you find most helpful in your life to sustain a balanced and effective lifestyle?
- A world without war will not just be the world as we know it but without the military industrial complex. How do you envisage this world? Be creative and imaginative. What one small thing can you do to bring this new world about?

## Notes

1.  Walter Wink, http://www.ekklesia.co.uk/content/cpt/article_060823wink.shtml
2.  Message of His Holiness Pope Francis for the Celebration of the Fiftieth World Day of Peace, 1 January 2017.
3.  Catholic Worker website, www.catholicworker.org
4.  Abolish War website, www.abolishwar.org.uk
5.  Campaign Against Arms Trade website, www.caat.org.uk
6.  CND website, www.cnduk.org
7.  Drone Campaign Network website, dronecampaignnetwork.wordpress.com
8.  Voices for Creative Nonviolence website, www.vcnv.org
9.  Our Journey to Smile website, www.ourjourneytosmile.com
10. Global Day of Listening website, www.globaldaysoflistening.org
11. Voices for Creative Nonviolence website, www.vcnv.org.uk
12. William Wordsworth, 'Lines Written a Few Miles Above Tintern Abbey'.

# OUR MISSION

# 14. The New Jerusalem: Building a Vision for the Common Good

## Simon Woodman

There is an important question to be asked, when it comes to considering a properly Christian response to the common good, and it is this: *'What, in the world, are we here for?'*

As Patrick Riordan demonstrates in the opening chapter of this volume,[1] there is a long trajectory of Christian engagement with philosophies of 'common good'; from the medieval Church's appropriation of Aristotelian concepts, to the development of Catholic Social Thought in the twentieth century. Of particular interest is the question of whether the Church's common good correlates with the common good of wider society beyond the Church, and of how these 'goods' relate to the self-interest of the individuals who comprise the Christian community. In other words, *'What, in the world, are we here for?'*

As with all interesting and important questions, this bears a little unpacking. Specifically, who might be referred to as 'we' here? Is it to be heard as applying to individual Christian believers, querying the purpose of personal existence? Or is it to be heard as applying to people at a congregational level, asking a collective group of Christians why they gather in their particular building, in their particular location? Or maybe it should be heard in a wider sense than this, perhaps as applicable to the Church universal, asking what the point is of Christian churches in general? Or maybe it should be heard at an existential level, as applying to all of humanity and asking what, if anything, is the point of human life itself? All of these are valid questions, and subsumed within them are whole disciplines of philosophy, ethics, ecclesiology and theology. So perhaps it might be helpful to narrow it down for the purposes of our enquiry into the common good. I'm going to suggest that it should be heard as being primarily directed at the Church in its universal sense – 'Why is there a church in the world?', and then secondarily as applying to the church at a congregational level – 'Why is *this* church *here* in *this* corner of the world?'

So, *'What, in the world, are we here for?'*

There is an old cliché that the Bible starts with a vision of a garden and ends with a vision of a city; and this can be a helpful way of thinking about the trajectory that Scripture takes, with its rollercoaster journey from a one vision of perfection to another, encompassing the vast sweep of human experience along the way. But another way of thinking about the Bible is that it is an attempt to explore, through story and history, through poetry and parable, what the purpose might be for God having called *some* people to be *his* people. This question of purpose is there in the moment of revelation given to Abraham, the spiritual ancestor of Jews, Muslims and Christians. In that moment of initial calling, the covenant that God made with Abraham was that his descendants would be the people of God, and that they would be a blessing to the whole earth (Genesis 12:1–9; 17:1–8). The purpose of calling one group of humans into a relationship with God was, from the beginning, that the blessing should go beyond that group. The outworking of this is surely that any form of religion that seeks to keep the blessings of their relationship with God to themselves and those like them is a betrayal of the covenant that God made with Abraham.

So, the first part of an answer to the question of, *'What, in the world, are we here for?'*, has to be that, at the very least, the Church is here to be good news to those who live beyond its own community. It is here to be good news to the lost, the lonely and the least; to be good news to those who are not like 'us'. Which brings us to the main point for this chapter: I propose that the Church (universal and local) is here, in this world, *to build a vision for the common good.*

Those who built the Tower of Babel were trying to build their way to heaven (Genesis 11:1–9), while those who built the tabernacle were trying to build a home for God on earth (Exodus 25:8–9). Solomon built his temple to keep God close to the seat of royal power (1 Kings 7:51), while Ezra rebuilt it as a symbol of ethnic exclusivity (Ezra 4:3). But all these attempts to build the Kingdom of God on earth ultimately failed, and the lesson from these stories is that God can neither be reached by human efforts, nor contained by human buildings. The good news of the New Testament witness is that God is encountered on earth, not through a sacred building or a tower of strength, but through the person of Jesus as he is revealed by his Spirit, through the people that bear his name. If the Church in the contemporary world is to think of itself as those people through whom Jesus is revealed, then the reason the Church is 'here' is not to build God a house, or to build power or strength, but to build a vision for the common good. The Church is here to be a blessing to those who are not part of it, to be 'good news' to all people. The Church is called to social evangelicalism, whose 'good news' is heard across all sectors and sections of society.

Jonathan Chaplin proposes that while other religious traditions such as Roman Catholicism and Anglicanism have developed profound theologies of the common good, the evangelical tradition has largely failed to do this, resulting in a sparsity of theological resources for evangelicals to articulate a vision for an alternative reality in anything other than spiritualised terms.[2] He notes that this has not prevented significant examples of evangelical social activism (such as the 'nonconformist conscience' of the nineteenth century), but that neither have these examples rooted themselves deep within the evangelical tradition. He locates the more recent recovery of evangelical social activism within the context of a sense of loss at the passing of 'the Christian country'. The desire to return to a nationalist narrative of Christian-inspired legislation is thus identified by Chaplin as a 'neo-Christendom assumption'[3] which interprets the role of the Church in national affairs as defending against the erosion of Christian privilege. By this model, it is Christians themselves who become the vulnerable and the weak, and in need of legal protection; as opposed to a vision of the common good where the Church is concerned with giving voice and protection to those others whom society would exclude or disadvantage. Against this, Chaplin points to theologians such as Stanley Hauerwas and John Howard Yoder, who have articulated a vision of the church as a radical alternative economic community, modelling a distinct vision of humanity focused around the teachings of Jesus. However, Chaplin's critique of this latter movement is that it encourages its adherents to 'work *apart* from the world, *for the sake* of the world'.[4] In other words, it is isolationist in its desire to be countercultural. This raises once again the question of what, *in the world*, is the Church for?

An answer may be discerned in the fascinating vision of the Church on the earth found in the biblical image of the new Jerusalem (Revelation 21:2). Many readers of this image have taken it as a vision of the future, something that will happen at some point far from now as a mysterious celestial city descends from the heavens to settle on a renewed earth. This is no mere theological abstraction, because if a Christian comes to believe that this present earth is going to go (quite literally) to hell, to be replaced in God's good time by a new earth and a new city for the purified elect to live in, then they have very little motive to act in ways that build the common good in the present. In some prominent streams of evangelicalism in the USA and elsewhere, it is not uncommon to find Christians so focused on heaven and the future that they will vote for politicians in the present whose policies are contrary to the common good.

In the light of this observation, I want to offer the image of the new Jerusalem as a model for Christian engagement in building a vision for the common good. If the new Jerusalem were merely a vision of the distant future, then one might reasonably ask what earthly use it is now for those who must live in the present? My contention is that it is much more likely that what the book of Revelation is offering here is a metaphor for the Church militant; a compelling picture which invites further reflection as to what it might mean to be the Church in the here-and-now, in *this* time and *this* place. By this understanding, the new Jerusalem is a picture of the people of God on the earth, a symbolic image designed to address the question of what, on earth, the Church is here for.

Consider the utility supplies in the new Jerusalem; specifically the supply of light and water. The text states that the city has no need for either the natural lights of the sun and the moon, or for the artificial light that comes from lamps (Revelation 21:22–26). Rather, the glory of God is its light, and its lamp is the Lamb of God. In fact, it has so much light that it shines brightly enough for all the nations to walk by its light. Similarly, the new Jerusalem seems to have a never-ending supply of fresh water, enough not only for its own citizens, but to quench the thirst of anyone who wishes to come and take the water of life as a gift (Revelation 22:17). This super-abundance of light and water is in stark contrast to all other human cities. The ancient city of Jerusalem itself had no natural water supply, and until relatively recent times was dependent on a tunnel bringing water in from outside the walls (2 Kings 20:20). Similarly, the supply of light to keep city streets safe at night was, until the invention of electricity and gas supplies, dependent on lamps and oil; as reflected in Jesus' famous parable about the virgins and their oil lamps (Matthew 25:1–13).

This consideration of light and water supplies introduces the concept of the economics of the common good. In any city, and in any society, there are certain things that it will make more sense to enact collectively. The lighting of the streets is a classic example, although the principle can be extrapolated across many areas of need and provision. The significant thing about street lights is that no *one* street light exclusively benefits any *one* individual. The system only works when all the lights are working for the benefit of all the inhabitants. It would make no sense to try and levy a charge on citizens only for the light they actually used, or to arrange to illuminate only the part of the pavement that someone was currently walking along. Similarly, one person's use of the light does not materially detract from any other person's use. This, in a nutshell, is the economics of the common good. The same is true of water supplies, sewage systems, public transport, and health care provision, to name but a few further examples.

Enlightened rulers down the centuries have sought to implement policies for the common good, from the building of Roman aqueducts to the health care and welfare reforms of the modern era. However, the difficulty such leaders have faced is that to do this requires a clear initial vision of the end result, in order that the bold economic steps to construct and offer a service for all, regardless of need or level of use, can be justified politically. For policies to be enacted for the common good, there first has to be a clear vision for the common good; and one of the key weaknesses of neoliberal capitalism has been that its driving vision has been towards the good of the individual, rather than for the good of all. The emphasis on free trade, privatisation, deregulation and fiscal austerity have, at best, placed the common good as a secondary function of the overarching vision of personal self-interest. Those who retain a hope for communitarian economics might well wonder where, in the twenty-first century, voices offering a coherent vision for the common good will emerge.

The image of the new Jerusalem as the city with enough light to shine across all the nations, and with enough water to supply the thirst of any who need it, invites a deeply politicised reflection on the Church's understanding of itself, in the world for the common good. *'What, in the world, are we here for?'* We're here for the good of all; in fulfilment of the covenant between God and Abraham. This is a spiritual vision, but it is a vision with some very practical out-workings. All too often churches have come to see themselves as existing in the world for their own benefit, with the Church in effect functioning as a closed-set club, admission upon request. Any benefits such churches offer to the wider world are often secondary, at best. The primary purpose of such club-churches may vary, from the basic Christian social church, to groups drawn together around a particular understanding of a theological issue, to single-issue churches focusing on anything from a specific style of music to a distinctive architectural style; but in all these the core operating principle remains the same. Too often the Church has adopted an individualistically centred approach to its existence in the world, rather than one which is focused beyond the primary church community. The Church has invented itself in the image of society, rather than seeing itself as existing in fulfilment of a covenant of universal benefit. At one level there's nothing wrong with these concerns; social interaction is a gift of grace, theological issues do matter, as do music and architecture; but there remains a significant problem with neoliberal-club-churches, which is that they primarily exist for the benefit of their own members. They build for themselves, rather than for the common good.

Many of the buildings we call churches exist because congregations have decided to build themselves a home. From parish church to nonconformist chapel, these structures provide somewhere for the people of God to come and worship their God. Those who attend tend to think of them as 'our church', where 'we' come to meet with God, encountering him in the sanctuary 'we' have built for him. However, this is not true of all church buildings. The great Methodist Mission churches of the London suburbs were built to offer transformation in the poorest and most deprived areas of the Victorian city, promoting the temperance movement in the face of the evils of alcohol addiction, and supporting the suffragette cause for the emancipation of women. They were built for the common good. Similarly, the church where I am privileged to minister in Central London was built not just to house a congregation who come to worship God on the Lord's day, but to be a place of Baptist mission to the centre of the city. The building was strategically placed on the boundary between wealth and poverty, between the squares of Bloomsbury and the slums of St Giles, with the express intention of bringing the two together in ways that would transform the city for good. In a different way, the Anglican/Roman Catholic parish system has at its heart the conviction that the church is there for the good of the entire parish, not just those who attend worship regularly. All the main traditions of Christianity offer the possibility for their ecclesiology to be brought to the service of the common good, just as they all contain the temptation to restrict themselves to those who consciously identify as part of their community.

The Church in all its forms, therefore, is the heir to a vision to build for the common good, just as it is comprised of the spiritual descendants of Abraham's vision of the people of God in the world for the blessing of all peoples. The Church is called to be the new Jerusalem, offering light and water to the community beyond the doors of whatever building it has constructed for itself. The question, of course, is what offering light and water might look like in a complex, technological, 24-hour Western society? What does it mean for the contemporary Church to build a vision for the common good? Where is the need in today's context? What would it mean for the people of God in our time to shine light into the darkest corners of society, exposing the oppressive systems and practices that enslave people's souls and bodies? What would it mean for the people of God in our context to offer refreshing water to those who are being poisoned by the polluted atmosphere of hatred and cynicism and despair?

Here it may be helpful to hear the word of Jeremiah to the exiles in Babylon. The Babylonians invaded Jerusalem about six hundred years before the time of Jesus, sacked the city and destroyed the temple, before carrying a swathe of the Jewish population into exile in Babylon. It was to these exiles, far from home, with no buildings of their own and no temple in which to worship, that Jeremiah wrote:

> 'Thus says the LORD of hosts, the God of Israel, to all the exiles whom I have sent into exile from Jerusalem to Babylon: Build houses and live in them; plant gardens and eat what they produce. Take wives and have sons and daughters; take wives for your sons, and give your daughters in marriage, that they may bear sons and daughters; multiply there, and do not decrease. But seek the welfare of the city where I have sent you into exile, and pray to the LORD on its behalf, for in its welfare you will find your welfare.'                    (Jeremiah 29:4–7 NRSV)

The call of God to those in exile in Babylon was to seek the welfare of the city of Babylon.

In the book of Revelation, where the image of the Church as the new Jerusalem is found, the name 'Babylon' is used as a codename for the Roman empire, and the picture the book paints is of the people of God there, in the midst of the Empire, for good, and for the common good. In Revelation's vision the gates of the new Jerusalem are open, its light shines brightly beyond its own walls, and its pure water is available for all. This is not a vision of the Church battened down, defensively protecting itself while entering survival mode. It is a vision of the Church militant, in the world for the good of all, courageously seeking the welfare of the city. For Babylon, read Rome, read London, read New York, read wherever the people of God are present in the midst of empire.

The people of God are not here, on the earth, called from among the nations, to build a temple in which 'they' can worship 'their God'. The people of God are not here to build a tower of strength, nor to build political power. They are not here to build walls around their communities to keep them safe from those who are not like them. Rather, the people of God are here, in the world, to throw open the doors of their communities, to shine brightly for the benefit of those beyond themselves, and to build a vision for the common good. The people of God are called to seek the welfare of the context to which they have been sent. This is not about building a new building, or even a new community; it's about building a new world. The people of God are here to learn, together, to see the world differently, to see the world as God sees it, and to speak and live into being an alternative way of being human before God. It is this new world which is light and water to those whose lives are in darkness and whose souls are parched.

It is no coincidence that many of the great welfare projects which dominated the twentieth century in the United Kingdom were born of a Christian vision for the common good, as has been noted by other commentators in this book. One important example of this was the influence of Catholic Social Teaching on the 'common good' subsidiarity principles of the European Union, in which each person is understood as connected to and dependent upon each other person. Recent political pressure from certain countries to break apart the EU speaks of a political failure to enact this vision in an embedded way within the nationalistically defined communities of Europe. In a similar way, the influence of Christian charity on the construction of the welfare state needs to be recognised, as does the impact of welfare cuts on the lives of those who might otherwise be in receipt of benefit. The contemporary widespread provision by churches of foodbanks, debt services, and homelessness initiatives are further examples of churches outworking in society the underlying Christian vision for the common good.

However, it should be recognised that there is a tension between a vision for national (or international) structures enacted for the common good, and a vision for localised initiatives that are responsive to immediate need. The first is about building systems of justice, while the second is about responding with mercy. The rise of foodbanks and the like, while at one level representing the Church's mission to the poor and the needy, also speaks of the failure of those very structures that an earlier generation built to ensure justice and welfare for all. The people of God sit between the local and the national (and indeed the international), and must operate across these spheres as they outwork their vision for the common good. The prophet Micah captures this tension between structural justice and localised mercy: 'What does the Lord require of you? To act justly and to love mercy and to walk humbly with your God' (Micah 6:8 NIV). It is not enough to just meet the immediate need, and neither is it enough to focus on enacting national reform. The Church is called to join the two together, for the common good. Virginia Moffatt makes a related point in her chapters above[5], noting the way in which 'common good principles' have shifted from the legislature to the charitable sector, as the financial constraints driven by the neoliberal consensus have combined to reduce the role of the state in ensuring the 'good' of its citizens. In this context, Simon Duffy[6] draws attention to the significance of biblical and Jewish examples of social welfare, before offering some proposals for what a rethought vision for the common good might look like in a contemporary context.

There is a literary device used by the author of the book of Revelation which gives an overall structure to the text. The device is this: he brackets the central visionary dream sequences with the real-world experience of his readers. The book begins with a series of letters addressed to seven churches, firmly rooting all that follows in the first-century context of Asia Minor. Then in chapter 4 he describes an open door into heaven, and steps through that door into the world of the vision (Revelation 4:1). From a rhetorical point of view, John's readers make the same step with him through the door; and those who keep reading his text find themselves journeying with him through the heavenly realm, encountering fantastical creatures that turn out to be symbolic representations of aspects of their earthly existence. So, for example, the beast and the great prostitute are symbols of the Roman Empire (Revelation 17), while the two faithful witnesses (Revelation 11) are symbolic of the faithful witness of the people of God. Towards the end of the book, John introduces his readers to the image of the new Jerusalem as a depiction of the Church, describing it as the bride of Christ (Revelation 21:9–10). The city descends from the visionary world of the heavens down to the earth of John's readers, and the rhetorical device introduced in chapter 4 is completed, as the people of God are returned from the pictorial world that they entered with him through the open door, back down to the earth of their lived reality, where they then have to engage the task of living faithfully and witnessing to the cause of the Gospel of Christ.

What the people of God discover is that, after journeying with John through the heavens, they then encounter the world differently. It is, from their perspective, 'made new' (21:5), it is a 'new heaven' and a 'new earth' (21:1). The world which is encountered by those who are 'new Jerusalem' is a new context, because it is encountered differently. The old world was one where the emperor was all-powerful and worshipped as a God, where the empire exerted absolute control over its citizens, and where the witness of the people of God was pointless and futile. The new world, which is the world seen through the visionary lens of Revelation, is one where imperial power is finite, where the empire is under judgement, and where the faithful witness of the people of God is the essential factor in the renewal of human society. The new world comes into being as the people of the new Jerusalem bear faithful testimony to the truth that they have seen, and live that truth into being in their midst.

However, the new Jerusalem does not sit easily in Babylon. The earth is not transformed the moment the heavenly city descends. Rather, this is a vision of the people of God as a migrant city of aliens; living in the world, but not of the world; living the new world into being in the heart of the old world, that the world may be transformed. Thus the issue of the relationship between the Church and the world in which it exists is made central to any vision of the Church.

To return to the question with which we started, 'What, on earth, are we here for?' The answer surely must be that the people of God are on the earth for the good of the whole earth. However, this assertion flies in the face of much that forms central dogma for many churches. For many Christians, salvation is about saving individuals from the hell that is to come by inviting them to repent of their sins. However, a vision for the common good reframes this understanding of salvation to one where the role of the Church is to save communities from the hells that they create and live under whenever they give free reign to individualistic ideologies. Repentance, by this understanding, becomes a call to the nations to turn away from the destructive ideologies of empire, and to turn towards the alternative way of being human embodied by the people of God, where the other takes precedence over the self. The call to worship Christ becomes a call to embrace the body of Christ, which is encountered as a community of benefit for all. This is a highly politicised understanding of the role of the Church in the world, where personal good is subsumed within common good. The book of Revelation is quite clear that within its visionary world, hell and death are no more, which means that there is no need for people to live their lives in fear of them. Rather, those who turn to Christ are freed to participate in the transformation of the world for good; which will involve challenging and rejecting all competing ideologies of salvation. As Jesus said, 'I am the way, and the truth, and the life. No one comes to the Father except through me' (John 14:6).

John's vision of the Church as new Jerusalem, in the world for the common good, extends beyond social justice programmes and political agendas, to embrace the entire created order. The water that flows through the city is described as the 'river of life', and John depicts a tree growing beside it which produces fruit all year round; he calls it the 'tree of life'. He then says that 'the leaves of the tree are for the healing of the nations' (Revelation 22:2). At one level this is a clear reversal of the Genesis 'fall' story, where the knowledge of good and evil is described as entering the world through the consumption of the fruit of the tree in Eden (Genesis 3:1–13). However, it is also an image of the people of God, rooted in the world, for the good of the nations. The allusion here is to the trees depicted in the book of Ezekiel (47:6–12), which describes a vision of a world transformed, with the dry and dusty land between Jerusalem and the Jericho brought to life, and the salt waters of the Dead Sea teeming with fish, its barren banks verdant with trees. Ezekiel's insight, consciously echoed in the book of Revelation, is that the coming of the Kingdom of God involves the transformation of the earth itself; it is about the salvation of all things, and the healing of the nations occurs as part of the process of the healing of creation.

As Ellen Teague notes in her chapter above,[7] the influence of humanity on the environment is so great that the current geological era might legitimately be regarded as the *Anthropocene*, with loss of biodiversity and the impacts of climate change affecting irrevocably the ecological systems that sustain life. Any vision for the common good that emerges from Christian theology must therefore speak truth to the powers that determine human environmental impact. As Edward Echlin goes on to observe, if there is to be a future, it must be green, with each person respecting the bioregion in which they live.[8]

The creation of the new earth, and the dawning of the new Jerusalem, are therefore not to be understood in terms of successful church growth, nor are they about personal or corporate achievement. Rather, the transformation of the earth comes about, as per Ezekiel's vision, through the pure clear water which flows from the temple in Jerusalem. It is the people of God themselves who are the source of life to the earth, and the blessing of God flows through them bringing renewal and refreshing to all. This isn't something that can be manufactured or performed, rather it is the gracious gift of the love of God, who invites his people to discover what it is to be truly loved for who they are, so that others may discover what it is to be truly loved for who they are. It is a call to empathy, and to a holistic understanding of the relationship between creation, creator, and all created beings.

Pope Francis has said:

> Indifference to our neighbor and to God … represents a real temptation for us Christians. Usually, when we are healthy and comfortable, we forget about others (something God the Father never does): we are unconcerned with their problems, their sufferings and the injustices they endure … Our heart grows cold. As long as I am relatively healthy and comfortable, I don't think about those less well off. Today, this selfish attitude of indifference has taken on global proportions, to the extent that we can speak of a globalization of indifference. It is a problem which we, as Christians, need to confront.[9]

The Church, universal and local, is here, on the earth, to be good news for all, to build a vision for the common good. Indeed, one might well observe that if the church fails to articulate heaven's perspective on the earthly situation, who 'on earth' is going to do it?

Simon Barrow,[10] in his article above, challenges churches to rediscover a politics that 'brings people together', noting that such a call to justice and love will stand in sharp contrast to the divisive rhetoric of the dominant nationalistic political discourse which is driven by 'disordered globalism' and 'unstable financialisation'. The key, for Simon Barrow, lies in a commitment to nonviolence, where the Church mirrors the example of Christ in forging alliances across boundaries, finding friends in unexpected places who will join in the task of building a vision for the common good. Savitri Hensman[11]echoes this call, emphasising the biblical imperative of justice as an injunction to encounter Christ in the poor, the vulnerable and the outcast. The outworking of this is that those who cross boundaries and borders as migrants and asylum seekers are themselves signifiers of the Christ who breaks down the barriers that divide humanity from itself and from encounter with God. It is in this context that Susan Clarkson[12] highlights the way in which the teachings of Jesus in the Sermon on the Mount deconstruct the dominant myth of redemptive violence which has determined so much of the international response to the immigration crisis of recent years.

So in a world of growing fear, with the whiff of fascism in the air, with growing suspicion of the other, and fear of the foreigner, with poverty and homelessness literally on the doorsteps of our churches, with mental health services in crisis at the very point where they are most needed, with social care and security facing cuts of catastrophic levels, maybe this is what, in the world, the Church is here for. It is called to look beyond itself, to take into action the conviction that in Christ every life matters, and that Christ always has a bias to the poor, the vulnerable and the marginalised. The Church is called to build alliances with others, to speak truth to power, and to hold to account those who hold power. It is called to engage politics and charity, to build communities of reciprocity, to run night shelters and day centres, to use its resources to see the marginalised included, the poor lifted up, and the vulnerable made strong.

The Church is therefore called to build a vision for the common good, where the absolute love of God for each and every person is at the heart of all that it does. It should be in and through the Church that utopian religion finds its pragmatic reality; the people of God are where dreams become real and visions get built. They are the outpost on the earth of the new world that that is coming. They are the people who live into being in their midst the reality for which they pray: that the kingdom will come, on earth as it is in heaven.

## Questions

- What do you think it would look like to see new Jerusalem built 'in England's green and pleasant land'?
- How can the Church be a 'blessing to all nations'?
- What should be the relationship between 'church' and 'politics'?
- Should the Church seek alliances with people from other faiths to work together for the common good?

## Notes

1. See Patrick Riordan, 'The history and principles of the common good' in this publication, pp. 11–26.
2. Jonathan Chaplin, 'Evangelicalism and the language(s) of the common good' in Nicholas Sagovsky and Peter McGrail (eds), *Together for the Common Good: Towards a national conversation* (London: SCM Press, 2015), pp. 91–106.
3. Ibid., p. 97.
4. Ibid., p. 102.
5. Virginia Moffatt, 'Rolling back the state', 'Rolling back the market', in this publication, pp. 85–98 and pp. 99–116 .
6. Simon Duffy, 'A new vision for welfare?' in this publication, pp. 71–84.
7. Ellen Teague, 'The threat of the Anthropocene', in this publication, pp. 145–57
8. Edward P. Echlin, 'Living within our bioregion: sharing planet earth', in this publication, pp. 158–67.
9. Pope Francis's Lent Message, 2015.
10. Simon Barrow, 'The uncommon good', in this publication, pp. 43–55.
11. Savitri Hensman, 'Crossing boundaries, overcoming barriers', in this publication, pp. 133–144.
12. Susan Clarkson, 'For ashes, a garland: embracing the vision of a world without war', in this publication, pp. 179–87.

# Further Reading and Resources

## What is the common good?

Patrick Riordan SJ, *A Grammar of the Common Good* (London: Continuum, 2008)

Patrick Riordan SJ, *Global Ethics and Global Common Good* (London: Bloomsbury, 2015)

Hilary Russell, *A Faithful Presence: Working together for the common good* (London: SCM Press, 2015)

Nicholas Sagovsky and Peter McGrail (eds), *Together for the Common Good: Towards a national conversation* (London: SCM Press, 2015), pp. 91–106.

## Service and society

Simon Barrow and Mike Small (eds), *Scotland 2021* (Ekklesia/Bella Caledonia, 2016)

Peter Beresford, *All Our Welfare: Towards participatory social policy* (Bristol: Policy Press, 2016)

Andrew Bowman *et al.*, *What a Waste: Outsourcing and how it goes wrong* (Manchester: Manchester University Press, 2015)

Gary Dorrien, *Reconstructing the Common Good: Theology and social order* (Maryknoll NY: Orbis Books, 1990)

Andrew Francis (ed.), *Foxes Have Holes: Christian reflections on Britain's housing need* (London: Ekklesia, 2016)

John Kay, *The Truth About Markets* (London: Penguin, 2004)

Andrew Marr, *A History of Modern Britain* (London: Pan Books, 2008)

Mary O'Hara, *Austerity Bites: A journey to the sharp end of the cuts in the UK* (Bristol: Policy Press, 2015)

Harry Leslie Smith, *Harry's Last Stand: How the world my generation built is falling down and what we can do to save it* (London: Icon Books, 2014)

Mo Stewart, *Cash Not Care: The planned demolition of the UK welfare state* (London: New Generation Publishing, 2016)

William Temple, *Christianity and Social Order* (London: Penguin 1942)

Simone Weil, *The Need for Roots: Prelude to a declaration of duties towards mankind* (London: Ark, 1987)

## People and planet

Hannah Arendt, *Origins of Totalitarianism* (New York: Houghton Mifflin Harcourt Publishing, 1951)

Richard Bauckham, *Living with other Creatures: Green exegesis and the Bible* (Milton Keynes: Paternoster, 2012)

Pope Francis, *Laudate Si'* (Papal Encyclical, June 2015)

David Hartsough, *Waging Peace: Global adventures of a lifelong activist* (Oakland, CA: PM Press, 2014)

Naomi Klein, *This Changes Everything: Capitalism versus the climate* (New York: Simon and Schuster, 2015)

Robert Murray, *The Cosmic Covenant* (London: Sheed & Ward, 1992)

Ched Myers and Matthew Colwell, *Our God is Undocumented: Biblical faith and immigrant justice* (Maryknoll, NY: Orbis, 2012)

Susana Snyder, *Asylum-seeking, migration and church: Explorations in practical, pastoral and empirical theology* (Farnham: Ashgate Publishing, 2012)

Guy Standing, *The Precariat: A new dangerous class* (London: Bloomsbury, 2011)

Niall Thomas, *The Figure of the Migrant* (Redwood City, CA: Stanford University Press, 2015)

Walter Wink, *Engaging the Powers: Discernment and resistance in a world of domination* (Minneapolis, MN: Fortress Press, 1992)

Chris Woods, *Sudden Justice: America's secret drone wars* (London: Hurst and Company, 2015)

## Our mission

Paul Mason, *Postcapitalism: A guide to our future* (London: Allen Lane, 2016)

Simon Woodman, 'Can the Book of Revelation be a Gospel for the Environment?' in Matthew J.M. Coomber (ed.), *Bible and Justice: Ancient Texts, Modern Challenges* (Chesham, Bucks: Equinox Press, 2011)

## Useful organisations

*Policy organisations*

Centre for Welfare Reform, www.cforwr.org

Ekklesia, http://www.ekklesia.co.uk/

The Equality Trust, https://www.equalitytrust.org.uk/

The Joint Public Issues Team, http://www.jointpublicissues.org.uk/

Praxis, http://www.praxis.org.uk/

Refugee Council, https://www.refugeecouncil.org.uk/

Tax Justice Network, http://www.taxjustice.net/

Tax Research UK, http://www.taxresearch.org.uk/Blog/richard-murphy/

Together for the Common Good, http://www.togetherforthecommongood.co.uk/

## Campaign and support organisations

BlackTriangle, http://blacktrianglecampaign.org/

Boaz Trust, http://boaztrust.org.uk/

Catholic Worker Farm, http://www.londoncatholicworker.org/CWfarm.htm

Child Poverty Action Group, http://cpag.org.uk/

Christian Climate Action, https://christianclimateaction.wordpress.com/

Citizen Network, www.citizen-network.org

Disabled People Against Cuts, https://dpac.uk.net/

Drone Wars UK, https://dronewars.net/

Fellowship of Reconciliation UK, http://www.for.org.uk/

Green Christian, http://www.greenchristian.org.uk/

Joint Council for the Welfare of Immigrants, https://www.jcwi.org.uk/

L'Arche UK, http://www.larche.org.uk/

London Catholic Worker, http://www.londoncatholicworker.org/

Movement for the Abolition of War, http://www.abolishwar.org.uk/

Migrant Rights Network, http://www.migrantsrights.org.uk/

Migrant Voice, http://www.migrantvoice.org/

Operation Noah, http://operationnoah.org/

Pax Christi UK, http://paxchristi.org.uk/

The People's Assembly Against Austerity, http://www.thepeoplesassembly.org.uk/

Voices for Creative Nonviolence, http://vcnv.org.uk/